Changing Norms through Actions

# Changing Norms through Actions

*The Evolution of Sovereignty*

JENNIFER M. RAMOS

OXFORD
UNIVERSITY PRESS

Oxford University Press is a department of the University of Oxford.
It furthers the University's objective of excellence in research, scholarship,
and education by publishing worldwide.

Oxford New York
Auckland  Cape Town  Dar es Salaam  Hong Kong  Karachi
Kuala Lumpur  Madrid  Melbourne  Mexico City  Nairobi
New Delhi  Shanghai  Taipei  Toronto

With offices in
Argentina  Austria  Brazil  Chile  Czech Republic  France  Greece
Guatemala  Hungary  Italy  Japan  Poland  Portugal  Singapore
South Korea  Switzerland  Thailand  Turkey  Ukraine  Vietnam

Oxford is a registered trade mark of Oxford University Press
in the UK and certain other countries.

Published in the United States of America by
Oxford University Press
198 Madison Avenue, New York, NY 10016

[Cataloging-in-Publication Data on file with the Library of Congress.]

ISBN: 978-0-19-992484-4 (hardcover); 978-0-19-992486-8 (paperback)

9  8  7  6  5  4  3  2  1

Printed in the United States of America
on acid-free paper

*To Duane, Mahal Kita*

# CONTENTS

ILLUSTRATIONS

Tables

Figures

# ACKNOWLEDGMENTS

I am ever mindful that it does take a village in endeavors such as this. Special thanks to Miko Nincic, a fantastic mentor and friend. I also appreciate helpful comments and encouragement from Donald Rothchild, Emily Goldman, Larry Berman, Dana Zartner, Kerstin Fisk, Leo Blanken, Molly Melin, Belgin San, Greg Love, Richard Fox, Jodi Finkel, John Parrish, and the anonymous reviewers at Oxford. For research assistance, I thank Jessica Lohmann, Michelle Larson, Ted Guerrero, Courtney Pickard, Talin Bagdassarian, Michael George, Lae-An Cantimbuhan, and Anne-Marie Boisseau. I also gratefully acknowledge the efficient and excellent work of Angela Chnapko, Erica Woods Tucker, and India Grey in turning this manuscript into a more polished work. Many thanks and love, as always, to my parents.

I am very thankful for the financial support I obtained to complete this project. I received funding from the Institute on Global Conflict and Cooperation; the Donald Rothchild Memorial Graduate Research Grant; the University of California, Davis, Department of Political Science Fellowship; the University of California, Davis Institute of Governmental Affairs; and the Loyola Marymount University BCLA Fellowship.

# CHAPTER 1 | Sovereignty
## History, Development, and Implications

La Souverainete, c'est quelque chose.

—CHARLES DE GAULLE

STATE SOVEREIGNTY HAS BEEN a central and enduring feature of international relations since the consolidation of the nation-state system. Yet, the content of sovereignty is changing as a result of the international policies of states that express the underlying beliefs about legitimate state behavior. These policies are often influenced by evolving international norms concerning states' rights and responsibilities in the global community, and their corresponding actions have important implications for the future of these norms and interstate behavior.[1] For example, although the norm of sovereignty and nonintervention are codified in the United Nations' Charter, under Article 2, recent history demonstrates that traditional sovereignty norms are continuously challenged by military actions taken to address major international issues. Thus, it is at the intersection of these policy domains and state sovereignty that we begin to unpack the complexities of this intensely debated, controversial concept called "sovereignty."

Scholars and politicians worldwide have much invested in how sovereignty is defined. State sovereignty is one of the most important norms, if not *the* most important norm, of international relations, encompassing states' external and internal rights and responsibilities. The norm determines, at any point in time, what policy domains lie within the purview of a state, and that of the international community. Traditionally, as long as a "state" was recognized as such by other states, it was accorded sovereign rights, including the right to conduct its internal and external affairs as it saw fit, without outside interference. For many years, states have coexisted on the basis of a norm of "absolute" sovereignty, according the state supreme authority over its people and territory, relative to the international community.

Currently, however, the concept of sovereignty is moving toward one in which states that cannot fulfill certain obligations to their citizens, and to the international community, forfeit the right to act autonomously in these domains, ceding that responsibility to the international community (see Deng et al. 1996). Today, states have obligations to fulfill *in order* to maintain their sovereign prerogatives, and others increasingly have the right to intervene in their affairs if these obligations are not met. We see this very clearly with regard to human rights. In the past, governments had wide reign over their citizens and were not subject to outside scrutiny. If humanitarian intervention did occur, it was focused on saving people who were part of the in-group, which during the nineteenth century meant European Christians, since potential interveners were Western states (Finnemore 2003). Now, for the first time in its history, the UN Security Council has deemed intervention legitimate in cases in which a state is guilty of gross human rights abuses, especially if they represent a threat to international peace and security. A case in point is the 2011 multilateral military intervention in Libya authorized by the United Nations Security Council Resolution 1973, which was designed to help protect civilians caught in the bloody civil war between the Libyan government and anti-Ghaddafi forces. If the international community has the right to intervene in a state not fulfilling its commitment to human rights, this implies a "contingent" norm of sovereignty; sovereignty is contingent upon certain levels of government performance.

What is perhaps most striking is the changing notion of sovereignty in Africa, which under the Organization of African Unity (OAU) held strictly to absolute sovereignty norms largely because of the legacy of colonialism. Despite atrocities in Uganda under Idi Amin, to genocides in Rwanda and Burundi, the OAU continued to prioritize the norm of absolute state sovereignty. However, in the newly formed African Union (2002), the OAU's successor, the founding charter embodies the "responsibility to protect" principle, which obligates states to respond to gross human rights abuses in other states. While the Union struggles to put this into practice, in cases such as genocide in Sudan or to protect civilians in the Libyan civil war[2], the fact remains that the absolute sovereignty of a state is no longer assumed.[3]

But *how* do understandings of norms—particularly long-held norms such as absolute sovereignty—change? In this book, I contend that the concept of sovereignty is moving toward one in which states that are unable or unwilling to fulfill their domestic and international obligations are forced to relinquish certain sovereign responsibilities to the international community. That is, states risk intervention by other states if they do not comply with generally accepted norms. I examine this proposition with regard to three of the most pressing international issues: counterterrorism, human rights, and the development of weapons of mass destruction (WMD). Since military intervention is a clear violation of the sovereignty norm, the intervention itself may imply that action taken on behalf of these other norms weakens the norm of sovereignty. However, I argue that it depends on the outcome of the intervention as to the extent to which sovereignty evolves. One would generally expect an arduous military intervention to exhibit *less* commitment by the intervener to the norms that it is based on. But the opposite may be true. Scholarship in social psychology on cognitive dissonance leads us to expect that such a situation would actually yield *more* commitment by the intervener to the norms that were used to justify the intervention. Thus, leading states are able to pursue their material agenda, but with norm evolution as the by-product of military intervention.

Not only do international norms change because of the evolution of ideas about the proper behavior of states but also as a result of state action. State actors justify their actions by relying on the norms accepted by other states in the international system. For example, the United States justified the recent intervention in Libya through appeals to human rights norms. However, one could argue that it was also in the self-interest of the United States to support a change in leadership in Libya. I assert that even when a major power acts primarily out of self-interest, with the normative argument being secondary, the action may have the *unintended* consequence of modifying the normative environment within which other states act.

## Contribution of the Book

Understanding the process of norm change, and of the norm of sovereignty in particular, is important for several reasons. First, there is little theoretical understanding of how political action shapes norms, and more specifically, how they are influenced by military intervention (Kowert and Legro 1996). Although a growing literature recognizes the impact of norms on state action, there is a deficiency in the literature on the ways by which such norms are shaped and maintained (Feldman 2003), including the role of state action in this process.

Military intervention offers an important avenue for understanding how the sovereignty norm evolves because intervention dramatically violates a state's sovereignty. This calls the sovereignty norm as currently defined into question and presents an opportunity for states to reconsider its contours. Since military intervention continues to be a tool of statecraft (Levite et al. 1994), often justified via self-defense broadly defined, it offers an interesting intersection of values by which to study sovereignty.

Second, while substantial research has investigated how norms and ideas shape military interventions (Jervis 1976; Van Evera 1984), and despite the fact that social interaction is inherently dynamic, no work has explicitly explored the reverse direction of causality: how intervention affects norms. In studying political phenomena, most scholars interested in the role of norms think of them as causes, rather than consequences (Goldstein and Keohane 1993; Hopf 2002; Jervis 1976; Van Evera 1984). This book seeks to address this shortcoming by accounting, theoretically and empirically, for norm evolution as a product of political action.

Finally, this research has practical implications for policymakers. If action taken by states may reinforce an existing norm or alter existing understandings of the norm, states must consider how their actions may change the rules of the game for the future. Shifting understandings of sovereignty (and how states relate to one another) have profound implications for the workings of the international system. How states and the international community understand their rights and obligations to one another is directly related to the possibility of international conflict and cooperation.

Changes in conceptions of sovereignty also are related to changes in other norms of state behavior and responsibility. For example, an emerging norm urges new democracies to accept international election monitoring to ensure free and fair elections (Santa-Cruz 2005). Before 1960, international election observation in sovereign states was unheard of. However, today almost 80 percent of all elections in developing democracies have international observers (Hyde 2006). Beyond satisfying domestic constituents, election monitoring signals to the international community that the state is serious about democracy and is worthy of the international aid and consideration it receives. Election monitoring became a more common practice after World War II, with the movement toward decolonization and the creation of the United Nations as a neutral party to oversee elections.

The international monitoring of the presidential elections in Iraq (2010), Nigeria (2011), Cote d'Ivoire (2011), Russia (2011), Libya (2012) and Egypt (2012) are some of the most recent examples of this norm in practice.

There is also an international norm concerning legitimate and representative government, reflected in the global norm of racial equality (see Klotz 1995). In South Africa, international pressure against the apartheid regime led to its eventual collapse. For years, the white minority government had enforced discriminatory policies of ethnic separation in almost all areas of life, including voting, education, health care, travel, and employment. The international movement against the government slowly spread, through isolation policies, like banning South Africa from competing in international sports events, implementing state laws making it illegal to invest in or do business in South Africa, and condemning South Africa at international conferences.

In sum, the evolution of the sovereignty norm is intertwined with changes in other norms as well, including norms governing human rights and democratic representation. Because state sovereignty is so central to the conduct of international relations, it is difficult to think of an international norm it does not interact with. As the normative fabric of the international system evolves, so too does the meaning of state sovereignty and vice versa. One might visualize this as a web of interconnecting norms, with state sovereignty at the center. These norms push and pull on one another, with profound implications for the conduct of international relations.

## Why Norms Matter

Changes in ideas about sovereignty matter because this norm guides both internal and external behavior. Within a state, norms structure decision-making by providing a "road map," narrowing (and clarifying) decision possibilities, and a way to make policy choices without perfect information (Goldstein and Keohane 1993). In this sense, ideas about the appropriate options for action limit which interests are pursued. Power and interests are only effective explanations of state behavior because of the norms and ideas with which they are constituted (Wendt 1999). While some argue that norms help states define their interests (Axelrod and Keohane 1985; Black 1999; Hopf 2002; Legro 1997; Risse, Ropp, and Sikkink 1999), others assert a more direct link between norms and state behavior (Kier 1995; Van Evera 1984). For example, Price and Tannenwald (1996) examine norms regarding the non-use of nuclear and chemical weapons to show how norms, not just material interests, guide state behavior. They demonstrate that chemical weapons taboos evolved at the international level and trickled down to the state level, while nuclear deterrence norms developed within a state (the US) and then spread to the international level. Both the nuclear and chemical weapons taboos became institutionalized as international norms, despite the obvious advantage of first use.

Just as norms serve as guides to actors, or "agents," they are also a structural feature of international relations. As part of the interactive process between structure and agency, states as agents not only draw upon the normative structure in their decision-making but also influence the content of the normative structure through political action. Normative structure is extremely important to the maintenance of the international order. Normative structure establishes "rules" for state conduct, creating expectations that facilitate international relations and reducing uncertainty, which breeds mistrust and misperception. With no consensus on appropriate state behavior, establishing a stable order in a world of anarchy becomes much more difficult, if not impossible. Moreover, without norms, an international community that pursued goals justified by the common good could not exist. For example, protecting the environment or regulating trade would pose insurmountable problems of coordination without common understandings to inform state behavior. We tend to take many of these norms for granted; indeed, it is difficult to imagine the world without them. This especially applies to the norm of sovereignty. And yet, in the span of human history, state sovereignty is a relatively recent concept.

## Emergence of Sovereignty

Although the norm of sovereignty can be dated to at least the thirteenth century, most discussions begin with the emergence of the modern state system in 1648, with the Peace of Westphalia.[4] Since that time, understandings of state sovereignty have evolved as the political context has changed, often via significant political events that challenge its current conception.

The initial understanding of state sovereignty emerged from the conclusion of the Thirty Years War (1618–1648), which marked a clash between the traditional and the modern political orders, as well as between religion and secularism, with the underlying goal of settling the question of political authority. As one legal scholar notes, the Peace of Westphalia "represents the majestic portal which leads from the old into the new world" (Gross 1948, 28). The break from medieval traditions of rule to modern conceptions of authority reflect a progression toward a more effective and efficient political system, with sovereign states as the primary actors. Unlike the modern state system, the feudal system of the medieval era resembled more of a web, than a hierarchy, of power relations. Political jurisdictions overlapped, power was decentralized and subjects often owed allegiances, and thereby taxes, to multiple authority figures. Rather than territory, authority derived from personal ties, inspired by the religious fervor of the time. The Catholic Church and the Holy Roman Empire struggled for dominance, though they also entertained a mutually dependent relationship, with kings acting as "Defenders of the Faith" and popes relying on royal support to stay in power (Philpott 1996).

As the struggle for power continued in the seventeenth century, a clear conceptual development occurred with the consolidation of statehood: the concept of sovereignty and authority became intertwined (Nincic 1970, 2). This resulted primarily from the legal wrangling between rulers and their lawyers over their legitimate political domains, underscoring the idea that sovereignty could not exist without authority as its primary attribute. Jean Bodin, the founder of the modern theory of sovereignty, asserted that it is the "absolute and perpetual authority of a state."[5] That is, sovereignty is the ultimate authority of a ruler over a given territory, which could not be compromised by outside influences (even the Church). According to Bodin, there was nothing above the state to set limitations on state behavior, *not even a higher moral law*.[6] Moreover, Bodin argued that state sovereignty continued beyond the life of its leaders. It remained an attribute of *state* power, regardless of changes in leadership.

The emergence of state sovereignty produced new legal and moral principles to guide international relations. In addition to Bodin, Thomas Hobbes was one of several great philosophers to direct his attention to state sovereignty in his classic work, *Leviathan*. He proposed answers to what sovereignty is and how it should function. In Hobbes's view, the state should wield its power over its citizens via a ruler (or assembly) and "direct their actions to the Common Benefit" (Hobbes 1914/1651). By "common benefit," Hobbes had in mind actions that benefited the state, not necessarily the international community. This was in direct contrast to another philosopher, Hugo Grotius, who advanced the idea of what we now know as international law.

Years earlier, Grotius had offered his views on a system of more humane international relations in *De Jure Belli ac Pacis* (1625), a society of states acting together for the common good. In contrast to Hobbes's focus on self-interested states with unrestrained authority, Grotius imagined an international community guided by common ideas about legitimate state behavior. He believed that laws infused with religious notions of morality, which states were obliged to respect through "mutual consent," would restrict them from provoking international conflict, which had so devastated Europe at the time of his writing (Grotius 1625/2001).

This version of sovereignty continued until the late eighteenth century, when events, in particular the French Revolution, gave voice to the idea that the state should be governed by the popular will of the people, not by whims of a ruler; the locus of authority, and thereby, sovereignty, was transferred from the ruler to the ruled. Demands for citizen equality and freedom within the state and its recognized legitimacy spilled over into states' external relations as well (Nincic 1970, 4). The changes in state-society power relations mirrored trends in interstate relations, as articulated in the Draft Declaration on the Rights of Nations (1795). In the eyes of international law, states had the right to independence from, and equality with, other states (Nincic 1970, 4). This implied the right of nonintervention of states, which Immanuel Kant articulated in his *Perpetual Peace* (1795). No state had the right to intervene in the internal affairs of another state (Kant, sect. 1, art. 5). In this view, if all leaders respected this tenet, there would be peaceful relations among states.

## Influence of Sovereignty over the Centuries

As the idea of a sovereign state spread, and more states appeared on the global scene, sovereignty became the dominant guiding principle of international relations. States jealously guarded their absolute right to conduct their internal and external affairs independently and sought recognition from other states of this prerogative. Sovereignty became associated with the right to wage war, and in this sense, states held an absolute and unlimited idea of sovereignty. Essentially, state behavior was based on this version of sovereignty, rather than guided by natural, moral, or religious tenets. As Politis writes, "The dogma of illimited sovereignty killed the theory of the just war" (Politis 1935, 19). The only requirement for waging war was that of being a sovereign state, and each state thereby had the right to decide whether it was in a state of war or a state of peace (Nincic 1970, 52). The bounds of sovereignty were such that almost any activity (internal/external) conducted by a sovereign state was viewed as legitimate, even under international law, though quiet debates about "just war" and "just cause" took place (Nincic 1970, 53). Virtually without constraint, war thus became a legitimate option for states to pursue their political goals.

As military technology became more destructive and populations grew weary of the consequences of war, states became concerned not only with their legal right to wage war but also with their ability to justify it on moral and political grounds (e.g., "self-defense," "duty to protect country's honor") (Nincic 1970, 54). Though the sovereign right to wage war remained a defining feature of statehood, discourse regarding the reasoning of state action highlighted the contradiction between an amoral legal right and moral justifications. States attempted to modify international perceptions of their behavior through changes in their discourse, but without any accompanying change in their behavior.

One of the dominant justifications for violating another state's sovereignty was a historical claim to territory. On this basis, France reclaimed Nice and Savoy from Italy, and France and Germany battled for their right to the Alsace-Lorraine region (Hill 1976, 41–43). Yet, because of the Peace of Westphalia, rather than being subsumed into an empire when wars ended, defeated states were allowed their existence as independent sovereign states (though some territory may have been taken). In fact, when Napoleon tried to challenge this with the empire-seeking Napoleonic Wars (1803–1815), in which France fought Britain, the Netherlands, Austria-Hungary, Spain, Russia, and Prussia, the end result was a reinforcement of state sovereignty, emphasized in the political negotiations at the Congress of Vienna (1815). Yet, somewhat paradoxically, the Congress also provided legitimacy to the principle that historical claims justified the retaking of territory (Hill 1976, 39). This loophole created an uneasy tension with sovereignty, which the Concert of Europe attempted to moderate.

As European imperialism abroad expanded through the nineteenth century, it became evident that state sovereignty was a concept of geographically limited application. In practice, it seemingly applied only to European states, which proved all too convenient for the colonization of Africa and Latin America. Power brought the ability to set the rules. Because indigenous populations were not considered as residing within a "state," and to whom the political concept of "state" was foreign, the colonizers could argue that the international rules of sovereignty did not apply. Thus, countries like France and Great Britain could take over these territories and still operate within the guidelines of the international (European-centric) community. Few areas of the world were left untouched by European power.[7]

Ideas about minority rights and the right of self-determination would periodically bubble to the surface of international relations, but the essence of sovereignty as defined in Europe remained unchanged. For example, although respect for minority rights was required in applications for statehood, exactly how this would be enforced after the fact of statehood was never specified. With no external accountability, states were unhindered in their treatment of minorities; it was during this time that the Armenians were massacred by the Turks (Philpott 1997, 36), and the international community took no action to thwart the genocide.

In the early twentieth century, states came a step closer to a new vision of sovereignty (Philpott 1997), as World War I compelled states to think about how to prevent future wars. In his now famous Fourteen Points (1918) speech, US President Woodrow Wilson advanced the idea of an international political body that would mediate conflict among states so that states would never experience the devastation of war again. In addition, he asserted the right to self-determination, arguing that groups within a state should have the freedom to govern themselves, if they chose. While the former objective gained support among other states (though ironically not from Wilson's own country), the latter did not resonate with other major powers at the time, in part due to the ongoing, though declining, practice of colonialism. At the conclusion of the war, the League of Nations was established as an intergovernmental organization, but without any mention of self-determination in its covenant.[8]

Another attempt at redefining sovereignty embodied in the League had to do with minority rights. Among many of the League's official duties was the task of enforcing minority-protection treaties. At last, the international community had a mechanism to hold states accountable; state responsibilities would not just be required, they would also be *enforced*. Unfortunately, this idealism was short-lived. Faced with an established tradition of absolute sovereignty in practice, even the League proved too weak and timid to confront violating states, as Hitler's New Order made all too clear (Von Frentz 1999; Fink 2004). Thus, while the movement toward limiting sovereignty had officially begun, it was not carried out in practice. This discrepancy was soon overshadowed by the onset of World War II (1939–1945).

In contrast to the era ending with WWI, the tragedies of World War II inspired rethinking of the legitimate rights of states and their corresponding obligations. The Second World War again brought devastation to people across the globe, instigated by Hitler's quest for German world domination. This war was like no other in modern history because of

Hitler's policy of systematically exterminating the Jewish people. The atrocities of the Holocaust resounded loudly in the human consciousness, and, upon the defeat of the Axis powers—Germany, Italy, and Japan—the international community vowed that "never again" would the world permit such inhumane treatment of a people, whether in peacetime or war.

To guard against the reoccurrence of such horrors, there needed to be a body outside of states that could hold states accountable and set standards for state behavior. This was theoretically achieved through the intergovernmental organization, the United Nations (UN), which arose out of the ashes of World War II and reflected strong improvements over the League of Nations, in that it included more countries and all of the major powers. Again, states committed to collective security and created laws that reached into the jurisdiction of states to protect minorities and human rights (Philpott 1997). Leaders would be held accountable for their domestic actions. For example, the charge of "crimes against humanity" signified to leaders that they could not hide behind the shield of sovereignty and would risk prosecution for such actions, as demonstrated in the Nuremburg trials of Nazi war crimes.

The UN, however, did face some of the same obstacles as the League of Nations. By virtue of being an intergovernmental organization rather than a supernational organization, the UN had no independent means by which to enforce core principles of the UN Charter. To compound the problem, the UN seemed to contradict itself by acknowledging the right to nonintervention of states, while also declaring a set of universal human rights (Nincic 1970). This ambiguity allowed states to justify their actions via absolute sovereignty, with little incentive to comply with international law when it contradicted national interests. At the same time, those states did risk international intervention since the decision-making body of the UN had some grounds to act against them. If the five permanent members of the United Nations Security Council (UNSC) agreed that a threat to international peace and security existed, then it was likely that the problem would be addressed.[9] Thus, the UNSC could serve as the enforcement mechanism and ultimate interpreter of the UN Charter.

The stage seemed set for a change in the norms of sovereignty in terms of what constituted appropriate state behavior. Yet few at the San Francisco conference, where the UN Charter was first drafted, foresaw the growing rivalry between the United States and the Soviet Union that would render the UN ineffective. The so-called Cold War essentially put a freeze on developments in state sovereignty for the next several decades.

# Sovereignty During the Cold War

During the Cold War, evolution of the norm of sovereignty was suspended. Despite strides made at the creation of the UN toward a norm of sovereignty that reflected basic human values, geostrategic politics precluded the concept's application in practice. While a contingent norm of sovereignty based on human rights existed in discourse, it failed to achieve the status that it has today. This was, in part, due to the nuclear standoff between the two superpowers, the Soviet Union and the United States.

Nuclear weapons raised the stakes in the political game between the Soviet Union and the United States, as both countries possessed the power to destroy each other's population, economy, and political systems, and security was in the foreground of interstate relations. In this period, the world was essentially divided into two ideological camps, communism (the Soviet bloc) and democratic capitalism (the West, led by the US). With various forms of aid, security guarantees, and active support of compliant regimes, each side sought to "buy" allies around the world. Whether in Africa, Asia, or Latin America, this meant that human rights abuses were often overlooked.[10] A few cases are illustrative: the West supported Mobutu Sese Seko of the Democratic Republic of the Congo (Zaire), despite his well-known human rights abuses, which included public executions of his political rivals; the United States continued to give military aid to the Philippines under Ferdinand Marcos's dictatorship, infamous for its corruption and human rights violations; and Chile also received support from the United States, though it committed systematic rights abuses for which its military dictator, Augusto Pinochet, was later brought to trial. As long as a regime remained loyal to its donor, little importance was given to its internal behavior. In fact, it was thought that intervening in a state would have signaled aggressive intentions to the other side, where none was intended. Because security trumped all other issues, there was no latitude to pursue "softer" issues, such as human rights abuses.

In this environment, neither side had much respect for the sovereignty of other states. As in the previous centuries, powerful states conducted their external relations as dictated by self-interest. Similarly, during the Cold War, sovereignty did not impede the superpowers from intervening in states within their sphere of influence and installing a more "friendly" government. For example, as a policy to contain communism and in tandem with the decolonization movement, the US took covert action to overthrow perceived pro-Soviet governments after democratic elections in Iran (1953), Guatemala (1954), British Guiana (1953–64), Indonesia (1957),

Ecuador (1963), Brazil (1964), Costa Rica (mid-1950s), Chile (1970–73), and the Dominican Republic (1965) (Van Evera 1991). Similarly, the Soviet Union quelled the reform movement of the Prague Spring (1968) in Czechoslovakia and a similar uprising in Hungary (1956) that sought to remove the country from the Soviet Union's grasp.[11]

Moreover, both sides were willing to use third-party states to conduct proxy wars. Instead of fighting each other directly and risk escalation to nuclear war, the Soviet Union and the United States would support different groups within a state involved in conflict. This occurred in a number of countries, including Korea (1950–1953), Vietnam (1964–1975), and Afghanistan (1979–1989). These proxy wars wreaked havoc on the social, political, and economic well-being of these states, and the effects can still be seen today.

As the Cold War thawed in the late 1980s and relations improved between the two blocs, such tactics were no longer necessary. With the collapse of the Soviet Union after 1990, the threat of World War III declined, and an opportunity for genuine cooperation on global issues emerged. Having long ignored looming international issues such as environmental degradation, global hunger, and disease, the international community could finally begin to work together to solve these problems without the impediments of a bipolar world. Under the circumstances, international organizations, namely the UN, could begin to function as intended. The end of the superpower rivalry meant that the deadlock in the UNSC, in which each permanent member had veto power, might be resolved. With all of these political changes, one significant, underlying question remained—what would state sovereignty mean in this "New World Order"?[12] Would sovereignty continue to be understood as it had during the Cold War, or would it be revised in accordance with pressing international issues?

## Current Political Debates on Sovereignty

The debate on sovereignty is not easily resolved or dispassionately argued. At its core is the question about the "division of responsibility" between the state and the international community; what falls to the international community, and what is reserved for the state? The answer is extremely important to the future of international relations, with implications for what is deemed legitimate behavior. States require an agreed allocation of rights and obligations between themselves and the international community, thus facilitating peaceful international interactions and minimizing uncertainty in an anarchic world.

Much of the political debate about these rights and obligations has taken place among the permanent members of the UN Security Council because of the UNSC's power to intervene in the internal affairs of other states, as well as the members' individual capability to act. Each member has a stake in how sovereignty is understood. The arguments on both sides are compelling. Those on the side of absolute sovereignty in all circumstances argue that anything less would open a Pandora's box of hegemonic interventions, justified under the cover of restoring international peace and security. In this view, violating sovereignty cannot be objectively justified, and thereby an intervention could not be legitimated.[13] On the other side, states argue that the international community cannot stand by while states fail to protect their citizens, as well as the international community (in some cases), from genocide or terrorism. Especially in the realm of human rights, with particular reference to the horrors of the Holocaust and the Rwandan genocide, the argument for contingent sovereignty is quite persuasive.

As norm-setters, powerful states are especially interested in how the debate plays out. China and Russia are often cited as the leading powers committed to the absolute notion of national sovereignty. In their view, regardless of whether a state is unduly repressive or guilty of gross human rights abuses, a state's sovereignty should be respected. Former Chinese President Jiang Zemin strongly opposed the argument that human rights should rank higher than sovereignty; he declared, "Dialogue and cooperation in the field of human rights must be conducted on the basis of respect for state sovereignty."[14] In fact, when the international community sought to remedy the grave human rights situation in Kosovo, President Jiang, referring to the absolute sovereignty norm, stated: "I hereby solemnly reiterate that the military actions against Kosovo and other parts of Yugoslavia violate the norms governing international relations."[15]

Moreover, from China's perspective, "Without sovereignty, there will be no human rights to speak of."[16] China's position is not that human rights abuses by a government are acceptable, but rather that it is an internal matter beyond the scope of the international community's reach. Even in the recent debate about a multilateral intervention on behalf of human rights in Syria, China "maintains that any attempt by the international community to help Syria solve its crisis must respect the sovereignty, independence and territorial integrity of the country."[17] Sovereignty supersedes all other considerations.

These views are mirrored by Russia, which is not surprising given that the two countries often support one another when it comes to the issue of sovereignty. Russia recognized China's sovereignty over Taiwan, supporting the one-China policy, while China supported Russia's sovereignty with regard to Chechnya. Like President Jiang, President Vladimir Putin questioned the motives of the West, when suggesting intervention in the internal affairs of another country. Russia's foreign policy statement in 2000 declared, "Attempts to belittle the role of a sovereign state as the fundamental element of international relations generates a threat of arbitrary interference in internal affairs."[18] Moreover, "Attempts to introduce into the international parlance such concepts as 'humanitarian intervention' and 'limited sovereignty' in order to justify unilateral power actions bypassing the UN Security Council are not acceptable."[19] President Putin argued within the context of the US-led intervention in Iraq (2003–2011), "If we allow international law to be replaced by the law of the first, in which the strong is always right, and has the right to do anything, then one of the most basic principles of international law will come into question: the inviolability of state sovereignty."[20] In light of recent debate about UN support for intervention in Syria, Russian Foreign Minister Sergey Lavrov declared: "Russia will seek respect for the sovereignty of states and noninterference in their internal affairs."[21]

There have been instances, however, when states traditionally opposed to infringements on sovereignty have supported actions that suggest some flexibility in their understanding of sovereignty. For example, China supported the international intervention in East Timor (1999). Moreover, it contributed to peacekeeping missions in several countries, such as Mozambique, the Western Sahara, Cambodia, and Iraq-Kuwait. More recently, China implicitly supported (through an abstention) a UNSC resolution to enforce a no-fly zone over Libya in 2011 amid mounting human rights abuses by its government forces. However, Chinese President, Hu Jintao, maintains: "China advocates full respect for every country's independence, sovereignty, unity and territorial integrity and does not approve of the use of force in international affairs."[22]

On the other side of the debate, major powers leaning toward a contingent norm of sovereignty include the US and the United Kingdom (UK). As US Secretary Rice in April 2007 pointed out:

The international system is experiencing a dramatic shift, one that we can trace through a series of humanitarian and political crises arising within nations, not necessarily between them; the failure of states from Somalia to Haiti, Bosnia to Afghanistan; and culminating in the events of September the 11th. As a result, we have been compelled to revise our old standard of sovereignty from mere state control to civil and global responsibility.[23]

This reflects the emerging consensus in the US that the norm of sovereignty is evolving. This movement began with the end of the Cold War and US involvement in Somalia, Bosnia, Kosovo, and Haiti. With regard to the brutality in Kosovo (1999), former President Bill Clinton argued for military intervention: "Ending this tragedy is a moral imperative."[24] Freed from Cold War geopolitical constraints, the US had the ability to engage these problems around the world. When it did not, the decision was strongly regretted. Former President Bill Clinton apologized to Rwandans for not intervening when genocide was occurring there: "We come here today partly in recognition of the fact that we in the United States and the world community did not do as much as we could have and should have done to try to limit what occurred."[25] From this perspective, the international community has a responsibility to protect citizens in states where their governments either lack the capability to act or engage in purposeful assault on their own people. In 2011, to prevent further human rights abuses and possibly massacres, US President Barack Obama justified the US role in the multilateral intervention in Libya: "To brush aside . . . our responsibilities to our fellow human beings under such circumstances would have been a betrayal of who we are."[26]

The United Kingdom has similar views:

> The U.N. needs new rules on when it can intervene to keep the peace within a state rather than between states. This is a real dilemma for an organization created to protect national sovereignty against threat. But it cannot be acceptable for oppressive regimes to claim the protection of sovereignty to carry out major violations of international law, such as genocide in Rwanda or ethnic cleansing in Kosovo.[27]

As early as 1999, former British Prime Minister Tony Blair began articulating potential criteria by which the international community could legitimately intervene in the affairs of a country to protect that domestic population.[28] While these comments were given within the context of the NATO-led intervention in Kosovo, Blair later expanded his "doctrine" from humanitarian considerations to security-related issues, arguing that "international terrorism post-9/11 and the spread of weapons of mass destruction require a further redefinition of the rights of a nation-state."[29]

Perhaps not willing to expand the concept of sovereignty that far, France is certainly amenable to the idea that human rights norms trump the norm of sovereignty. Though France believes that the United Nations Security Council has ultimate authority over decisions that would violate sovereignty, former President Chirac declared, with regard to Kosovo, "any military action must be requested and decided by the Security Council [but] the humanitarian situation constitutes a ground that can justify an exception to the rule, however strong and firm it is."[30] Reaffirming this view, perhaps more strongly, former President Nicholas Sarkozy spearheaded the 2011 military intervention in Libya, and President Francois Hollande has stated that an armed intervention in Syria is certainly an option, especially considering the Houla massacre.[31] For France, protecting human rights is more important than protecting states' rights to sovereignty.

In sum, these leading powers' perspectives reveal an emerging "sovereignty divide." Because sovereignty is at the very core of statehood, changes to it have significant implications for all players in the international system. Being recognized by other states as a sovereign member of the international system means that a state can participate in the community of states, empowered with the privileges and obligations that sovereignty brings. Yet, what it means to be a sovereign state is not only debated in the empirical world of politics but also among scholars of international relations. Having discussed the political debates on sovereignty, I now turn to the theoretical debates in the academic literature.


## Academic Debates on Sovereignty

During the Cold War, much of the literature in international relations rested on the parsimonious explanations of realism (Morgenthau 1948), later refined by neorealism (Waltz 1979). Realism and its variants have traditionally been used to explain state military actions. This school makes two primary assumptions: (1) anarchy dominates the international system; and (2) states are self-interested, unitary actors (Waltz 1979). States, as rational actors, seek power and security in order to survive in the international system (Jervis 1976; Oye 1985; Walt 1987; Waltz 1979). Geostrategic interests and economic concerns are the primary motivations for state behavior and in particular, the use of force.

Regardless of the motives they assign to states, whether to enhance power or security, both realism and neorealism assume absolute state sovereignty, the ability of a state to "decide for itself how it will cope with its internal and external problems" (Waltz 1979, 96). As a consequence, sovereignty is "one [principle] that will not be dislodged easily, regardless of changed circumstances in the material environment" (Krasner 1988, 90).[32] However, the theory implies that sovereignty is contingent on the power of a state. In a world in which "the strong do what they can, the weak do what they must" (Thucydides 1910), some states are more sovereign than others. While realism and neorealism are useful to our understanding of the causes of conflict, they do not allow for any mechanism by which change can occur in international relations and thus offer little insight into how the rights and obligations of states vary across contexts.

The other major strand of literature, neoliberalism and its variants, while sharing some assumptions with realism/neorealism, acknowledge the possibility of change, if only indirectly (Keohane and Nye 1977). Scholars of this school are primarily interested in explaining cooperation among self-interested states, which has led to a plethora of analyses focused on international regimes and organizations. Cooperative developments in the international system, like the evolution of the European Union, pose important questions concerning the nature of sovereignty, since they challenge mechanistic, power-based models of state interaction. However, the scholarship that does engage these questions tends to consider sovereignty as a matter of state control, rather than state authority (Thomson 1995). Moreover, even if this approach recognizes the potential for change in the nature of sovereignty, it largely focuses on structure, with little regard for agency.

The idea that humans, as agents, contribute to the maintenance and creation of social reality, or social facts, is one of the core tenets of the constructivist school. In this perspective, concepts like sovereignty are variables, not constants. Constructivism takes seriously the logic of appropriateness, which refers to what states ought to do, given social conventions or rules, procedures, and principles for members within a particular group context (Finnemore 1998; March and Olsen 1998). While not *dis*regarding material interests, constructivists offer a compelling explanation for state actions by emphasizing the role of identity, norms, and ideas (Black 1999; Hopf 2002; Legro 1997; Risse, Ropp, and Sikkink 1999).

In explaining varying conceptions of sovereignty, these scholars rely on the ability of actors to shape intersubjective understandings of sovereignty (Biersteker and Weber 1996). For example, some argue that the definition of sovereignty fluctuates according to dominant ideas in the international system. Barkin and Cronin (1994) argue that the post–World War II era stressed *state* sovereignty, rather than the nation-based definition, in reaction to the extreme nationalism of Nazis. This could be one reason that during this period sovereignty trumped individual rights. Similarly, others assert identity as the engine of change, in that changes in collective identities drive changes in the constitutive rules of sovereignty (Hall 1999). If the most salient identity of citizens is that regarding the state (i.e., patriotism), then sovereignty will be defined in terms of the state. In contrast, if the group identity becomes the most important, it will be reflected in a sovereignty that focuses on the rights of the group.

These contributions and other constructivist research offer important insights for understanding state sovereignty and its evolution. They illuminate an important part of the story by demonstrating the influence of ideas and identities on conceptions of sovereignty. However, there is one missing link—action. Without action taken on its behalf, we cannot know what sovereignty really means at any given point in time. Leaders in the international community can argue that states have certain obligations to fulfill, as in the area of protecting human rights, but without actions to bolster these claims, this discourse remains empty rhetoric. In other words, the concept of sovereignty (as with any concept) is necessarily grounded in action. As argued in the following chapter, the meaning of sovereignty is dependent on the actions taken on its behalf. Political actions have the ability to shape ideas about sovereignty. We know that changes to sovereignty have occurred when we see both changes in related actions and their corresponding discourse.

## Outline of the Book

In the next chapter, I develop the theoretical framework for the book, in which I address change as a function of both structure and agency. In terms of structure, I first discuss the conditions necessary for norm change to occur, which are derived from an evolutionary perspective. These conditions are that the norm must be prominent in the international system, it must be compatible with other norms, and it must face structural conditions conducive to change (Florini 1996). To address agency, I then draw on cognitive dissonance to specify the mechanism by which change occurs. Clearly, states with a preponderance of power have a disproportionate say in which norms get propagated within the international community because they have the capability to act on behalf of a norm, if they wish. However, I argue that even when a major power acts primarily out of its own self-interest, with the normative argument being secondary, the action may have the *unintended* consequence of modifying the normative environment within which other (minor power) states act. The theory proposed in this book offers a counterintuitive explanation for these phenomena. One would generally expect an arduous military intervention to exhibit *less* commitment to the norms that it embodies. But the opposite may be true. Insights from social psychology, and cognitive dissonance in particular, lead us to expect that such a situation would actually yield *more* commitment to the norms that were used to justify the intervention. Thus, leading states are able to pursue their material agenda, but with norm evolution as the by-product of military intervention. I conclude chapter 2 with a discussion of the empirical approach taken to investigate my theoretical arguments. I rely on content analysis of United Nations Security Council speeches and case studies of policy responses (including inaction) by leading states (China, Russia, United States, United Kingdom, and France) in issue areas at the top of the international agenda in the post–Cold War era: global terrorism, human rights, and weapons of mass destruction.

The next three chapters focus on the empirical examination of the theory presented, each taking on a different policy domain. Chapter 3 examines state sovereignty in the context of global terrorism. The war in Afghanistan was the first time a global coalition intervened in a state on behalf of counterterrorism. In reaction to the terrorist attacks on the World Trade Center and the Pentagon in 2001, the UN Security Council unanimously adopted Resolution 1373, which "obliges all States to criminalize assistance for terrorist activities, deny financial support and safe haven to terrorists and share information about groups planning terrorist attacks." In other words, in the interest of international peace and security, states have the responsibility to the international community to uphold certain standards of internal behavior in the realm of counterterrorism. As demonstrated by the military intervention in Afghanistan shortly after the resolution, states that fail to comply risk the possibility of external interference and at its most extreme, foreign military intervention. The chapter investigates how the rights and obligations of states have changed (or not) in this regard by focusing on leading states that intervened militarily in Afghanistan, the United States and the United Kingdom, and then contrasting them with two major powers that did not intervene, China and Russia.

In sum, the chapter finds support for its expectations. First, the extent to which a contingent norm of sovereignty is accepted by a state depends, at least in part, on the process and outcome of the military intervention, including the domestic political costs and benefits, for the intervener. Second, leading states that are not directly involved in the military intervention will moderately change their views toward contingent sovereignty, as the cases of Russia and China demonstrated, due to their nonculpability and self-interest in this issue area. What seems clear, regarding the states examined, is that an event like 9/11 acts as a *contributing* condition for norm evolution, but an action such as military intervention provides the actual *mechanism* by which changes in states' understandings of sovereignty occur.

Chapter 4 is concerned with the intersection of human rights and sovereignty norms. With the establishment of the International Bill of Human Rights in the second half of the twentieth century, the "responsibility to protect" individuals from threats to their existence and dignity creates a tension with the principle of sovereignty (Deng et al.1996; Evans and Sahnoun 2002). The chapter explores the humanitarian crisis in Somalia and the extent to which military intervention (1992–1993) on behalf of human rights affected the norm of sovereignty. Though the mission was initially successful, it later encountered significant difficulties from Somali warlord Mohamed Farrah Aidid. The chapter examines the extent to which understandings of sovereignty in this issue domain changed before and after the intervention by focusing on the United States and France as interveners, and China and Russia as noninterveners. The examination demonstrates that France and the United States placed greater emphasis on sovereignty as contingent on compliance with human rights norms after the intervention than before, even though the mission was ultimately a failure. For the two nonintervening states, their culpability in this area largely explained why they held to a strict code of absolute sovereignty.

The issue area of chapter 5 is weapons of mass destruction. Chapter 5 explores the policy domain of weapons of mass destruction within the context of Iraq. Conceptually distinct, though related to terrorism, weapons of mass destruction are another controversial matter for sovereignty. Some states argue that it is their sovereign right to produce weapons of mass destruction, but, at the same time, they are pressed by international obligations *not* to. For example, former French president Nicolas Sarkozy asserted in his first major foreign policy speech: "Iran could be attacked militarily if it did not live up to its international obligations to curb its nuclear program."[33] Although the US-led intervention in Iraq was conducted without the backing of the UN Security Council, it certainly demonstrates the plausibility of this claim. The United States had argued that the international community had a right to intervene to prevent Iraq's further development of weapons of mass destruction. Although such weapons were never found, the chapter investigates how the US-led war in Iraq has shaped understandings of state sovereignty by analyzing the cases of the primary interveners, the United States and the United Kingdom, and comparing them with the cases of France and Russia as noninterveners. The chapter asserts that the military intervention in Iraq provided a potential impetus for change toward contingent sovereignty. However, because of the false premises of the intervention (i.e., the failure to find WMD), the predictions were not borne out. Rather, the evidence showed that the action reinforced absolute sovereignty in the cases of the interveners. As for the noninterveners, state culpability and self-interest were found to be important predictors of attitudes toward sovereignty, providing support for the desire of a state to maintain cognitive consistency.

To conclude the book, I first consider the theoretical contribution of this study, which rests on two ideas: first, the usefulness of a social psychological approach in explaining phenomena in international relations, and second, the role of action in shaping ideas. Next, I synthesize the results of the empirical chapters and draw out the major themes throughout the investigation. I compare and contrast the changes in conceptions of sovereignty across the cases and discuss the implications of this research for norm change more broadly, as well as how the findings might be extended to lesser powers. Following this, I consider the extent to which contingent soverignty is desirable for international peace and security in the international system. I then explore current events in light of the evolving concept of sovereignty, and offer some thoughts on some possible limitations in its evolution. I end with some thoughts for foreign policymakers to consider.

# CHAPTER 2 | Accounting for New Visions of Sovereignty

There remains now the one question concerning an honorable cause for waging war . . . which is undertaken for no private reasons of our own, but for the common interest and in behalf of others. Look you, if men clearly sin against the laws of nature and of mankind, I believe that any one whatsoever may check such men by force of arms.

—ALBERICO GENTILI, *De Jure Belli Libri Tres*, 1598

AS THE WORLD FACES a multitude of challenges, from genocide to nuclear weapons development, military intervention is one policy response that states or international organizations (e.g., the United Nations) consider. Yet, the consequences of these actions on ideas about the "rules of the game" do not always generate much interest or concern, though their implications for the international system and its future are significant. As discussed in the preceding chapter, state sovereignty is a pillar of international relations, the foundation on which states' rights and obligations in the international community are constructed. It produces a level of certainty in state interactions, so that states can conduct foreign relations as sovereign equals. But amidst changing international contexts, we expect that reigning conceptions of sovereignty would, as most norms do, evolve as states engage the issues of the day. Rather than taking the usual approach of examining how norms influence political policy, I investigate the reverse causal direction by asking how political policies and their related actions influence the development of norms, with the underlying premise that it is through action that previously unarticulated ideas may become sources of explicit general principles that guide state behavior.

I propose a counterintuitive theory to explain how changes in understandings of sovereignty might occur, specifically, as a consequence of military intervention. Military intervention is often considered the ultimate violation of a state's sovereignty, and it is at the intersection of these two concepts, military intervention and sovereignty, that the meaning of each is revealed.[1] Here, I focus solely on how military intervention shapes understandings of sovereignty, given the presence of conditions conducive to normative change. Drawing largely from insights of social psychology's cognitive dissonance, I argue that an arduous and costly intervention yields *stronger*, rather than weaker (as a cost-benefit approach would suggest) allegiance to an understanding of state sovereignty as one in which certain international standards of behavior must be met.

## Normative Evolution as Reflection of Action

A theory focused on change must take into account the contextual features of the environment within which change occurs, as well as the individual-level mechanism(s) that drives the change. As I am interested in how norms change, and since norms (and normative structures) are part of the social structure that both guide and are shaped by social agents, I begin with the insights of *structuration theory*, which presents a holistic approach to social explanations. Explanations based only on agents (or actors) fail to contextualize the agent within a given environment and the influence that the environment may have on the choices made by the agents (Adler 1997; Hay 2002). For example, classical realism is largely agent-focused in that it accounts for war in terms of human nature (Morgenthau 1948; Thucydides 1910). At the same time, structure-based explanations ignore the power of individuals to influence the environment and are unable to explain changes in structures (Adler 1997; Hay 2002). Neorealism, a derivative of classical realism, focuses on structure to explain conflict in the international system (Waltz 1979), but it ignores aspects of agency that cannot be accounted for by structural processes. Largely for that reason, neorealism was sharply criticized for failing to predict changes to the international system (e.g., the end of the Cold War).

The goal of structuration theory is to reconcile agent-based explanations with structure-based accounts of social phenomena. Structuration theory offers a dynamic understanding of how the world works, as most influentially articulated by Anthony Giddens (1984). It attempts to explain how certain social outcomes are possible, given the mutually dependent factors of structure and agency. By terming his theory "structur*ation*," Giddens reveals the core of his assumptions; "structure" is not a static notion but rather a *process* (1984). In reconceptualizing structure as a duality, Giddens attempts to move away from traditional conceptions of structure that are fixed and ventures toward one in which agents (actors) have the power to alter the structure within which they act, consciously or not.

Structuration theory views agents and structures as co-determined; one cannot causally separate the individuals from the context (across time and space) within which they act. While structure refers to the rules governing society that arise from social interaction, it concerns more fundamentally the concepts embodied in actions. For example, widely accepted and abiding ideas within a society about the meaning of social justice or the proper structure of authority may qualify as social structures. Structure *may thus be* composed of the ideas that are held by actors that then guide their behavior.

As such, these actors have a "transformative capacity" by which they are able to shape the structure (Giddens 1984). Since they act on their beliefs, they contribute to the creation or reproduction of the structure of ideas that guided them in the first place. This iterative process leads to the routinization of actions because the ideas behind them are reinforced as each action takes place (Searle 1995). In this perspective, actors are knowledgeable and therefore able to influence the constitution of ideas through their actions.

A concrete example of structuration is found in the development of language, which is a structure that emerges, not from a predetermined plan, but from actions viewed as attempts to communicate via sound. Language arose as a mechanism to communicate based on sounds and the meanings each signified. This evolved into a specific linguistic structure, in which language took on rules known as grammar. The grammar then regulates that language, which is constantly being reinforced as it is used. In a more general sense, everyday practice gave rise to a structure, which reproduced the practice. In turn, language shapes behavior, via the intersubjective meanings it creates. In this sense, the structure both enables and constrains the practices of the agents.

## Influence of Actions on Ideas

Though scholars tend to study the effect of ideas on actions, there is precedent for studying the reverse causal direction. In fact, pragmatist philosophers have long theorized that the only way to study the relationship between ideas (e.g., sovereignty norms) and actions (e.g., military intervention) is by looking at how actions shape ideas. According to John Dewey, ideas only take on meaning if they produce observable outcomes (Dewey 1929). Actions are viewed as evidence of what people really believe, or as economists would say, "revealed preferences." If we talk to someone who is antiglobalization, but does nothing to this end, it is unclear whether that person is being earnest. However, if we see that same person protesting the World Trade Organization, we then know that this person is antiglobalization. In the context of this study, this means that the act of military intervention reflects real beliefs; it is a manifestation of what states believe, transcending rhetoric, although the actor herself may also help shape and create beliefs. This in no way implies that only one belief is embodied in military action. In practice, we know that military interventions reveal different kinds of ideas about what states value, from material to moral interests, as well as beliefs about the proper conduct of states in the international community.[2]

Similarly, William James believed that the truth of an idea is revealed by events associated with it (1907). What is "true" depends on the context of the situation. The concepts that survive are those that are useful for a society at that specific time. In his view, experience continually tests and determines the content of a society's values. This suggests that military intervention, *the action*, encourages states to constantly reassess their understandings of sovereignty. If the military intervention reveals that the current sovereignty norm is not useful to a state, it will adapt a new version of sovereignty with a better fit to the context. In contrast, if the intervention reaffirms current conceptions of sovereignty, then the state will have no incentive to change it. In this way, sovereignty as a concept is in flux.

## Sovereignty Defined

What is sovereignty? It is generally agreed that (absolute) sovereignty can be broadly defined as "supreme authority within a territory" (Philpott 2001, 16). Absolute sovereignty assumes that a government's policies are legally protected by international law and that external actors cannot seek to modify those policies. For many years, since its codification in the Peace of Westphalia, absolute sovereignty has served as the dominant norm in the international system. Yet, sovereign authority can be less than absolute, and thus I conceive of sovereignty in the political sense as a continuum (Rosenau 1995, 195), from absolute sovereignty in the

| Absolute | Contingent | World Government |
|:--------:|:----------:|:----------------:|
| ◆------------------------------------◆------------------------------------◆ | | |

FIGURE 2.1 Sovereignty Continuum

Westphalian tradition to world government, in which states exercise little independent authority over their internal affairs. More conservatively, world government does not necessarily mean a global Leviathan, but a "federation, a union of separate states that allocate certain powers to a central government while retaining many others for themselves."[3] Between these two poles, one may locate "contingent sovereignty."[4] With contingent sovereignty, a state is required to maintain certain standards of political performance, wherein external intervention is allowed when these standards are egregiously violated (ICISS 2001; Jackson 1990; Keren and Sylvan 2002). As depicted in Figure 2.1, the closer we move in the direction of world government, the more numerous and stringent the sovereignty contingencies become.

Sovereignty has no meaning in and of itself. Rather, it is an intersubjective process involving the existing rules of the international system (structure) and state actors (agents). A change in one affects the other, producing a dynamic relationship. Any conception of sovereignty thus reflects a process, rather than a constant state. For example, the action (military intervention) of a state can influence the rules of the international system and in turn the subsequent behavior of states. It is at the interstate level, relations between states, where sovereignty resides. A state cannot be sovereign unless it is recognized as so by other states (Ashley 1984; Miller 1984; Jackson 1990). Moreover, "an independent political community which merely claims a right to sovereignty . . . but cannot assert this right in practice, is not a state properly so-called" (Bull 1977, 9).

## Two Sides of the Same Coin: Rights and Obligations

Sovereignty refers to a set of both rights and obligations concerning a legally constituted state; these are opposite sides of the same coin. States have rights that dictate which of their actions are legitimate in the eyes of the international community. At the same time, they have obligations to uphold and on which their sovereign rights rest. Rights and obligations vary over time, according to the international context, making sovereignty an evolving norm. Rights and obligations may be positive or negative, in the sense that positive rights and obligations encompass what a state is allowed to do, whereas negative rights and obligations dictate what a state

TABLE 2.1 Changes in Conceptions of Sovereignty

| Before the end of the Cold War (traditional view) | | |
|---|---|---|
| | Right | Obligation |
| State | X | |
| International Community | | X |
| After the Cold War (evolving view) | | |
| | Right | Obligation |
| State | | X |
| International Community | X | |

cannot be obliged to do. For example, a state has a right to file a complaint with the World Trade Organization (positive right), but a state also has the right not to grant citizenship to foreign nationals (negative right). A state is obliged to comply with international treaties (positive obligation), but a state also has no obligation to become a signatory (negative obligation).

Sovereignty also can be viewed through the lens of a state (self) and the international community (other). As I described in chapter 1 in the history of sovereignty, and as table 2.1 illustrates, there has been a shift in sovereignty along these dimensions. Formerly, a state had the *right* to conduct its affairs as it saw fit, behind the shield of sovereignty. Other states had the *obligation* to respect the sovereignty of that state, thereby reinforcing their own state sovereignty.

As the Cold War faded and new challenges appeared on the global scene, a gradual change in conceptions of sovereignty emerged among major powers. As seen in table 2.1, there is an incipient trend, in which a new "division of responsibility" imposes revised "rules of the game" for individual states and the international community. States now have *obligations* to fulfill in order to be sovereign, and the international community has a *right* to intervene in the internal affairs of states under certain conditions.

As discussed in the previous chapter, in the 1990s, unhindered by Cold War geostrategic constraints, we saw growing evidence of states' willingness to intervene in the affairs of other states, in support of an emerging normative consensus on legitimate state behavior (Finnemore 2003). As Martha Finnemore notes, in Europe, NATO intervened in the former Yugoslavia on behalf of Albanian Kosovars and Bosnians threatened by ethnic cleansing. In Asia, the UN militarily attended to the crisis in Cambodia and helped rebuild the country. In the Middle East, the US, Britain, and France resorted to force to protect the Kurds from persecution in Iraq (Finnemore 2003, 52). In many of these cases, the decision to intervene reflected changing ideas not just about the use of force, as Finnemore argues, but also about state sovereignty,[5] which increasingly assumes that states must fulfill certain obligations to be recognized as full sovereigns, while the international community has the right to intervene when the state cannot fulfill its duties.

To explore the evolution of the norm of sovereignty, I look at conditions necessary for change in conceptions of sovereignty at the systemic level, as well as the mechanism of change at the state level. A multilevel theory is useful for providing context and detail to the questions of interest, and it more closely mirrors the real world with its multiple layers and moving parts. Working at only one level of analysis leaves an incomplete picture of how norms change, because change involves both the actor and the structure within which the actor operates. While analyzing the interaction of agent and structure presents more challenges for the analysis, it offers a more satisfying account of the richness and complexity of social phenomena.

## Necessary Conditions for Normative Change

Evolutionary models provide a useful starting point for thinking about necessary conditions for the norm of sovereignty to change. These models, traditionally found in the biological sciences, have been helpful in understanding change in the political world, in areas such as foreign policy analysis (Farkas 1996), states' involvement in interstate conflicts (Maoz 1989), and the formation of global institutions (Modelski 1996).[6] I draw on evolutionary theory and ideas about "punctuated equilibriums" to develop a theory of change in sovereignty norms by identifying the conditions necessary for change. In the following section, I specify the mechanism, cognitive dissonance, by which this occurs.

Though evolutionary models are gaining attention within political science, many scholars remain unfamiliar with them. At the most basic level, an evolutionary model simply explains how one type of information triumphs over another, void of any normative claims. Central to this model are identifying the kind of information transmitted, the mechanism(s) for transmission, and the selection mechanism that controls how quickly the information is communicated (Farkas 1996, 348; Maynard Smith 1978; Dawkins 1989). For example, in explaining the evolution of patriotism, Johnson (1997) argues that patriotism is "a predisposition to altruistic behavior on behalf of a system as a whole" (47) that "helps groups of humans pursue their interests" (83) and is transmitted through nepotism and reciprocity. When a group is threatened, patriotism will trump other predispositions, such as partisanship. This theory of the evolution of patriotism broadly resembles theories on the evolution of genes.

Comparing the most common objects of evolutionary models, genes, with the focus of this study, norms, we find compelling parallels, as Ann Florini (1996) points out. Both genes and norms instruct certain behavior within their respective organism given certain environmental conditions (Florini 1996, 367). Moreover, both genes and norms communicate future behavior through inheritance, in the form of either cultural transmission or biological reproduction. Finally, genes and norms are constantly in competition with their respective cohort for prominence in the process of natural selection. Given these similarities, it is reasonable to think that an evolutionary model might have something to offer for an understanding of norm development (Florini 1996).

Florini (1996) advances an underappreciated perspective of norm evolution using insights from population genetics.[7] While the analogy between norms and genes is not perfect, because humans enjoy some free choice, the evolutionary model is useful in suggesting what most mainstream theories of international relations ignore—how change occurs. Florini (1996) suggests that three factors explain how norms are selected: prominence, coherence, and environmental conditions. Each condition is a necessary, but not sufficient, part of the story. In terms of genetic evolution, prominence means that genes must have the opportunity to reproduce. For norms, prominence refers to the ability of a norm to gain a foothold among the many competing norms in the international system. This normally occurs when a norm entrepreneur promotes the norm (Finnemore and Sikkink 1998; Nadelmann 1990; Mueller 1989) and/or the "mutant" norm occurs in a major power (Florini 1996, 374; Price and Tannenwald 1996; Ikenberry 1993). What follows from prominence is the emulation of the new norm by other states, compelled by self-interest or reputational concerns, among others.[8] With respect to the norm of sovereignty under investigation here, I expect to see the rising prominence of a preference for contingent sovereignty, driven by the great powers, alongside norm entrepreneurs, such as the United Nations.

The second condition necessary for norm change is coherence, which relates to the legitimacy of the norm. When a foundation already exists in which the norm can "settle in" to, the new norm is more likely to survive. In order for a norm to change, or evolve, there must be a supportive normative structure (a good fit with other genotypes) within which the new norms can be incorporated or reprioritized.[9] In this sense, the new norm cannot change into something that goes entirely against current societal norms (the gene pool). This recognizes that norms do not occur within a vacuum but exist through the social interaction of states. During this process, the new norm either gains legitimacy or is cast aside. This presents quite a challenge for new norms, "because most existing norms are codified in international law, emerging norms must make the case that they are logical extensions of the law—or necessary changes to it" (Florini 1996, 377).

The final necessary condition is the environment, or the circumstances faced by the population of norms. In other words, are there material and ideational conditions that will serve to strengthen a particular norm? Such conditions may range from technological capabilities to distributions of state power to communication resources. In order for a norm to survive—and thrive—the environment should be hospitable to the spread of the norm. For example, the advent of new media and the rise of human rights norms provide an environment conducive to the proliferation of democratic norms in the Middle East. At the same time, the extent to which democratic norms diffuse depends on individual actors to drive the change within this "ripe" environment.

To review, the prominence of a norm, the coherence of the new norm with other established norms, and environmental circumstances are all necessary conditions for the evolution of norms. Before going further, though, let me highlight one *contributing* condition that I will highlight here. While not a necessary or sufficient condition for normative change, specific events that occur as shocks to the international system serve as contributing conditions that may also compel actors to change their behaviors and beliefs about the world, given that the necessary conditions are met. While evolutionary theory considers change a gradual process, it may be that large-scale events that impact the global system encourage rapid and discontinuous change, in one of many possible directions. This has often been characterized in the institutionalist literature within political science as a "punctuated equilibrium" (Hall 1999; Pierson 1996; Skocpol and Ikenberry 1983). Punctuated equilibrium implies that there are long periods of relative stasis, with short bursts of massive change (Goertz 2003, 132). Indeed, scholars of species evolution (Berggren and van Couvering 1984; Gould and Eldredge 1977) are now moving away from traditional notions of evolution and finding increasing evidence of a punctuated equilibrium in evolutionary biology (Hay 2002, 160; Gould and Eldredge 1993). However, as Hay writes, a more apt description of this occurrence is "punctuated evolution" (2002, 163). In this way, one captures the prospect for change between and because of crises. "Evolution" suggests gradual change while the "punctuated" acknowledges the potential impact of a shock to the environment to create change.

Moreover, adding the "punctuated" to the evolutionary theory of norm change allows us to consider the influence of actor-induced events in international relations. As contributing conditions for change, these are events that are generally large in scale, humanly dramatic, and have a global reach. They generally demand remedial action. 9/11 is one striking example in recent memory that few would debate. Unfortunately, there are numerous other examples, such as the 1994 Rwandan genocide, the 2007 terrorist bombings in London and Glasgow, the 2004 train bombing in Madrid, the WWII atomic bombing of Japan, and the current humanitarian crisis in Darfur. Though these events present opportunities for change on a number of issues (e.g., protecting human rights, limiting nuclear weapons), change is not inevitable.

Events may encourage normative change by highlighting an issue that was previously sidelined by other policy pursuits. This happens for several reasons. First, with advances in media technology, citizens around the world are instantly linked to the crises in once distant lands. Second, because these crises are shocking to human sensibilities, they grab the attention of policy elites and their citizenry, and encourage them to consider policy options to address the crisis. The event, in essence, forces itself onto the policy agenda. In seeking to remedy the crisis, if the policy chosen is incongruent with current state or international norms of behavior, norm change may occur through political attempts to justify the new policy. These justifications contribute to the reshaping of the normative structure.

Since events may spark a powerful chain of policy choices, we must look at the major powers making the decisions behind these choices. These actors have the ability to maintain the status quo or induce change in the normative assumptions of international relations: "It is the powerful that are generally at the origin of norms" (Goertz and Diehl 1992, 639). Similarly, I argue that changes in sovereignty occur based on the actions of leading states in the international community.[10] As noted in the previous chapter, these states set the rules of the game for international relations. Previous attempts to modify sovereignty, as in the minority-protection treaties of the League of Nations, found little success because major states were not willing to acknowledge this *in practice*. Even if small states sought to change a norm, they would have to build a consensus with the major powers in order for that norm to change.

Why focus on leading states? At a minimum, the content of sovereignty varies depending on the "consensus among coreflective statesmen" (Ashley 1984, 273), or transnational elites (Meyer 1980). Some assert that these leaders must be the European or great powers (Bull and Watson 1982; Thomson 1995). For example, previous studies have shown that new norms, such as state control over nonstate violence (Thomson 1990), depend on leading states' practices in order to become universalized. Thus, I focus on leading states, defined as states that have the capability and will to intervene, and therefore a potential impact on conceptions of state sovereignty in the international community.

Increasingly, though not without controversy, the leading states are considered to be the permanent members of the UN Security Council, among others.[11] As China noted, "The Security Council . . . play[s] a leading role" in the maintenance of international peace and security.[12] In addition, the actions of the Security Council are supposed to reflect the voice of the international community. Regarding sanctions against Libya's recent human rights abuses, the United States remarked: "The Council's action . . . sends the clearest possible signal that the international community will not tolerate such conduct."[13] Moreover, it is now more common to judge the legitimacy of a military intervention on the approval of the UN Security Council. For example, the US-led war in Iraq was seen as an illegitimate military action because it was not approved by the UN Security Council. I therefore focus on conceptions of sovereignty held by the permanent members (and veto players) of the UN Security Council: the United States, the United Kingdom, China, Russia and France.

## Cognitive Dissonance

So far, I have discussed necessary and contributing conditions for a new norm to take root within the normative structure. Although this normative structure *guides* state behavior, it is also *shaped* by state behavior. Thus, I attend now to one way in which states influence this structure through their actions. Though guided by punctuated evolutionary theory, in contrast to biological organisms, I must take into account the ability of humans to make choices and to reason. I therefore draw on cognitive theories, since a state's decisions can be regarded as the collective decision of its key decision-makers (Snyder et al. 1962, 65), and hence, subject to psychological analysis.[14] Whereas the evolutionary model would suggest that norm reproduction occurs mainly through individual emulation (horizontal reproduction[15]) of successful states' behavior, I am interested in determining how the "successful" states reinforce or modify existing norms. Emulation may reflect norm change in states with less prestigious status, but whom do you emulate if you are one of the leading states?[16] I propose that a cognitive dissonance model more closely reflects the real-world mechanisms of norm change for the leading powers.[17]

Within a complex and uncertain international environment, leading states may change their conception of certain norms only after knowing the outcome of a behavior based on that norm. In this way, a norm may come into being without the explicit rational calculation of the leading states. This proposition rests on cognitive dissonance theory, which explains how our ideas may be influenced by our actions. Developed by Leon Festinger (1957), the theory begins with the observation that relevant cognitions, or pieces of knowledge, can either be consonant or dissonant. If consonant, they create no psychological tension because they are mutually implied. However, if the cognitions clash, or are not mutually implied, they create psychological discomfort for the person or social entity, which one will seek to lessen by avoiding information that accentuates it or by changing the cognition. In addition, one will exaggerate the benefits of the chosen decision and downplay the drawbacks, while applying the reverse to the alternatives not chosen (Shultz and Lepper 1996).

The classic example of cognitive dissonance is the chain smoker who learns that smoking is bad for his health (Festinger 1957). The smoker has two options to reduce the dissonance. First, the smoker can quit smoking so the behavior matches the cognition regarding health. Second, the smoker may rationalize that smoking is not so bad and that it enhances his pleasure in life, disproportionately to the risk. Such examples also abound in political life. For instance, citizens who voted for President Clinton and then learned of the Monica Lewinsky scandal, may have rationalized their support for Clinton by trumpeting his political achievements, while deeming irrelevant his personal life. Or, US legislators who initially supported the Iraq war in 2003 and were then faced with the mission's declining success, either withdrew their support or intensified their efforts justifying the war. In both examples, people resolve cognitive dissonance by bringing their beliefs in line with their previous actions.

Cognitive dissonance has a long tradition in psychology and has sparked a number of research paradigms. This is mainly because Festinger's original theory was cast in "very general, highly abstract terms" (Harmon-Jones and Mills 1999, 5). A number of research paradigms in cognitive dissonance research have since been developed. These include the free-choice paradigm (Brehm 1956; Shultz and Lepper 1996), the belief-disconfirmation paradigm (Burris, Harmon-Jones, and Tarpley 1997; Festinger, Riecken, and Schachter 1956), and the effort-justification paradigm (Beauvois and Joule 1996; Aronson and Mills 1959). Each explores how cognition interacts with motivation and emotion within a cognitive dissonance framework.

One particularly interesting line of research has focused on the condition of forced compliance and cognitive dissonance. This research further refines and specifies the mechanisms by which people bring their previously dissonant cognitions in line with one another. When someone behaves discordantly with her beliefs or attitudes, dissonance is aroused. However, promises of reward or threat of punishment help alleviate psychological tension caused by dissonance (Harmon-Jones and Mills 1999, 8). These new cognitions aid in justifying the given action so that a person achieves cognitive consistency. Several experiments support these conclusions. In one experiment, scholars found that the smaller the reward for saying what one does not believe, the more the opinion changes to agree with what was said (Festinger and Carlsmith 1959). In another experiment focusing on punishment (the "forbidden toy" experiment), scholars found that the less threat of punishment, the less positive one is about something, and the more threat of punishment, the more positive one is about something (Aronson and Carlsmith 1963).

Cognitive dissonance theory is especially applicable to cases of military interventions because of the tension between two competing cognitions, sovereignty norms of nonintervention, on the one hand, and enforcing international peace and security, on the other hand. Because of this tension and a host of other domestic and international concerns, the decision to intervene is not taken lightly. Research has shown that in such cases, when a decision is especially difficult to make, greater dissonance occurs than when one is faced with an easier decision (Brehm 1956). Moreover, scholars have suggested that "social psychological mechanisms, such as cognitive dissonance," contribute to changes in social purpose and thereby shifts in normative understandings (Finnemore 2003, 67).

Resolving dissonance has important implications for how states reconcile the norm of sovereignty with military action that violates it. For example, in the context of humanitarian military intervention, state sovereignty as a concept that *includes* obligations to protect human rights cannot exist merely as an idea in a vacuum; it becomes meaningful only when action is taken on behalf of human rights. Depending on the outcomes of the military intervention, this action may contribute to the idea that human rights norms trump absolute sovereignty norms; absolute sovereignty and sovereignty contingent on compliance with human rights norms cannot coexist because they are competing cognitions that imply different sets of rules that guide state behavior (Festinger 1957; Brehm 1956). In a state's view, one norm must necessarily dominate the other.

The use of cognitive dissonance theory assumes an elite-driven process, in that leaders shape the content of public information (Converse 1964; Zaller 1990, 1992). As Converse asserted, belief systems diffuse from elites to the masses since elites often serve as the source of ideologies (1964). Moreover, the masses are not likely to hold readily accessible opinions on any given topic, and so they rely on cues from elites (Zaller 1992). This is especially likely to occur when these topics involve matters "out of reach, out of sight" (Zaller 1992, 8). As I am interested here in states' conceptions of sovereignty, which are clearly removed from an average individual's direct observation and/or understanding, the assumption of a top-down process seems reasonable.

Given that leaders' primary goal is to stay in office (Mayhew 1974), they need to construct a legitimizing public narrative for their actions. This must be consistent throughout their tenure, because inconsistent cues will likely lead to public distrust and a delegitimation of a leader's policies. To maintain legitimacy in the eyes of their publics, leaders need decision outcomes to reaffirm the rationale for their decisions. Especially in situations that threaten to call leaders' competence into question, such as continuing a losing conflict overseas, I expect leaders to justify their decisions by emphasizing the norm that prompted the action, in order to minimize cognitive dissonance among their constituency. This occurs because leaders, to protect their legitimate right to rule, will seek to reduce the dissonance that their public encounters trying to reconcile the *value* of the norm with the *cost* that adherence to the norm comes with. In the course of politics, leaders as individuals may be acclimated to a certain level of dissonance that their publics are not. I thus focus on cognitive dissonance as it relates to the leaders' justifications for their publics, rather than any dissonance that occurs for the leaders themselves.

## Attributes of Intervention: Costs and Success

Because I am interested in how the process of military intervention affects the sovereignty norm, I focus on two important pieces of information about the intervention: its costs and success. By costs, I mean both the casualties and the political liabilities created at home for the intervener.

I regard success in terms of the degree to which the intervention's objective has been achieved. Taken together, the costs and success of an intervention, via cognitive dissonance, aid in forming specific expectations about the conditions under which contingent sovereignty will be reinforced or challenged.

Why costs and success? Within the rational choice paradigm, scholars regularly employ models that incorporate the likely costs and the probability of success to predict the policy choices of decision-makers (Bueno de Mesquita 1981, 2000; Allison and Zelikow 1999; McDermott 1992). In these models, "the decision maker uses a maximizing strategy in calculating how best to achieve his goals" (Bueno de Mequita 1981, 31). The decision-maker evaluates different options and then selects the "alternative that offers the best combination of a high probability of success and low cost" (Ray 1998, 123). In general, a rationalist would expect that a policy yielding minimal results would be shelved, while a student of cognitive dissonance would predict that the decision-maker might reinforce her commitment to the policy in the same situation, because doing so relieves the psychological tension posed by the dissonant cognitions. Rationalist approaches overlook the fact that, in addition to weighing pieces of information, decision-makers also typically work in a complex political environment that may alter the internal decision-making processes of individuals. Decisions are not simply a result of a mechanical process but rather the results of an individual's cognitive interaction with information. Thus, while both approaches may use the same criteria (costs and success) to form expectations, there is a sharp divergence between their expectations.

## Cognitive Dissonance and Intervention

Whereas a rational choice, cost-benefit analysis suggests that an intervener would reconsider the normative purpose underlying a costly and difficult intervention, a cognitive dissonance approach asserts otherwise.[18] Why? The justification for military intervention rests on the belief that, in the current setting of international normative evolution, certain principles of state behavior trump the norm of sovereignty. If a state fails to carry out the basic duties prescribed by the normative order, the international community may be justified in engaging in military intervention to remedy the problem—implying a norm of contingent (rather than absolute) sovereignty. Under such conditions, then, the dominant cognition is one of desirable intervention because its purpose upholds the normative order.

At the same time, a few other cognitions associated with the intervention—notably its costs and the outlook for its success—must be considered, and these may be consonant or dissonant with the dominant cognition, the one justifying contingent sovereignty. In other words, they may or may not point in the same direction when it comes to justifying the intervention. If dissonant (the intervention is excessively costly or the outlook for its success is dubious), continued support for acting in a spirit of contingent sovereignty may require a fortified justification. We might, then, expect that the interveners would commit themselves even more strongly to the norm of contingent sovereignty, to make the intervention cognitively acceptable in the face of problems with costs and/or success (see Heider 1958). That is, the higher the costs and/or the murkier the prospects for success, the more strenuously the case justifying contingent sovereignty must be made, emphasizing that the need to set right the target state's failures supersedes the need to respect a norm of *absolute* sovereignty.[19] These justifications help resolve cognitive dissonance, leading to cognitive consistency, in which psychological tension is eased.

## Noninterveners and Normative Change

Minimizing cognitive dissonance is also a goal for leaders of nonintervening states. These leaders seek to maintain cognitive consistency among their masses. However, noninterveners may or may not change their understandings of sovereignty, depending on their domestic circumstances. I will first discuss situations in which change in these understandings may be possible, before outlining my expectations for when change is unlikely to occur.

There are at least two scenarios that may induce change for noninterveners that are leading states. The first is a situation in which contingent sovereignty fits with the values a state espouses. Such a change would be entirely consistent with a value system that places compliance with international obligations in a particular issue area as a priority—even over absolutely sovereignty. The second case leans on a self-interest explanation: a state seeks to maximize its own welfare; supporting changes in conceptions of sovereignty may not be wholly associated with the normative values embodied by contingent sovereignty, but rather, at least in part, driven by the benefits derived from lip service to the contingent norm. In either case, I expect a state to adhere to contingent sovereignty *but less firmly* than a state involved in a military intervention. As a nonintervener, the state's position carries little risk; it has not committed any financial or human investment in the norm, as the intervening state has done. Change is, however, *possible* because it allows a state to maintain cognitive consistency; the contingent norm of sovereignty is consistent with that state's value system. Still, while change is possible, it is uncertain how far changes in conceptions of sovereignty would occur because the state is not putting action behind its new conviction.

However, leading states may choose not to become involved in an intervention because of their culpability in the normative issue area the intervention highlights. It may be that they practice internal policies that violate international laws and norms, which could warrant external remedial intervention. For example, if a state harbors terrorists, it would not support a counterterrorism intervention against another state. Rather, the state would advocate for absolute sovereignty, avoiding cognitive dissonance that would have resulted had the state favored intervention.

An interesting puzzle is why major powers such as Russia and China resist humanitarian intervention in weak states when they themselves face little risk of intervention, despite their own human rights abuses at home. It seems quite obvious that no other state would threaten an intervention against them. I suggest that, at least in part, such states hold tightly to absolute sovereignty as an international norm not for fear of a humanitarian intervention on their territory but to maintain cognitive consistency—discourse-consistent actions.

## Investigative Approach

Having discussed the theoretical contours of this project, I turn now to the details of my preliminary investigation of my propositions within three policy domains. As explained, I am primarily interested in changes in understandings of sovereignty by leading states within the context of military intervention, though I consider cases of inaction for comparative purposes.

### Analysis of Speeches

The method of analysis will be a structured, focused comparison, a form of comparative case study (George and Bennett 2005, see ch. 3). Because it is difficult to conduct a comparative study with the precision of a controlled experiment, structured, focused comparisons offer the next best solution. A structured, focused comparison enables the researcher to draw causal inferences, analyze causal mechanisms, and investigate the process by which an outcome occurs. This method relies on systematic investigation of each case, by asking the same questions throughout, which enables the researcher to standardize the data collection. The key questions throughout the intervention cases in this study, for both interveners and noninterveners, are as follows: How does a state view the norm of sovereignty, in a particular issue area, before and after the intervention? What is the outcome of the intervention in terms of costs and success? I thus concentrate on certain aspects of the intervention, rather than the complete history. For the purposes of this book, I am only interested in how sovereignty norms intersect with various issue areas within the context of military intervention. My goal, and the overall intention of structured, focused comparisons, is to generate "useful generic knowledge of important [foreign policy] problems" (George and Bennett 2005, 67).

While conducting these comparative case studies, I examine the discourses that surround the interventions to ascertain state positions on sovereignty. I analyze the speeches given at the UNSC by the permanent members. This provides me with several advantages. Focusing on the UNSC allows me to collect speeches from leading states, while holding the venue and audience constant. In addition, the public nature of these speeches allows me to collect evidence on the justifications leaders utilize in the international community.[20] The justifications reveal the norms that are considered legitimate to reference. Moreover, this forum is particularly relevant because many look to the UN, and the UNSC, as legitimizing bodies that play an important role with regard to the creation and reproduction of norms.

One advantage of analyzing speeches, or content analysis, is that "language is essentially constitutive of institutional reality" (Searle 1995, 59). Content analysis highlights the significance of communication in constructing social reality (Holsti 1969; North et al. 1963). In short, it examines what is said along with who is speaking and who is being spoken to. While some have refuted that every discourse has a corresponding practice (Fischer 1992), others demonstrate that the reverse may be true—every practice has a corresponding discourse (1991; 1997). This implies that the act of intervention is associated with specific discourse that justifies and contextualizes the action. As one scholar observed, "fundamental modernist concepts such as . . . sovereignty . . . would not have been comprehensible before the development of appropriate terms of social discourse" (Ruggie 1990).

Some criticize the use of speeches as appropriate evidence because they may not reflect underlying motivations of the speech giver. However, I am interested in how the intervention is discussed because it relates directly to the normative context. In speeches, speakers will draw on the shared values that exist in the international community to contextualize their comments. Thus, I will be able to ascertain the standards of behavior and beliefs that exist at the global level and how they change over time.

## Measuring Changes in Conceptions of Sovereignty

In the speech analyses, the main variable of interest is changes in conceptions of sovereignty. This variable represents movement away from or toward contingent sovereignty. To capture absolute and contingent sovereignty, I create four categories: states' rights, state's obligations, international community's rights, and international community's obligations.[21] The first refers to speeches that advocate absolute sovereignty. If a speech emphasizes the sovereign right of states to nonintervention and the obligation of other states to respect that, then the dependent variable would be coded "absolute sovereignty." For example, a statement such as "but the war on terrorism starts within each of our respective, sovereign borders" reflects notions of absolute sovereignty.[22] The latter three categories refer to support for contingent sovereignty, reflecting states' obligations to comply with the norms of the international community, the international community's right to interfere in a state's internal affairs, and the international community's responsibility to help states meet their obligations. For each category of sovereignty, I first establish a proportional baseline in the preintervention period and then substantively compare it with the discourse after (or during, if ongoing) the intervention.

Because the UN Security Council speeches are arranged by topic, I search UNBISnet, the online United Nations Bibliographic Information System by policy domain. UNBISnet is an online catalogue of United Nations documents and publications, which includes bibliographic records, voting records, and an index to speeches; it is available at http://unbisnet. un.org/. I use additional search terms, when necessary, to gain the maximum number of relevant speeches. As each issue area presents its unique challenges, these terms are further specified within each empirical chapter. Since I am interested in the intersection of conceptions of sovereignty and a particular issue, each speech must meet two qualifications: first, the speech must be within the chosen policy domain, and second, the speech must also mention sovereignty as depicted in one or more of the four categories described earlier.

## Costs and Success of Intervention

The key explanatory variables are the success and the costs of the intervention, as well as the culpability of the leading power in that issue area. Regarding success, I investigate the extent to which the political objective(s) of the mission has been achieved from the perspective of the intervener. More often than not, success is not a dichotomous variable but is best measured as a continuum. For example, it could be that the goal of removing a regime is accomplished, but that establishing a stable government is not. This is elaborated on in each of the empirical chapters, in specific relation to the case. As for costs, I consider them in several ways: casualties, financial costs, and domestic backlash, as seen in public opinion polls on the military intervention.

## Culpability

In order to tease out the effects of military intervention, and the possible effect of the event that led to the intervention, on sovereignty discourse, I also analyze discourse for noninterveners. Since the potential for change may be limited by a nonintervener's culpability, I also explore the extent to which a state's record in the given policy domain is consistent with its sovereignty perspective. This variable is dichotomous, ranging from culpable to nonculpable states, and is detailed further in the subsequent empirical chapters. Where available, I derive an understanding of culpability based on a state's signatory and ascension status to the relevant international treaties and conventions. In addition, depending on the issue area under investigation, I also obtain data from relevant monitoring agencies, such as Human Rights Watch, Amnesty International, and the Arms Control Association, as well as reputable news reports pertaining to a country's culpability (e.g., *New York Times,* BBC, and CNN).

## Study Parameters

The period under study is the post–Cold War era, chosen to control for international structural conditions. This allows for a reasonable degree of constancy in the international environment, with the United States having a preponderance of power. Examining cases in different policy arenas, but under similar structural conditions, allows a greater level of confidence in any conclusions drawn from the empirical findings.

As mentioned earlier, I investigate conceptions of sovereignty and military intervention in three issue areas: global terrorism, human rights abuses, and

TABLE 2.2  Cases of Military Intervention by Issue Area

| GLOBAL TERRORISM | HUMAN RIGHTS | WEAPONS OF MASS DESTRUCTION |
|---|---|---|
| AFGHANISTAN | SOMALIA | IRAQ |
| Interveners: United States, United Kingdom<br>Noninterveners: Russia, China | Interveners: United States, France<br>Noninterveners: China, Russia | Interveners: United States, United Kingdom<br>Noninterveners: France, Russia |

weapons of mass destruction. The specific cases are denoted in table 2.2. These cases represent interventions that challenge decision-makers with information that is discordant with the initial decision to intervene, in that the interventions have varying levels of costs and success for the interveners. The interveners for each case were selected by using the states with the highest level of troop commitment. Noninterveners were chosen based on a random sample of the remaining UNSC permanent members. Within the context of each issue area, I examine the necessary and contributing conditions for changes in the understanding of sovereignty to occur, and I then analyze the discourse surrounding the intervention by both interveners and noninterveners. The following discussion provides a brief overview of the cases.

Regarding global terrorism, I examine the effects of the Afghanistan intervention (2001–) on the norm of sovereignty. In November 2001, a multilateral coalition intervened in Afghanistan to hunt for Osama bin Laden and other al Qaeda operatives, to punish them for the attacks on the United States on September 11, 2001. Afghanistan's external and internal sovereignty were thus undermined because of the Taliban regime's affiliation with al Qaeda.[23] The Taliban failed to cooperate with the United States and the international community in bringing them to justice, choosing instead to allow the terrorists safe haven. One of the significant aspects of this intervention is that it represents the first time the international community banded together to intervene in another state's internal affairs because of its failure to comply with international counterterrorism norms. States that harbor and support transnational terrorist networks or refuse to help capture terrorists within their territory may now be subject to international military intervention. This case examines the extent to which this intervention furthered this contingent understanding of sovereignty by investigating views from key players: the United States and the United Kingdom as interveners, and Russia and China as noninterveners.

I then investigate changing understandings of sovereignty as they relate to human rights norms. In Somalia, a US-led coalition intervened in 1992 to address humanitarian needs and establish order amidst political chaos. Though the mission was initially successful, it later encountered significant difficulties against Somali warlord Mohamed Farrah Aidid, which forced the retreat of both the United Nations and the United States. This humanitarian intervention also represents a first—it united countries around moral concerns rather than geostrategic interests. "Invocations of sovereignty to justify the obstruction or denial of relief assistance to needy populations no longer command primacy over the needs of persons at risk" (Deng et al. 1996, 28). With a focus on the United States and France as interveners, and China and Russia as noninterveners, I analyze if and how the intervention in Somalia influenced understandings of sovereignty.

At the intersection of sovereignty and weapons of mass destruction, the 2003 invasion of Iraq demonstrated that states seeking to develop such weapons are not immune to foreign invasion by powerful states. Although the lack of evidence later established the falsehood of the initial justifications for war, it nonetheless pointed to what was believed to be a legitimate justification for war by the interveners to stop the development of weapons of mass destruction. The US-led coalition argued that there was evidence to implicate Iraq and, therefore, deemed an intervention necessary to remedy Iraq's supposed violation of international norms. Again, an intervention for such purposes reflects a precedent in the international community; there had been no previous military attempts by a *coalition* of states to thwart a state's progress in this area. Yet, in contrast to the other two cases of intervention in this book, the Iraq war failed to garner the approval of the UN. Within this context, I examine the consequences of the intervention for states' understandings of the norm of sovereignty for both interveners, the United States and the United Kingdom, and noninterveners, Russia and France.

In sum, this preliminary investigation of the evolution of the norm of sovereignty focuses on three issue areas, counterterrorism, human rights, and weapons of mass destruction, which also have normative and legal obligations. When states failed to meet those responsibilities, military interventions by the international community were undertaken. Given that necessary conditions for normative change are met, I argue that these interventions contribute to the redefining of the norm of sovereignty, particularly when they are costly and difficult for the intervener, as leaders are forced to repeatedly justify their decision to intervene. In an effort to untangle the influence of the event that spurred the intervention and the effect of the military action itself, I examine changes (or lack thereof) in understandings of sovereignty by noninterveners as well. I expect that, depending on their culpability and self-interest, they may espouse views of contingent sovereignty, though less stridently than interveners. As demonstrated in the following chapters, much of the debate about the right of military intervention reduces to the varying conceptions of sovereignty that states hold, which, in essence, is a dispute about the rights and obligations of states vis-à-vis the international community.

# CHAPTER 3 | Sovereignty and Counterterrorism

All nations of the world must be united in their solidarity with the victims of terrorism, and in their determination to take action—both
against the terrorists themselves and against all those who give them
any kind of shelter, assistance or encouragement.

—KOFI ANNAN, UN Secretary General, 2001

THE WAR IN AFGHANISTAN was the first time a global coalition intervened
on behalf of counterterrorism.[1] As former US Secretary of State Colin
Powell expressed, "And so, in defense of shared values and out of a sense
of shared vulnerability, the world answered President Bush's call for a
great global coalition against terrorism."[2] The Taliban-led regime in Afghanistan had failed its international obligations to thwart terrorism, a
failure forced to the forefront by the events of 9/11. There had been increasing global condemnation of the Taliban's affiliation with the terrorist organization al Qaeda.[3] Prior to 9/11, the UN Security Council had
passed two resolutions sanctioning the Taliban regime for protecting
Osama bin Laden and al Qaeda. After 9/11, new justifications for military
interventions surfaced, which renewed the debate on sovereignty. As part
of this discussion, a meaningful redefinition of sovereignty is emerging:
states must now fulfill certain counterterrorism obligations *in order* to be
sovereign.

Indeed, in reaction to the terrorist attacks on the World Trade Center
and the Pentagon in 2001, the UN Security Council unanimously adopted
Resolution 1373, which "obliges all States to criminalize assistance for
terrorist activities, deny financial support and safe haven to terrorists and
share information about groups planning terrorist attack." In other words,

in the interest of international peace and security, states now have a responsibility to the international community to uphold certain standards of internal behavior with regard to counterterrorism. As demonstrated by the military intervention in Afghanistan shortly after the resolution, states that fail to comply risk external interference and, at the most extreme, foreign military intervention.

But how did this new vision of sovereignty emerge? Given the necessary structural conditions are met (as discussed in chapter 2), I expect that the more problematic an intervention is for the intervener, the greater its allegiance to sovereignty contingent on a state fulfilling its international counterterrorism responsibilities. Moreover, interveners will more adamantly support contingent sovereignty than noninterveners. Using comparative case studies and content analysis of UN Security Council speeches by two of the leading interveners, the United States and the United Kingdom, and two noninterveners, Russia and China, I examine these states' views on sovereignty within the context of the global war on terror, both prior to and during the intervention in Afghanistan.[4]

This chapter is structured as follows. I first provide an overview of the international development of counterterrorism norms and laws. Next, I discuss the presence of the necessary conditions, as well as a contributing condition, for changes in conceptions of sovereignty to occur. I then begin the analyses of the United States and the United Kingdom before moving on to investigate Russia and China. I conclude with a comparative analysis of the cases and a discussion of their implications.

## Counterterrorism and the International Community

Although the past twenty years have seen an increase in high-profile terrorist activity, such as attacks against the United States at the World Trade Center (1993), at the United States' embassies in Kenya and Tanzania (1998), and on the *USS Cole* (2000), terrorism is not new to the international system. It can be traced at least to the Roman Empire (Carr 2002), and it has affected many parts of the world, from bombings in Northern Ireland to suicide attacks in the Middle East. To date, there has been at least seven regional conventions concerning terrorism.[5] Though terrorism was a recurring phenomenon, there was no general consensus within the international community on the associated rights and obligations of states. Primarily, this had to do with the problem of defining terrorism and the role that ideology and politics played in this regard (Clunan 2006). Nonetheless, terrorism has been on the agenda of the UN General Assembly since 1972, but its Ad Hoc Committee on International Terrorism reported only a few times (1973, 1977, 1979) before it was disbanded. The committee was brought back to life in 1996 but provided largely symbolic acknowledgement of the terrorist threat without any enforcement mechanism.

Yet, as early as 1963, the United Nations was the source of a number of treaties on specific terrorist activities, from hijacking to bombings.[6] Partly because of the Cold War, the focus of the treaties was more on individual perpetrators, rather than on the responsibilities and obligations of state actors. Only recently have the conventions against terrorism more explicitly articulated states' obligations to combat terrorism. For example, the 1997 International Convention for the Suppression of Terrorist Bombings and the 1999 International Convention for the Suppression of Financing of Terrorism call for state action to prevent terrorist activities. However, the consequences to states of not abiding by their obligations were unclear. A handful of countries that had signed one or more of the antiterrorism treaties were considered state sponsors of terrorism (including Iran, North Korea, and Sudan). Though some states were targets of economic sanctions, the sanctions were primarily symbolic disapproval, providing little, if any, motivation to change (Nincic 2005).

After 9/11, the war against terrorism was regarded as a collective fight for international peace and security. Since then, several UN treaties and resolutions have provided the framework for global action, with surprising commitment by the majority of states. For example, the 2005 Convention for the Suppression of Acts of Nuclear Terrorism recognizes the dangerous link between nuclear weapons and terrorism and calls on states to develop national legal frameworks to address possible transgressions and to share relevant information with international investigations.[7] The Russian deputy UN ambassador also emphasized, "It's the first time that an anti-terrorist convention has been developed on the basis of preventing—that is, not after the fact but before the terrorist acts which are criminalized by this convention."[8]

To aid in these and other counterterrorism efforts, the UN secretary-general created the Counter-Terrorism Implementation Task Force, which coordinates efforts throughout the UN system and beyond, including representatives from the International Monetary Fund (IMF) and INTERPOL. Recently, the United Nations Global Counter-Terrorism Strategy (a resolution and an annexed Plan of Action) represents the first time states have agreed on a common strategy. The Task Force is charged with aiding member states in complying with this global strategy.

Within this framework for comprehensive counterterrorism measures, states now have an obligation to fight terrorism wherever it may occur, even if it crosses state borders. This may imply that a state failing to do so compromises its right to sovereignty. However, we know that the UN, states, and other entities can create rules, but they are less meaningful without action to enforce them. The process of military intervention on behalf of international counterterrorism treaties and conventions therefore reveals the extent to which sovereignty is redefined in practice. When an intervening state prioritizes counterterrorism norms over absolute sovereignty to justify its actions, it entrenches a new version of sovereignty in its discourse.

## Conditions Conducive to Changes in Sovereignty

As illustrated in the previous discussion of developments within the United Nations on the evolution of counterterrorism conventions, counterterrorism increasingly requires active state compliance with legal obligations to the international community. These developments are occurring amid conditions favorable to changes in the norm of sovereignty. This evolution toward a contingent norm of sovereignty (sovereignty conditional on states meeting their counterterrorism obligations) is possible because the three conditions necessary for normative change—prominence, coherence with other norms, and environmental conditions—are present in the global system (see chapter 2).

In terms of prominence, counterterrorism has been high on the post-9/11 agendas of the international community *and* individual states, especially those states involved in the war in Afghanistan and those that have suffered terrorist attacks on their own soil. From Madrid (2004) to London (2005) to Mumbai (2008) to Aleppo (2012), states have found common ground in the fight against terrorism. The emerging counterterrorism norms, indicating the rights and obligations of states in this issue area, are facilitated by the voices of leading states seeking to enforce this threat to suit their interests. This results in the prominence of a contingent norm of sovereignty in the international system, which implies a state's obligation to comply with counterterrorism norms or risk international intervention. The competing norm of absolute sovereignty may be outweighed by the imperative security needs (e.g., self-defense) of both the international community and individual states.

With regard to coherence with other norms, the move toward a contingent notion of sovereignty within the realm of counterterrorism is compatible with developments in other norms that are a part of the normative structure of international relations. For instance, upholding human rights norms now goes beyond a responsibility to protect one's own citizens and includes an obligation to foreign nationals. Both human rights norms and counterterrorism norms are concerned with harm to innocent civilians, regardless of citizenship. With the increasing focus on the protection of *individuals*, and not states, these norms find common ground and challenge absolute sovereignty in similar ways. State sovereignty is contingent on certain levels of government performance in these areas. Along the same lines, if we consider norms regarding legitimate governance as another component of the current normative structure, we find that sovereignty contingent on counterterrorism norms is also compatible with democratic norms, which encompass the protection of individual rights of political and social freedoms. Perhaps one of the most enduring norms, which counterterrorism norms are closest to in kind, is a state's right to preemptive self-defense. Because terrorism presents a security threat that may challenge a state's survival, states harboring terrorists may be putting their sovereignty at risk. As such, preemptive self-defense inherently provides for legitimate violations of sovereignty. As it becomes more salient in the fight against transnational terrorism, the norm of preemptive self-defense contributes to the erosion of absolute sovereignty.

Just as a contingent norm of sovereignty is compatible with others norms in the international system, so too are the environmental conditions. In contrast to the bipolar Cold War environment, the current system allows more freedom for states to pursue common goals, such as prevention of environmental degradation. With regard to counterterrorism, states previously had an obligation to respect sovereignty, even if a target state harbored terrorists. For example, South Africa was frequently suspected of state-sponsored terrorism during the Cold War and implicated in several major incidents, including the 1961 airplane crash in Zambia that killed UN Secretary-General Dag Hammarskjold. Given the chilly Cold War climate, these activities were mostly overlooked in the interests of the ideological war and the balance of power. Yet with the end of the Cold War and the rise in terrorist attacks on major powers by nonstate actors (though sometimes state sponsored), transnational terrorism has replaced nuclear-armed superpower rivalry as *one of the major* threats to international peace and security (especially when coupled with weapons of mass destruction). According to the new rules of the game dictated by the leading powers, absolute sovereignty is no longer a shield behind which terrorists can hide. China, Russia, the United Kingdom, and the United States all agree that the international community must play a role in the fight against global terrorism.

In sum, the existence of these conditions make changes in conceptions of sovereignty, in the context of the global war on terrorism, possible. Emerging counterterrorism norms are prominent in the international system, as well as compatible with the current normative structure. The global environment provides favorable conditions for states to pursue a transnational agenda, as the major powers confront common, international threats.

## Intervention in Afghanistan

Drawing on the theory presented in chapter 2, I examine the cases of the two major interveners in Afghanistan, the United States and the United Kingdom. As leading states in the international system, I expect their experiences in Afghanistan to drive their understandings of sovereignty and in turn, to influence sovereignty norms in the global arena. As they come to adopt a certain notion of sovereignty, their positions promulgate that vision, especially since both have been major participants in the debate between the global imperatives of counterterrorism versus respecting state sovereignty. I begin with the United States.

### United States

Driven by the 9/11 attacks, the United States intervened in Afghanistan with two objectives: remove the Taliban regime from power and eliminate al Qaeda and the Taliban as terrorist threats (including capturing Osama bin Laden).[9] The first task was successfully accomplished, though the Taliban continue to challenge this. On October 7, 2001, the United States and the United Kingdom began aerial bombing, as troops from the Afghan Northern Alliance and NATO engaged their targets on the ground. Operation Enduring Freedom destroyed communications, electricity supplies, and terrorist training camps in and around Afghanistan's major cities. By November, the Taliban had left Kabul, the capital city, and an interim Afghan government began to form, headed by Hamid Karzai in 2002. However, with a clear resurgence in Taliban activity, this can only be assessed as a partial success. For example, they continue to challenge the authority of the Hamid Karzai government through repeated attacks against Afghan civilians and foreign security forces.

The second objective has proved more difficult. While Osama bin Laden was found and killed in May 2011 in Pakistan, this came after ten years of searching. In December 2001, the hunt for Osama bin Laden focused on the mountainous region of Tora Bora, though to no avail. Many believed he slipped over the border into Pakistan. Redoubling their efforts, the international coalition took on the Taliban and Al Qaeda in the Shah-i-Kot Valley and Arma mountains in Operation Anaconda. This operation lasted a total of sixteen days, from March 2 to March 18, 2002, though it did little to destroy Taliban and al Qaeda forces. After recruiting and reorganizing, the Taliban and al Qaeda came back strong in 2003.

The severity of their threat was recognized in official strategy documents since the war in Afghanistan began,[10] as well as in various public statements by US officials. In 2005, a US senior general in Afghanistan warned, "Taliban and al Qaeda insurgents remain a grave threat to Afghanistan."[11] In 2008, the director of national intelligence reported, "Al-Qaeda and its terrorists affiliates continue to pose a significant threat to the United States."[12] In December 2009, President Obama admitted "the situation in Afghanistan has deteriorated."[13]

With al Qaeda finding safe haven along Afghanistan's border with Pakistan and the Taliban controlling large areas of Afghanistan, President Obama decided to send an additional 30,000 troops to "reverse the Taliban's momentum" and eliminate al Qaeda's refuge.[14] With a promise to begin US troop withdrawals after eighteen months, President Obama acknowledged the waning public support for the war and its increasing cost in both human and financial terms. Though met with "some success in clearing insurgents from their strongholds, particularly in central Helmand," 2010 proved a difficult year.[15] A 2010 Pentagon report stated that Taliban tactics were becoming more sophisticated, and their reach was expanding—despite major US offensives.[16] In fact, the report notes that attacks rose by 70% since 2009, and other sources confirmed the instability as well.[17] A UN official working in Afghanistan noted, "in the course of 2010, the security situation in many parts of the country has become unstable where it previously had not been so. There is violence happening in more parts of the country."[18]

The United States achieved a major victory in 2011 with the death of Osama bin Laden. Subsequently, President Obama announced a dramatic plan for troop withdrawal, despite warnings from military officials that it may jeopardize recent gains.[19] However, from 2001 to 2010, the war had been arduous. Tangible evidence of the waning success of the mission can be seen in the increasing number of terrorist attacks by the Taliban and al Qaeda. Initially, the intervention was very successful, but as time went by, less so. There were no attacks once the intervention began in October

2001, through the end of the year, and in 2002, there were only twelve attacks. However, that number jumped sharply in 2003 to sixty attacks, remaining at that level through 2004 (fifty-four attacks). The following year, in 2005, attacks doubled to 120, steadily rising in the subsequent years to 304 attacks in 2010 (see figure 3.1).[20]

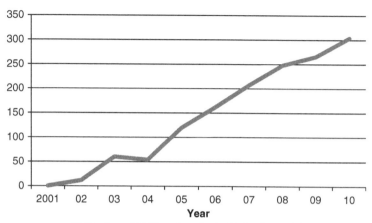

FIGURE 3.1  Al Qaeda and Taliban Attacks in Afghanistan, 2001–2010.

SOURCE: National Consortium for the Study of Terrorism and Responses to Terrorism (START).

Coinciding with the rise in attacks, the costs to the United States have also increased. Financially, the war has cost billions of dollars, steadily rising over the course of the war from $20.8 billion in 2002 to $93.8 billion in 2010 (see figure 3.2). Cumulatively, the United States spent at least $650 billion from 2002 to 2010.[21]

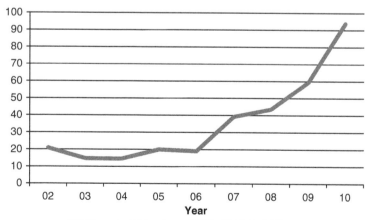

FIGURE 3.2  US Costs in Afghanistan, 2002–2010 (in billions of dollars).

SOURCE: Amy Belasco. 2011. "The Cost of Iraq, Afghanistan, and Other Global War on Terror Operations since 9/11." *Congressional Research Service*. March 29. http://www.fas.org/.

In terms of public opinion, the percentage of Americans that believed the war in Afghanistan was a mistake increased from 9% in November 2001 to 25% in 2004.[22] This upward trend persisted: 34% in 2008 agreed the war was a mistake, and 43% in 2010.[23] Similarly, when the American public was asked, "Do you favor or oppose the US war in Afghanistan?" 48% opposed the war in 2006, rising to 63% by the end of 2010.[24]

At the same time, the number of American casualties had increased (concurrent to the rise in US troops on the ground).[25] As depicted in figure 3.3, the number of casualties per year remained consistent through the early years, averaging 50 deaths per year, but then spiked in 2005 and 2006 to 98 and 99 deaths, respectively. Casualties continued to climb, from 117 in 2007 to 499 in 2010. The cumulative losses up to 2010 were 1,446 soldiers, representing 63% of the coalition's total losses.

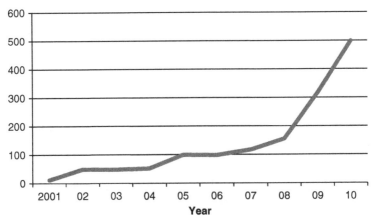

FIGURE 3.3 US Casualties In Afghanistan, 2001–2010.

SOURCE: icasualties.org. "Operation Enduring Freedom." http://icasualties.org/oef/.

Because costs increased and success apparently decreased over the period of 2001–2010, the American justifications for the war in Afghanistan, in terms of sovereignty, should strongly reinforce a contingent sovereignty norm, compared to the pre-9/11 discourse.[26] As the war continues, there should not be any reference to the right of Afghanistan to conduct its affairs as it sees fit, but more focus on the responsibility of a state to its own citizens and citizens around the world for the sake of international peace and security. This should be complemented by discourse bearing on the international community's obligation and increasing responsibility to deal with this problem, if Afghanistan is unable or unwilling to do so. I expect this to contrast with American views on sovereignty and counterterrorism before the war, which would express greater recognition of the rights of states to conduct their affairs without outside interference, though limited, perhaps, by the need for states to comply with international law.

## US' Stated Views on Sovereignty Before Intervention

Prior to 9/11, the United States described terrorism as an important concern to all states, requiring international condemnation of states that sponsored terrorism. In this period, the United States emphasized state compliance with international obligations as well as the international community's obligation to maintain international peace and security. This can be seen in the United States' views regarding one of the most memorable terrorist attacks in recent history. In 1988, terrorist bombs brought down Pan Am flight 103 over Lockerbie, Scotland. As the investigation progressed, mounting evidence pointed to the involvement of the Libyan government. The immediate perpetrators were two Libyan nationals, who Libya refused to hand over. The United States argued that Libya had an international obligation to turn over the suspects to international authorities.[27] In addition, the United States maintained that the international community must exercise its duty to ensure that Libya met its international responsibilities. Though the United States did not assert that the international community had the right to intervene in Libya's affairs, nowhere did the United States mention Libya's prerogative as a sovereign state.

Similarly, the United States argued that Sudan was violating its international obligations when it allowed Egyptian terrorists safe haven after they attempted to assassinate Egyptian president Hosni Mubarak in 1995. The United States ambassador to the UN, Madeleine Albright, argued, "The Government of the Sudan, which must bear responsibility for the acts it allows its guests to perform, also has the responsibility to extradite those guests to face justice."[28] Thus, Ambassador Albright acknowledged a state's obligation to enforce counterterrorism measures within the state and to comply with international conventions against terrorism. In the same speech, she also mentioned that the international community condemned Sudan for not having met one of the "minimum" obligations (extradite criminals) of a state that wants to live in "peace with their neighbors." For this failure, Sudan faced international condemnation and isolation. Furthermore, the international community "is prepared to apply measured, incremental pressure on the Government of Sudan until it meets fully its obligations."[29] By "pressure," Ambassador Albright implied the use of sanctions, which have been traditional tools of retaliation for the "bad" behavior of states. In addition to emphasizing the utility of sanctions against states that harbor terrorists, the United States also urged other states to sign numerous counterterrorism conventions.[30] The United States asserted somewhat vaguely, "all of us have the responsibility to act accordingly."[31]

What is possible in the realm of punishment for a state's failure to comply with international obligations is implicitly constrained by sovereignty norms. In US discourse, we find the United States encouraging cooperation in matters related to terrorism, while refraining from discussing the explicit right of the international community to step in. For example, in the context of the US embassy bombings in Kenya and Tanzania, the United States declared: "We call upon Member States to support the ongoing investigations."[32] This reflects a strategy of encouraging cooperation, without compelling it. This kind of discourse continues after the sanctions were placed against the Taliban regime in 1999. The United States implored: "It is incumbent upon all of us in the community of nations to stand together and to stand strong."[33]

The statements and their associated beliefs for the pre-9/11 period can perhaps most easily be illustrated through content analysis (see figure 3.4). As figure 3.4 illustrates, prior to 9/11, the United States believed strongly that states had certain obligations to the international community, reflected in 89% of its speeches. Of particular note, there is

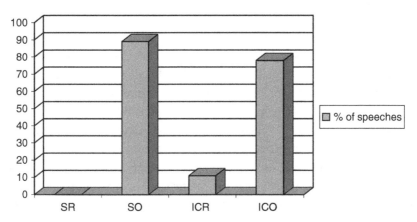

SR = State Rights, SO = State Obligations, ICR = International Community's
Rights, ICO = International Community's Obligations

FIGURE 3.4 US' Conceptions of Sovereignty Before Military Intervention

no explicit mention of respecting state sovereignty or the rights of states. With regard to the international community, the United States placed great value on the obligation of all states to fight terrorism together (in 77% of speeches). As a threat to international peace and security, counterterrorism presented an appropriate policy pursuit for the international community, with the possibility of a *right* to supersede state's prerogatives (in 11% of speeches). Taken together, these indicators present a baseline for comparing post-9/11 beliefs to assess any changes in views of sovereignty, to which I now turn.

US' Stated Views on Sovereignty During Intervention

Have American views on sovereignty continued unchanged or moved toward a firmer belief in contingent sovereignty? I first describe statements made as the war carried on and then consider the results of the content analysis.

The day after 9/11, the United States asserted that it would make no distinction between terrorists and those who harbor them.[34] In this sense, host states are considered as culpable as the terrorists they protect, and therefore subject to the same punishment. Initially, however, the United States was reluctant to let go of the traditional sovereignty norm: "the war on terrorism starts within each of our respective, sovereign borders."[35] At the same time, the United States argued, "all states now have the legal, as well as political and moral, obligation to act against it."[36] This implies that in the pursuit of terrorism, nothing is off-limits—not even violations of sovereignty. Taken together, early statements by the United States form a conflicting picture of the rights and obligations of states and the international community. This is not surprising, given the changes affecting the sovereignty norm at the time. We should not expect an immediate change, but rather a gradual move toward a contingent norm, especially as the war in Afghanistan waged on.

Indeed, as the military intervention in Afghanistan continued, the discourse began to change to one of responsibility of states at home *and* abroad. There was much discussion about how states were obligated to "weave counterterrorism" into national law, as well as international institutions.[37] We begin to see statements concerning external obligations, for states to work with other states. Furthermore, the Counter-Terrorism Committee (CTC) is introduced as an international monitoring body to oversee state implementation of international conventions against terrorism, a body that the United States continues to emphasize its support for.[38]

In fighting terrorism, the United States maintained that the international community is "charged with a heavy responsibility" and that Resolution 1373 "is generating a worldwide juridical transformation" in the rights and obligations of states.[39] The United States repeatedly emphasized the obligations of states to implement domestic legislation regarding counterterrorism and suggested that states would be pressured to comply if the Counter-Terrorism Committee review finds them lacking. In fact, the United States asserted that the Security Council is instrumental in overseeing the implementation of international obligations.[40] This was not an insignificant change in the meaning of sovereignty. In the context of fighting terrorism, the United States supported responsibilities to bring national laws into accordance with international laws. For example, states are obliged to freeze assets of suspected terrorists, share intelligence information, and tighten airport security, among other things.[41] These developments reach into realms of traditional state authority, such that even a state's laws become subject to international scrutiny. This clearly goes beyond the scope of the traditional bounds of sovereignty.

Content analysis offers more tangible evidence (see figure 3.5). There was some movement within the absolute and contingent sovereignty categories, though only one represents a substantially large change. This change occurs within the category of international community's rights and represents a meaningful change in the direction of contingent sovereignty, as expected.[42] Specifically, the United States mentions the *rights* of the international community with regards to states' affairs in almost half its speeches

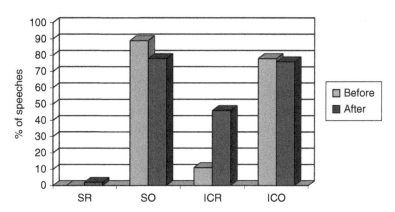

SR = State Rights, SO = State Obligations, ICR = International Community's

Rights, ICO = International Community's Obligations.

FIGURE 3.5 US' Conceptions of Sovereignty Before and During Military Intervention

(46%), up from 11% in the pre-9/11 period. This finding is further buttressed by the fact that the United States made little mention of states' rights.

Changes in the other categories were not as large but deserve brief mention. The United States held strongly to its belief in the obligations of the international community to lead the war on terror. In terms of total speeches, such statements remained about the same, from 78% to 76%. Speeches discussing the obligations of states slightly declined from 89% to 78%. One explanation could be that the number of states that were parties to international counterterrorism conventions increased, so that there was less need to emphasize this. In that case, the United States has turned to an increased emphasis on the international community's rights in fighting terrorism, especially since global terrorism is a threat that states alone cannot deal with. Thus, the only solution is to work together, even if it means that the international community takes on rights formerly accorded to the state.

In sum, the evidence supports my expectations. As the United States continued an increasingly costly and unsuccessful war in Afghanistan, the more it reinforced its commitment to contingent sovereignty to relieve this cognitive dissonance. In particular, stronger beliefs regarding the international community's rights pervade the American speeches given in the post-9/11 period, compared with the previous years.

## The United Kingdom

Although the attacks of 9/11 took place in the United States, the United Kingdom has been one of the main supporters of the war in Afghanistan. It began the war with similar objectives to those of the United States: remove the Taliban regime from power and eliminate the al Qaeda threat.[43]

The cost of the war in Afghanistan to the United Kingdom has increased over time.[44] In terms of casualties, the United Kingdom averaged one casualty per year for the first five years.[45] However, in 2006, the United Kingdom lost 39 troops (see figure 3.6). The sharp increase in the number of casualties coincided with a rise in Taliban and al Qaeda attacks, reemerging as serious threats to accomplishing the UK's political objectives. Unfortunately, casualties continued to rise, with 42 deaths in 2007 and 51 deaths in 2008. These numbers doubled in subsequent years to 108 casualties in 2009 and 103 in 2010.

The political costs at home of the war in Afghanistan have also increased. In October 2001, 62% of the public backed the war.[46] Later on, in September 2006, public support wavered at 31%.[47] A few years later, in 2009, 58% believed the war "unwinnable," and a majority of the British public viewed

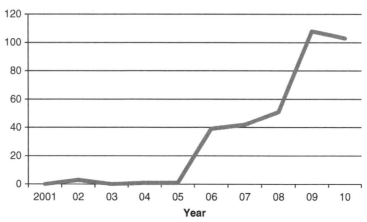

FIGURE 3.6 UK Casualties in Afghanistan, 2001–2010.

SOURCE: icasualties.org. "Operation Enduring Freedom." http://icasualties.org/oef/.

"the risks and the sacrifice as unacceptably high."[48] Moreover, at least half the voters wanted troops withdrawn immediately.[49] In 2010, 77% of British voters supported the withdrawal of all troops from Afghanistan.[50]

The financial cost of the war in Afghanistan was relatively low in the first few years. Between 2002–2006, the costs fluctuated between a high of £311 million in 2003 and a low of £46 million in 2004. The United Kingdom renewed its efforts, though, as casualties and the number of terrorist attacks alarmingly increased. In 2007, costs soared to £742 million and continued to rise over the subsequent years, reaching £4200 million in 2010 (see figure 3.7).

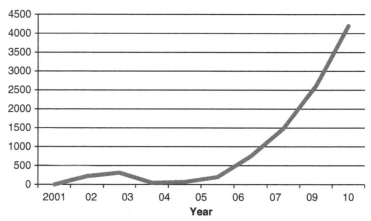

FIGURE 3.7 UK Costs in Afghanistan, 2001–2010 (in millions of pounds).

SOURCE: UK House of Commons Defence Committee. 2011. "Operations in Afghanistan." July 6. http://www.publications.parliament.uk/pa/cm201012/cmselect/cmdfence/554/55406.htm#a28.

As noted in the US case, from 2001 to 2010, the extent of success in Afghanistan was low. As figure 3.1 indicates, the Taliban attacks did not decline or stabilize but rather increased as the war went on. A 2007 report of the British House of Commons Defense Committee revealed "things are going badly, alarmingly wrong in Afghanistan."[51] A number of indicators were cited, including "too many Afghans are being killed," "there are too few troops on the ground to win," and "Afghan security forces are a disappointment." A few years later, British Colonel Stuart Tootal admitted, "There is a real risk that we could lose the war in Afghanistan."[52] Echoing early admissions of lowering expectations in Afghanistan, in 2010, General Sir David Richards, UK chief of the defense staff, declared, "The West can only contain, not defeat, militant groups such as al Qaeda."[53] Though the period from 2001 to 2010 is marked by a fledging mission, one major success did occur in 2011—the death of Osama bin Laden. Soon after, Prime Minister David Cameron announced that he would begin to withdraw troops from Afghanistan and acknowledged that the United Kingdom would continue to pursue a major strategic and military relationship with Afghanistan.[54]

In the period from 2001 to 2010, the United Kingdom's involvement in Afghanistan resulted in an increasingly costly, low-success war. I therefore expect, as in the US case, a strong reinforcement of contingent sovereignty in United Kingdom discourse, compared with the discourse prior to the war. This means that I should see an increase in references to obligations of states to follow international norms as embodied in the counterterrorism conventions, in addition to increased mention of the international community's obligation and right to monitor state's internals affairs if they were not capable or willing to pursue terrorists.

Moreover, given the United Kingdom's experience with terrorist attacks on its soil, it should be more willing to change its views on sovereignty, in the direction of contingent understanding. Contributing to this expectation is the fact that the United Kingdom actively pursues and prosecutes suspected terrorists, both at home and abroad, and is a party to all twelve conventions and protocols relating to terrorism. The following section establishes a baseline for comparison.

UK's Stated Views on Sovereignty Before Intervention

In reviewing statements regarding sovereignty in the realm of counterterrorism policy, several incidents illustrate British thinking on sovereignty prior to 9/11. These include the airliner bombing in 1988 by Libya, the attempted assassination of the Egyptian president in 1996, and the Taliban's links to international terrorism in the late 1990s. Before discussing the results of content analysis of the speeches, I provide a summary of representative statements surrounding these events.

The Pan Am bombing over Lockerbie, Scotland, provides a point of departure to investigate British views on sovereignty. In its discourse, the United Kingdom emphasized the obligation of states to comply with international laws. In this case, it asserted that Libya must comply and hand over the suspects implicated in the bombing.[55] In addition, the United Kingdom argued that international law is above national law. While there may be national laws that prohibit extradition, "there is no rule of international law which precludes the extradition of criminals."[56] The United Kingdom frequently mentions the obligations of a state to the international community, as well as the obligation, and sometimes even the right, of the international community to take charge when a state is unwilling.[57]

Similarly, in 1996, after the assassination attempt on Egyptian President Mubarak, the United Kingdom condemned Sudan for not extraditing the three suspected terrorists, which placed it out of compliance with international obligations. In drafting the subsequent UN Security Council resolution, the United Kingdom declared, "One of the principal demands of this draft resolution and the previous resolutions is the requirement for Sudan to ensure that the three suspects wanted in connection with the assassination attempt . . . are brought to justice."[58] The focus was on Sudan's obligations to the international community; Sudan must "comply with the demands of the Security Council and the OAU."

In 1999, when discussion at the UNSC turned to sanctioning the Taliban regime, UK Ambassador Greenstock remarked, "Terrorism is condemned by all States, each in its own way."[59] With this statement, Greenstock implied that states were still free to choose how they dealt with terrorism and there was no unified response from the international community to such acts. While the United Kingdom reaffirmed the role of the UN in promoting international cooperation against terrorism, it did not go further in specifying an obligation of the international community to interfere in state's affairs. However, it did argue that states were obliged to follow their international obligations as codified in the international counterterrorism conventions. As the United Kingdom strongly reminded the UNSC, "The Conventions establish an international legal regime, based on the principle of universal jurisdiction, which imposes on State parties the requirement to prosecute or extradite suspected terrorists."[60]

Content analysis of UK speeches clearly points to an emphasis on states' obligations as well as the international community's obligations in the struggle against terrorism (see figure 3.8). In just over half the speeches (56%), the United Kingdom discusses states' obligations to the international community and an even higher percentage of speeches mentioning the obligations of the international community to eradicate terrorism (67%). However, only a very small percentage of speeches addressed the *right* of the international community to interfere in states' affairs (11%). While this evidence points to an already strong belief in contingent sovereignty, at least one speech also refers to respecting state sovereignty. Thus, the United Kingdom has not entirely let go of absolute sovereignty in this policy arena.

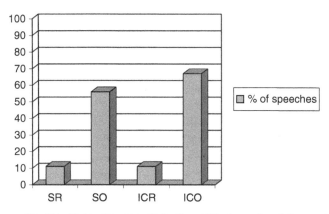

SR = State Rights, SO = State Obligations, ICR = International Community's Rights, ICO = International Community's Obligations

FIGURE 3.8    UK's Conceptions of Sovereignty Before Military Intervention

To what extent will the United Kingdom continue these beliefs after 9/11 and during the war in Afghanistan? The next section examines British discourse after 9/11 by first looking at a sampling of statements related to sovereignty and then comparing the content analysis of this period with the baseline established earlier.

UK's Stated Views on Sovereignty During Intervention

In response to the attacks of 9/11, the United Kingdom broadly asserted that "we must all respond globally,"[61]. What this meant in more tangible terms became apparent in UNSC Resolution 1373 (2001), which was "an historic event: the first resolution to impose obligations on all States to respond to the global threat of terrorism."[62]

As the intervention continued, the United Kingdom emphasized the obligation of states to incorporate international laws on counterterrorism into their own legislation, as well as to share information across borders about potential security threats.[63] Moreover, the United Kingdom stressed support for the Counter-Terrorism Committee, encouraging it to pressure governments to implement and enforce counterterrorism measures.[64]

Moreover, the United Kingdom believed that states cannot be passive in the fight against terrorism but must take the initiative.[65] As United Kingdom Ambassador Greenstock put it, "It is your choice, Member States."[66] Though this one statement recalls traditional sovereignty, it is overshadowed by the continuous references to states' obligations to the international community and that community's obligation to interfere in noncompliant states. The following remark is characteristic of statements by the United Kingdom in this regard: the UNSC "must ensure that the duties imposed by the UN counter-terrorism law-SC Resolution 1373 (2001) are vigorously enforced in every Member State."[67]

In terms of the Council's general obligation with regard to terrorism, the United Kingdom noted that "the Security Council has a responsibility to ensure that every Member State of the UN takes action to combat this threat to international peace and security."[68] Thus, the United Kingdom advocated a more systematic approach to monitoring member states through the CTC and demanding that states cooperate with the CTC.[69] Again, the United Kingdom referenced the potential use of force to combat terrorism, which challenges state sovereignty: "The fight against terrorism needs to be sustained, effective and efficient. Combating and defeating terrorism requires concerted and wide-ranging action. Military action may be necessary."[70]

In the United Kingdom's discourse on terrorism, there is increasing emphasis on the obligation of the international community to pursue terrorists, regardless of state borders. There is also a focus on holding states accountable for their inaction and scrutinizing their domestic affairs. In a sense, since "terrorists have no boundaries," neither do states: we must "take action against those who incite, preach or teach this extremism, wherever they are in whichever country."[71] And with this perspective, the United Kingdom continues to reinforce the importance of CTC visits in member states to evaluate their counterterrorism measures.[72] In efforts to fight terrorism, "We must all play our part within and beyond the UN to reduce this risk."[73] The United Kingdom implores states to follow through on their domestic and international responsibilities and reminds them that the international community will not stop until every state is in compliance.[74] After all, "terrorism remains one of the greatest challenges to international peace, stability and security."[75]

British discourse in the post-9/11 period clearly reflects stronger views of contingent sovereignty in the realm of counterterrorism (see figure 3.9).[76] As the content analysis reveals, 40% of the speeches support the international community's rights, up from 11%. In 89% of the speeches, the United Kingdom asserted the obligation of the international community to take action, compared with 67% of previous speeches. The United Kingdom emphasized states' obligations to the international community significantly more, from 56% to 83% of the speeches. Further reflecting an increased commitment to contingent sovereignty, the United Kingdom made no reference to a belief in absolute sovereignty.

The results are consistent with my expectations. Because of the war's increasingly high cost and low success, I predicted that the United Kingdom would move away from support of absolute sovereignty and would increase its commitment to a contingent view of sovereignty. While these results are suggestive, one might argue that it is difficult to disentangle the impact of the war in Afghanistan and the bombings in London in July 2005. This would be an interesting point for further investigation. However, there is still evidence from the onset of war up to the July 2005 attacks that suggests the process of military intervention in Afghanistan contributed to the strong

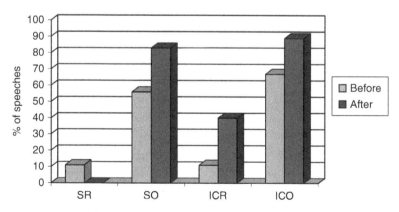

SR = State Rights, SO = State Obligations, ICR = International Community's
Rights, ICO = International Community's Obligations.

FIGURE 3.9 UK's Conceptions of Sovereignty Before and During Military Intervention

reinforcement of contingent sovereignty, and that this trend continued through the end of the time period under study.

## China and Russia: Change Too?

### China

In both regional and international forums, China has denounced terrorism: "China will not give in to terrorism . . . and will continue to play its due part in the fight against terrorism."[77] "Terrorism constitutes a grave threat to world peace and security."[78] China has been generally supportive of the global war on terror, increasingly cooperating with other countries as per its international obligations. For example, China helped create a regional antiterrorism agency in Tashkent, and it has engaged in joint counterterrorism exercises with Russia and neighboring countries, under the auspices of the Shanghai Cooperation Organization (SCO), an intergovernmental security organization founded in 2001.[79] Similarly, China has cooperated with the United States on counterterrorism. China allowed the establishment of a US Federal Bureau of Investigation Legal Attache Office, with which it has coordinated counterterrorism investigations. Moreover, China engaged in joint exercises with the United States to train its security forces, including air marshals and port authorities. Given China's political actions and that it is party to eleven of the twelve international counterterrorism conventions and protocols, I consider China a nonculpable state in this policy domain.

This is not surprising, since China also considers itself to be a victim of terrorism. Shortly after 9/11, Chinese officials asserted that the United States was not alone in this struggle. China faced similar dangers because of the "East Turkestan" militant force in its Xinjiang region that has international terrorist ties.[80] Thus, China has an interest in complying with and supporting international efforts against terrorism.[81]

But how far is China willing to change? China has long been a strong believer in absolute state sovereignty, illustrated by its human rights rhetoric (see, for example, Chen 2005). I would expect China to be among the most resistant countries to changes in sovereignty conceptions, especially because it did not participate in the military intervention in Afghanistan and did not experience the devastating attacks of 9/11 firsthand. However, because this is an issue that resonates with Chinese interests and since China is not a state supporter of terrorism,[82] I would expect subtle changes in how Chinese officials discuss the rights and obligations of states and the international community on this issue. I might find that China grants more authority to the international community on this issue and emphasizes that states must meet their international legal obligations. However, I would be surprised to find that China supports violations of state sovereignty on behalf of an antiterrorism agenda.

China's Stated Views on Sovereignty Before 9/11

To establish a baseline of China's views of the intersection of state sovereignty and terrorism prior to 9/11, several incidents of terrorism of broad international concern are illustrative. The focus of this attention fell on three states: Libya, the Sudan and Afghanistan. Before discussing the results of the content analysis of the associated speeches, I summarize the discourse, using representative statements to show how sovereignty was conceived.

After the Pan Am airline bombing in 1988 over Lockerbie, Scotland, Libya was suspected of harboring the responsible terrorists and of masterminding the tragic event. Libya refused to cooperate with the international community in bringing the criminals to justice. China responded by condemning terrorism and urged the international community to comply with the United Nations Charter in determining which actions were appropriate to address this problem.[83] To China, this meant respecting state sovereignty. While China supported UNSC Resolution 731 (1992), encouraging Libya to comply with its international obligations, it is clear that China did not favor further international action toward Libya. In the next two resolutions concerning sanctions against Libya—UNSC Res. 748 (1992), 883(1993)—China abstained. The Chinese discourse surrounding these decisions mentioned nothing about Libya's obligations to international law or the international community's obligation to push further into Libya's internal affairs.

Chinese discourse on the terrorist assassination attempt on the president of Egypt in 1996 also indicates an adherence to absolute sovereignty. While China acknowledged that the attempt was an act of terrorism, it expressed "reservations" about asking Sudan to stop its support of terrorist activities.[84] China urged the international community to not rush to judgment, despite the strong evidence that three suspects were hiding in Sudan. China preferred to not interfere in the internal affairs of the Sudan and held the view that it was up to the Sudan to decide what should be done. China later abstained from voting on a UNSC resolution calling for sanctions against the Sudan, expressing the belief that the international community could encourage states to cooperate but not compel them.[85]

However, with regard to Afghanistan, China was more willing to use sanctions as a response to terrorist activities by the Taliban, aided by Pakistanis.[86] China cited the sanctions as a "last resort" and emphasized that UNSC Resolution 1267 (1999) called for the international community to respect the sovereignty of Afghanistan. China also called on all states to cooperate in the fight against terrorism but omitted any reference to a specific obligation: "we call upon countries around the world to offer meaningful, speedy and effective cooperation in the fight against terrorism."[87] China offered itself as an example, noting that in July 2000, it joined with neighboring countries to cooperate regionally on terrorism. In doing so, those states were committed to never allowing "their territories to be used for activities aimed at harming State sovereignty."[88] That is, states must guard their sovereignty from within by not letting their territory be used for terrorist activities. In addition, China also implicitly warned that an international fight against terrorism must respect external borders.

In sum, these statements suggest that Chinese views on sovereignty have tended toward the absolute notion. Content analysis of Chinese speeches at the United Nations Security Council provides confirmatory evidence (see figure 3.10). In the post–Cold War world prior to 9/11, on the topic of terrorism, 38% of the time Chinese speeches included calls to respect the rights of states, and 38% of the time the speeches mentioned the obligations of states to follow international law. At no point did China assert a right of the international community to intervene in the internal affairs of a state, though about 13% of the time China recognized that the international community had some kind of obligation to help prevent terrorism.

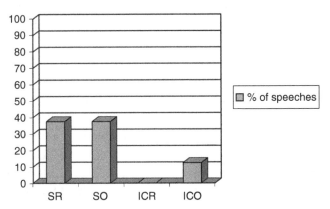

SR = State Rights, SO = State Obligations, ICR = International Community's

Rights, ICO = International Community's Obligations

FIGURE 3.10 China's Conceptions of Sovereignty Before 9/11

Thus, China seemed to believe that the international community has an obligation to let individual states deal with issues as they saw fit, though the international community can try at times to guide these decisions. In reference to the antiterrorist conventions, China noted that "these should be earnestly and effectively implemented."[89] States have some obligation to abide by the rules of the international system, but sovereignty remains the reigning norm. The extent to which China's understanding of sovereignty continues or changes is the next subject of investigation.

China's Stated Views on Sovereignty After 9/11

I begin this section by providing a summary of statements that characterize China's views on sovereignty in the post-9/11 world. This is followed by a discussion of the results from content analysis and an assessment of how my expectations match the empirical reality.

Shortly after the attacks on the United States, China reiterated its condemnation of terrorism and encouraged states to work together to fight terrorism as outlined in the international conventions against terrorism.[90] By supporting the implementation of the conventions, China implicitly acknowledged that states have obligations to fulfill in this arena. Moreover, China recognized that the international community had to play a "leading role" in the fight against terrorism. Not only were states obliged to cooperate, but the Security Council should lead the effort.[91]

That states have international counterterrorism obligations became a recurrent theme in Chinese speeches, from November 2001 on.[92] Moreover, China noted the importance of regional cooperation as well as international cooperation in the antiterrorist fight.[93] Recognizing the fight against terrorism as "a new task for the Security Council," China confirmed the obligation of the international community to address terrorism as a threat to international peace and security.[94] Furthermore, China continued to reiterate its support for the newly formed Counter-Terrorism Committee, from January 2003 on.[95] China had no reservations about an international body monitoring states in this way, even if it includes visits on the ground. This implies both a right and obligation of the international community to intervene in matters normally accorded to the state.

However, alongside its affirmation of both states' and the international community's obligations to counter terrorism, and its recognition that "terrorism remains a major threat facing the international community," China sometimes reminds the international community that they should abide by the "purposes and principles of the United Nations Charter and the fundamental norms of international law," by which China means absolute sovereignty.[96] China occasionally notes the importance of respecting states' authority: "Counterterrorism efforts should . . . fully respect the independence, sovereignty, and territorial integrity of States."[97]

The content analysis suggests that while China may continue to hold on to the notion of absolute sovereignty, this belief is much weaker than in the period prior to 9/11 (see figure 3.11). Interestingly, only 15% of the time did China refer to respecting states' rights, down from 38% in the previous time period.[98] At the same time, though, references to a state's obligations to the international community stayed about the same, decreasing only slightly from 38% to 33%. What is most interesting is China's increased support for the international community's obligations, and the important role of the Security Council in enforcing international law. Prior to 9/11, China mentioned these beliefs in only 13% of the speeches, but after 9/11, over half the speeches refer to the Security Council's obligations (67%).[99] In tandem with this dramatic increase, China claimed in 15% of the speeches that the international community has a right to intervene in states' affairs, primarily through the monitoring mechanism of the UNSC's CTC.

As expected, in this policy domain, China leans toward a contingent view of sovereignty. While maintaining about the same level of emphasis on state obligations, China asserts the absolute notion of sovereignty to a lesser degree than before. Rather, China increasingly affirms the international community's responsibility to ensure that states follow counterterrorism norms. It appears that China is in the midst of being pushed toward contingent sovereignty by the international antiterrorism campaign, yet pulled back by its historical leaning for absolute sovereignty in dealing with global issues in general.

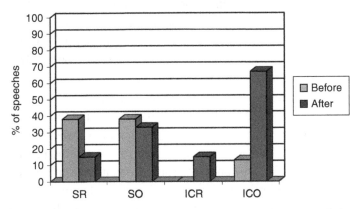

SR = State Rights, SO = State Obligations, ICR = International Community's

Rights, ICO = International Community's Obligations.

FIGURE 3.11  China's Conceptions of Sovereignty Before and After 9/11

## Russia

Russia has been an important force in the fight against terrorism. Having experienced deadly terrorist events within its borders, Russia has supported counterterrorism measures both domestically and abroad: "The effort will never work unless we unite the whole international community in a common front against terrorism."[100] To this end, Russia has engaged in a number of multilateral efforts. As mentioned in the case of China, Russia is party to the regional security organization, SCO, and has conducted joint counterterrorism exercises with China. It is also actively engaged in counterterrorism cooperation, such as intelligence sharing, with the United States, primarily through the United States-Russia Working Group on Counterterrorism. Russia has spearheaded the creation of an antiterrorism rapid-reaction force with members from the Commonwealth of Independent States (CIS). In addition, Russia is an active member of the international community. For example, Russia served as the chair of the UN Counterterrorism Committee from 2004 to 2005. In terms of fulfilling its legal obligations, Russia has integrated UN resolutions into domestic law and is party to eleven of the twelve international conventions relating to terrorism.

Russia has faced repeated attacks from alleged separatists turned global jihadists in the North Caucasus and in Moscow, spurring its resolve in the fight against terrorism at all levels.[101] For example, after the 2002 terrorist attack by Chechen rebels in a Moscow theater, Russia introduced a resolution before the United Nations Security Council that condemned the attack and reiterated states' duty to cooperate with Russian police in the matter. Although Russia may have friendly relations with states that sponsor terrorism, it unequivocally condemns terrorism as a tactic. Thus, the evidence points to Russia as a nonculpable state.

Given Russia's nonculpability in this area, I expect that it would view sovereignty in similar ways to China. First, Russia also is not involved in the ongoing military intervention in Afghanistan, and the effects of 9/11 for Russia are indirect, in that the attack did not occur on Russian soil. Yet, Russia has ever more reason to support a contingent notion of sovereignty because of the large-scale terrorist attacks within its borders, such as in Kaspiysk, Moscow, and Grozny, which are linked to terrorism in European and Muslim countries through the Chechen rebels. In addition, counterterrorism gives Russian leaders opportunities to consolidate power and implement policies that stray from democratic principles.[102]

While Russia previously supported absolute sovereignty as a general principle, it may lean toward a larger role for the international community in policing terrorism across countries after 9/11. I expect that Russia would hold stronger beliefs about the obligations of states to the international community's laws regarding counterterrorism and would emphasize the role of the international community in the fight against terrorism to a greater degree than prior to 9/11. Moreover, I posit that Russia will begin to mention the rights of the international community in the post-9/11 period, and not just its obligations as it did in the previous period. The following section establishes a baseline for comparison.

Russia's Stated Views on Sovereignty Before 9/11

As with China, to establish Russia's views on sovereignty prior to 9/11, I examine its discourse on several terrorist attacks that garnered international attention. These include the terrorist bombing of Pan Am Flight 103 (1988); the attempted assassination of the Egyptian president (1996); and terrorism linked to the Taliban regime in Afghanistan (1998–2001), such as the US embassy bombings in Africa. I first review representative statements from the related speeches, before discussing the results of the content analysis.

With regards to Libya's suspected involvement in the airline bombing of Pan Am Flight 103, Russia repeatedly condemned terrorism but reminded the international community to follow the "principles and norms of international law" in dealing with this issue.[103] Russia was wary of the infringement on sovereignty that could occur during efforts to bring the suspects to justice. While it encouraged Libya to turn over the suspects by voting for all three resolutions related to this incident—UNSC Res. 731 (1992), 748 (1992), 883 (1993)—including sanctions against Libya, Russia refrained from mentioning Libya's obligation to the international community; rather, it declared that it "hopes that Tripoli will treat the resolution . . . with all due seriousness."[104] Russia seemed to believe that the international community was right in sanctioning Libya but accorded equal weight to giving Libya space to exercise its sovereignty.

With reference to Sudan's harboring of terrorist suspects, Russia again declared that terrorism is deplorable and that states should cooperate on the issue of international terrorism.[105] As with Libya, Russia stated that it "hopes that the Government of Sudan . . . will take real steps" toward cooperating with other countries in the airline bombing case.[106] Furthermore, Russia "encourages the Government of the Sudan to respond fully and effectively," though it admitted that the UN Security Council was not the responsible party to ensure this.[107] Russia believed that there was no authority above the state. The international community should cooperate on terrorism issues but has no obligation to interfere in states' affairs.

This position displayed some movement, however, when confronted with the Taliban regime in Afghanistan in 1999. Acknowledging the "growing consolidation of terrorist structures throughout the world," Russia observed that the United Nations was increasingly responsible for helping the international community deal with this threat.[108] Moreover, Russia became more adamant that states fulfill their obligations to the counterterrorism conventions.[109]

Taking these statements together, it appears that before 9/11, Russia believed that states and the international community shared responsibility for fighting terrorism. However, in specific instances, Russia was sensitive to the offending state, respecting its sovereign authority. Though Russia voted to sanction all three states, the discourse revealed that it was reluctant to apply sanctions, and would not support an escalation of action for the sake of international peace and security. Thus, though Russia believed that the international community has a responsibility to fulfill, this did not imply that the international community had the right to interfere within states' internal affairs.

Content analysis makes this development clearer (see figure 3.12). In 25% of the speeches in this period, Russia endorsed respecting the rights of states. Russia also emphasized obligations of states to the international community in 25% of its speeches. While Russia failed to articulate anything concerning the rights of the international community to further involve itself in the affairs of a state, Russia did maintain that the international community had a responsibility to see to it that states were fulfilling their obligations (50% of the speeches). To see if Russia changes its views after 9/11, I turn to an investigation of statements made since the terrorist attacks on the United States.

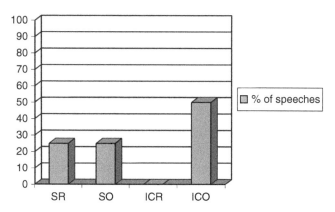

SR = State Rights, SO = State Obligations, ICR = International Community's
Rights, ICO = International Community's Obligations

FIGURE 3.12 Russia's Conceptions of Sovereignty Before 9/11

After the 9/11 attacks, Russia immediately condemned them as an act of terrorism and lent its full support to the United States. As Russia reminded members of the Security Council, in 1999, "on the initiative of Russia, which had suffered massive attacks by international terrorists—the Council began to comprehensively consider the problem of terrorism as a threat to international peace and security."[110] Russia spoke of the need for international solidarity because in the age of globalization, "one country's grief becomes the grief of the entire international community."[111] It expressed its satisfaction with the new role that the Security Council was taking in "creating a global system to counter terrorism."[112] In addition, Russia emphasized that Resolution 1373 (2001) was not just an *appeal* to states, but it *imposed* obligations on states: "far from being a declaratory appeal, it imposes the obligation on each State to lead a decisive struggle against international terrorism."[113] This reflected Russia's increasing belief that states had certain obligations to fulfill and that the international community also had an obligation to see that states followed through.[114]

In statements regarding the Counter-Terrorism Committee, Russia asserted that it "must be an effective mechanism of international compliance."[115] Russia was unwavering in its view that such a monitoring system was necessary, which meant that states no longer had ultimate authority in this domain. While it was careful to note that "the CTC should not function as a repressive body," Russia also asserted that the "CTC must help states with effective implementation of obligations,"[116] emphasizing its critical role in the fight against global terrorism.[117] Encouraging all states to comply with this UN counterterrorism body, Russia also openly scolded states that failed to complete their national reports that were required by the CTC.[118]

Russia was mindful of the implications of the encroachment of the counterterrorism regime on state sovereignty, something which it largely supported: "we are witnessing a process to establish, under the auspices of the United Nations, an unparalleled global structure to counteract the threat of terrorism."[119] Furthermore, Russia stressed that serious action may need to be taken in the fight against terrorism: "we are fully aware of the Security Council's readiness and ability to exercise its Charter authority to protect international peace and security in the face of the threat of terrorism."[120]

Russia constantly urged the Council to "redouble" and "intensify" its efforts against terrorism, insisting that the Council "take more decisive action."[121] This view was espoused early on, as it reflected Russia's immediate self-interest. In 2002, Russia took action against Chechen terrorists in the Pankisi Gorge of Georgia.[122] Fueled by counterterrorism imperatives in the international community, Russia claimed that it now had an international right to take unilateral military action, indicating the trumping of counterterrorism over state sovereignty.[123] At the same time, Russia also recognized the central role of the international community against terrorism: it is "our common responsibility to eliminate terrorism . . . the United Nations must continue to provide political and moral leadership, and to coordinate counterterrorism efforts."[124]

To express Russian views during the 9/11 era in more concrete terms, the content analysis illustrates that Russia placed little value on state sovereignty when it came to counterterrorism (see figure 3.13). Russia referred to absolute sovereignty in only 3% of the speeches after 9/11, compared with mentions in 25% of speeches in the period prior.[125] Furthermore, Russia placed greater emphasis on states' obligations to fight terrorism and comply with international laws (from 25% to 51%), as it more than doubled its discussion of states' obligations. In terms of the international community's rights and obligations, Russia also demonstrated a change in its beliefs. Russia came to view the international community as having a right to intervene in states' affairs (from 0% to 38%) and believed much more strongly that the international community has a responsibility to lead the war on terrorism, helping states to achieve compliance with international norms and laws (from 50% to 78%).[126]

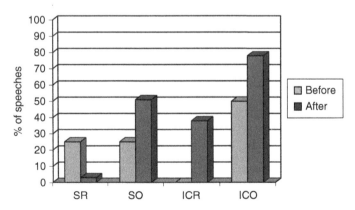

SR = State Rights, SO = State Obligations, ICR = International Community's Rights, ICO = International Community's Obligations.

FIGURE 3.13   Russia's Conceptions of Sovereignty Before and After 9/11

How did the empirical reality match my expectations? I expected that Russia would move toward the idea of contingent sovereignty, emphasizing the obligations of states and the international community in the fight against terrorism. Because Russia was a nonculpable state, I did not expect Russia to hold onto absolute sovereignty in this policy domain. These expectations were borne out in the analysis. The evidence suggests that Russia strongly believes in contingent sovereignty for states because it asserted not just an obligation for states to comply with counterterrorism measures, but a *right* of states to intervene in the internal affairs of states.

## Discussion and Conclusion

Although the cases differ in degree, they point to similar trends in the direction of contingent sovereignty. Table 3.1 summarizes the results and aids in comparing states' beliefs about sovereignty before and after 9/11. The states participating in the military intervention in Afghanistan indicate shifts in their understandings of the rights and responsibilities in combating terrorism. Both the United States and the United Kingdom demonstrate the greater value placed on the rights and obligations of the international community since 9/11 and the onset of the war in Afghanistan.

Even China and Russia show signs of movement toward the contingent understanding of sovereignty. I had expected that despite China's reputation as a champion of absolute sovereignty, its nonculpability and self-interest in this policy arena would predict a moderate reinforcement of contingent

TABLE 3.1 Conceptions of Sovereignty for Interveners and Noninterveners

| | STATES' RIGHTS | | STATES' OBLIGATIONS | | INTERNATIONAL COMMUNITY RIGHTS | | INTERNATIONAL COMMUNITY OBLIGATIONS | |
|---|---|---|---|---|---|---|---|---|
| | BEFORE | AFTER | BEFORE | AFTER | BEFORE | AFTER | BEFORE | AFTER |
| **Military Intervention** | | | | | | | | |
| United States | 0 | 2 | 89 | 78 | 11 | 46** | 78 | 76 |
| United Kingdom | 11 | 0** | 56 | 83* | 11 | 40* | 67 | 89 |
| **Noninterveners** | | | | | | | | |
| Russia | 25 | 3** | 25 | 51 | 0 | 38** | 50 | 78* |
| China | 38 | 15 | 38 | 33 | 0 | 13 | 13 | 67** |

NOTE: Numbers indicate percent of total speeches that mention a given category. The total number of speeches for each country is as follows (before; after): US (9; 41); UK (9; 35); Russia (8; 37); China (8; 39). Statistically significant changes indicated by $*p < .10$; $**p < .05$.

sovereignty. Though China still makes mention of the need to respect state sovereignty in the post-9/11 period, it too has an interest in seeing some change in the traditional norm of sovereignty. While China has significantly increased its support for the obligations of the international community (showing the largest leap of the states studied in terms of international community obligations), it is not to the same degree as the other states under investigation. Interestingly, references to *states'* obligations by China and Russia are much lower than the two state interveners, the United States and the United Kingdom. At the same time, though, Russia is very similar to the interveners in its emphasis (or lack thereof) on states' rights, international community rights, and international community obligations. One explanation might be that Russia engaged in a brief military intervention of its own in Georgia in 2008. While it was not fought for counterterrorism purposes, the conflict did involve Russia's violation of Georgia's sovereignty.

The changes in understandings of sovereignty found in this study suggest ways in which the normative structure that governs international relations is influenced. The outcome of the British and American military intervention affected not only the increasing prominence of contingent sovereignty, which was given high profile by the actions of two major powers, but also contributed to the coherence of contingent sovereignty with other norms. Both states successfully packaged a sovereignty contingent on compliance with counterterrorism norms together with human rights and democratic norms. For example, states that adhered to basic human rights tenets would provide less fertile ground for the appeal of terrorism. However, as the United States and the United Kingdom continued their fight against terrorism in Afghanistan, it was not clear that the discourse regarding these norms was reflected in practice. Some argue that the United States tolerates repressive regimes, if they cooperate with the global war on terrorism (e.g., Pakistan). Others debate the humane treatment of prisoners of war at Guantanamo Bay. As such, counterterrorism supersedes not just absolute sovereignty but also respect for human rights and democratic principles. Though I posited earlier that prioritization of contingent sovereignty would affect environmental conditions, with the expectation that the democratization trend, and thereby human rights norms, would continue as a consequence of the war in Afghanistan, it seems that the military response to 9/11 by the United States and the United Kingdom has done little to affect global conditions in this regard.

Those states not involved in the intervention, but willing to place counterterrorism norms over absolute sovereignty, were expected to contribute to the prominence and coherence of contingent sovereignty with other norms. As the analyses shows, both Russia and China illustrate these expectations. Not only did these leading states contribute to the prominence of contingent sovereignty through reiteration of counterterrorism norms, but they also tied contingent sovereignty to other legitimate norms, such as norms of self-defense and international (and national) security.

In sum, this chapter has investigated changes in sovereignty conceptions in the context of the global war on terrorism. It found general support for the expectations. First, the extent to which a contingent norm of sovereignty is accepted by a state depends, at least in part, on the process and outcome of the military intervention. Second, states that are not directly involved in the military intervention will moderately change their views, depending on their culpability and self-interest. Moreover, what seems clear in all cases is the importance of an event like 9/11 as a contributing factor to the process and conditions necessary for change, which then allow for an action, such as military intervention, to propel normative change.

# CHAPTER 4 | Sovereignty and Human Rights

... if humanitarian intervention is, indeed, an unacceptable assault
on sovereignty, how should we respond ... to gross and systematic
violations of human rights that affect every precept of our common
humanity?

—KOFI ANNAN, UN Secretary-General, 2000

THE GRADUAL EROSION OF traditional notions of sovereignty appears in
tandem with the rise of the human rights regime. Not only has the body of
international human rights law expanded since the inception of the United
Nations (1945), so too has the number of international organizations and
movements on behalf of human rights. Collectively, they represent a direct
challenge to the notion of absolute sovereignty. By calling for a fundamental shift from protecting states' rights to individuals' rights, human rights
advocates compel the international community to consider its own rights
and responsibilities vis-à-vis states and individuals. At the same time, such
deliberations are made all the more urgent by crises in which grave violations of universal human rights occur. In these situations, there is often a
demand for the use of force to halt the abuses. In stark contrast to the
politics of the Cold War, military intervention is now seen as a viable
option, as the 2011 international intervention in Libya demonstrated.

Such actions illustrate the fact that the norm of unconditional sovereignty is progressively being replaced by a norm of contingent sovereignty,
in which a state's sovereignty depends on compliance with its international
human rights obligations. But how do these changes occur? As I argued in
chapter 3, the extent to which a contingent norm of sovereignty is adopted
by a state depends on the circumstance of the action taken on its behalf—in

this case, military intervention on behalf of human rights. Given that the necessary structural conditions are met, I expect that the more arduous and costly the intervention for the intervener, the greater the commitment to sovereignty contingent on a states' fulfilling its internationally recognized human rights obligations. Moreover, interveners will adhere more strongly to contingent sovereignty than noninterveners. Using comparative case studies and content analysis of UN Security Council speeches by two of the leading interveners, the United States and France, and two noninterveners, China and Russia, I investigate one of the first instances of humanitarian intervention in the post–Cold War era: the international intervention in Somalia.[1] I examine their discussions of sovereignty as they relate to human rights prior to, during, and after the intervention.[2]

In the following sections, I provide a brief background on the evolution of human rights in the international community, as well as a discussion of the conditions that made new understandings of sovereignty possible. I then begin the examination of conceptions of sovereignty by the United States and France, within the context of their intervention in Somalia. For comparative purposes, I then investigate the views of China and Russia, which supported but did not participate in the intervention. Finally, I offer a comparative analysis of the cases and a discussion of their implications.

## Norms Regarding Human Rights

The genocide during World War II spurred the international community to create a set of human rights standards to complement the United Nations Charter, eventually resulting in the Universal Declaration of Human Rights (1948). In 1946, the United Nations Commission on Human Rights (UNCHR) was created to monitor and report on human rights abuses. In its early years it contributed to what is now called the International Bill of Human Rights (IBHR). By producing two treaties, the International Covenant on Civil and Political Rights (1966) as well as its two Optional Protocols, and the International Covenant on Economic, Social and Cultural Rights (1966), the commission created mechanisms to enforce the Universal Declaration of Human Rights. Together, all three documents constitute the International Bill of Human Rights, the foundation for worldwide human rights. Increasingly, national and local tribunals cite principles found in the IBHR, elements of which can be found in charters of regional organizations, including the Organization of African Unity and the European Union.[3]

Throughout its sixty years, the UNCHR was fairly successful, given the Cold War climate prevalent during most of its existence. It helped improve human rights in individual countries and contributed to the institutional capacity of the United Nations as it sought to promote and protect human rights (Scannella and Splinter 2007). Yet, it was increasingly plagued by criticism for having members with questionable records and politicizing human rights, ultimately resulting in its dissolution.[4] In March 2006, it was replaced by the UN Human Rights Council, which embraced the mission of the UNCHR but revised its operating procedures and composition to address criticisms of the UNCHR. While the new council still contends with some of the same issues as its predecessor (members with troubling human rights records and political bias), the fact that efforts were made to reinvent this international body on human rights reflects the importance of its purpose. However, the council remains hampered by its ability to act in cases of gross human rights abuses. When use of force is deemed necessary in such situations, the international community is largely dependent on the UN Security Council, which has the authority to sanction military action. Horrific crises, such as the genocide in Rwanda and ethnic cleansing in Bosnia, compelled heated debates on the right of military intervention by the international community to halt mass atrocities.

In efforts to quell these disputes, in 2000, the government of Canada commissioned a report by international scholars to help create a set of intervention principles for the international community. This commission, the International Commission on Intervention and State Sovereignty, redefined state sovereignty as the "responsibility to protect" (R2P). This concept was revolutionary because previously the debate had centered on the right of intervention, and the commission reframed it as one of responsibility to protect, changing the perspective from a potential intervener to the point of view of those in distress. In essence, when states fail to protect, the international community must act.

The commission's report, *The Responsibility to Protect* (2001), outlines several specific principles, beginning with the responsibility to prevent atrocities before they occur. By devising early-warning detection systems, the international community can potentially avert or minimize large-scale human rights abuses. In the case that the international community becomes aware of a crisis, there exists a responsibility to react. Suggested actions range from sanctions to the use of military force. Finally, the international community holds the responsibility to rebuild. This last principle includes not only a commitment to disarmament and reconciliation in the affected country, but also the encouragement of an economy that sustains development. Widespread support for these elements of "responsibility to protect" culminated in their unanimous adoption at the 2005 UN World Summit. In states unwilling or unable to fulfill their obligations to their citizens, the responsibility for those citizens shifts to the international community. Under these circumstances, the "choice for the state then becomes one of endeavoring to discharge its responsibilities or otherwise risk forfeiting its sovereignty" (Deng et al. 1996, 28).

## Conditions Conducive to Changes in Sovereignty

Before focusing on the intervention in the Somali humanitarian crisis, it is first important to demonstrate that international conditions were conducive to a revised understanding of sovereignty. Not only was there a contributing condition, the crisis itself, but all three of the necessary conditions (prominence, coherence with other norms, and environmental conditions) were met to facilitate changes in state understandings of sovereignty as one conditional on states' meeting human rights standards.

In the time surrounding the Somali intervention, human rights norms were a prominent feature of the international system. As the growing body of international human rights law illustrates, the international community moved from a general affirmation of human rights in the Universal Declaration of Human Rights to their more specific articulation in the form of treaties designed to protect particularly vulnerable populations and to uphold standards of human rights protection for states.[5]

Another reason that suggests that normative change is possible rests on the coherence of contingent sovereignty with other norms. Conceptions of sovereignty as dependent on meeting human rights obligations also complemented democratic norms, which were on the rise with the demise of the communist Soviet Union. A democratic society is one in which there is respect for political and civil liberties as well as economic and social rights, all of which are considered part of the more general notion of human rights. Thus, support for human rights is tied to an endorsement of democracy.

Perhaps the most important factor that allowed for the possibility of normative change was the end of the Cold War. While establishing a set of fundamental human rights in the International Bill of Human Rights, the international community made little progress toward enforcing these rights during the Cold War. Hampered by political divisions among the permanent members of the UN Security Council, in whom veto power rested, human rights abuses within states were largely ignored for the sake of geopolitical interests. Consider the 1965–66 horrific massacre of at least 500,000 people in Indonesia as Suharto's anticommunist regime rose to power. Even when intervening states *could* claim that an intervention was intended to stop gross human rights abuses, they chose not to. Such was the case when Vietnam intervened in neighboring Cambodia. The United Nations turned a blind eye to the genocide occurring there (1975–1979). This large-scale killing stopped when Vietnam intervened in 1978, but not before 1.7 million Cambodians lost their lives to the tyrannical leader, Pol Pot, and the Khmer Rouge.[6] However, rather than citing humanitarian justifications, Vietnam legitimized the intervention with reference to self-determination principles (Finnemore 2003, 77). It clearly felt that this argument would have more currency in the international arena than would a defense of human rights. Surprisingly, those states that did view the situation in Cambodia as one of gross human rights violations *condemned* Vietnam's action as a violation of state sovereignty (Finnemore 2003, 78). Thus, absolute sovereignty remained unchallenged; while states valued human rights, they valued sovereignty more.

With the collapse of the Soviet Union, the Cold War ended, making international conditions conducive to possible military intervention by the international community if a state violated human rights norms. The fact that humanitarian intervention was openly discussed and debated at international forums in the 1990s indicates that states were willing to consider the possibility of such intervention, a significant change from the Cold War milieu (Gillespie 1993; Mills 1998). With the so-called CNN effect, citizens from around the world came face to face with the horrors of mass killings. The growing transnational moral consciousness, driven by a range of actors, demanded that human rights top the international agenda, making it politically possible for state leaders to consider intervention abroad for reasons other than national security.

The decision of the United Nations to support a military intervention at the time of humanitarian crisis in Somalia in the early 1990s represented one of the international community's first steps toward the doctrine of "responsibility to protect." This crisis was considered a critical test of how the international community would cooperate within the new world order. An internal crisis became one demanding an international solution. In striking contrast to Cold War politics, not only did the crisis make the UN Security Council's agenda, but it received broad support from states, including all permanent members of the UNSC. The intervention in Somalia thus provides an opportunity to examine changes in conceptions of sovereignty in a context freed from superpower rivalries.

# Humanitarian Intervention in Somalia

The civil war in Somalia began in the early 1980s when clans in the south grew weary of the increasingly repressive tactics of their country's president, Siad Barre. Opposition spread to the north, leading the country to civil war. Rather than uniting against President Siad Barre, the clans fought one another *and* the regime. For years, the president had pitted clan against clan to distract them from his ailing regime. Now these efforts would destroy the Somali people and the regime. The violence became so great that President Siad Barre and his supporters were forced to leave the country in 1991, escalating the struggle to fill the power vacuum. Somalia collapsed into a state of anarchy, and alongside the civil war, severe droughts caused mass starvation and signaled the first humanitarian crisis in the post–Cold War world. As the United Nations reported:

> By 1992, almost 4.5 million people, more than half the total number in the country, were threatened with starvation, severe malnutrition and related diseases. The magnitude of suffering was immense. Overall, an estimated 300,000 people, including many children, died. Some 2 million people, violently displaced from their home areas, fled either to neighbouring countries or elsewhere within Somalia. All institutions of governance and at least 60 per cent of the country's basic infrastructure disintegrated.[7]

## Help is Here? United States and France

### United States

The United States' involvement in the humanitarian efforts in Somalia began in August 1992, as the famine worsened and international relief organizations were overwhelmed with the logistics of transporting and distributing food to the Somalis. The food supply was threatened by looting at distribution centers, so the United States helped remedy this by airlifting food from Kenya directly to Somali villages. This operation was designated Provide Relief and sought to enhance the efforts of UNOSOM, the United Nations Operation in Somalia. This soon proved inadequate, as the warring political groups attempted to gain control over the food supply by stealing and killing those who got in the way. In this situation, food became a symbol of power. But simply transporting the food safely into the country was not enough. The supplies also needed to be *distributed* in a secure environment. Because of this, the United States implemented Operation

Restore Hope, which meant the deployment of thousands of US troops to secure relief supplies and end the starvation. In December 1992, the UN Security Council legitimized the US-led Unified Task Force (UNITAF) through Resolution 794.

The initial US objective was to secure the transportation and distribution of food in Somalia. According to President George H. W. Bush, the mission was "to create a secure environment in the hardest-hit parts of Somalia so that food can move from ships overland to the people in the countryside . . . devastated by starvation."[8] When this was accomplished, the mission would be turned over the United Nations. By March 1993, this goal was largely obtained for the immediate future. The security environment had greatly improved, and the famine had been curtailed.[9] Violence within the capital city decreased, and relief supplies reached remote areas of the country.[10] Though the United Nations Secretary-General Boutros-Ghali pressed the United States to disarm the warring clans, the United States was firm in its commitment to a solely humanitarian mission.[11]

Having achieved the humanitarian goal, Operation Restore Hope ended on May 4, 1993, and the United Nations took over with about 25,000 troops (roughly replacing the number of US troops) from its member countries.[12] The new goals of the United Nations, embodied in United Nations Operation in Somalia II (UNOSOM II), were to restore law and order through disarmament and reconciliation.[13] The United States, as a member state, contributed a small contingent to this next phase.

As it turned out, the United States' achievement was a temporary band-aid; the violence continued, overwhelming the United Nations' mission. Shortly after the transition from US command, UN troops were massacred in June 1993, the first of several such attacks. Realizing the inadequacy of the present security forces, the Special Representative of the United Nations Secretary-General, Admiral Howe, asked the United States for a specialized task force to aid in finding the parties responsible. The suspected leader of the attacks was General Aideed, a powerful clan leader vying for control of the country. Though the request was originally declined, because of increasing attacks on American troops in August, US Special Forces (Delta Force and US Army Rangers) were deployed.

The new US objective was to capture General Aideed.[14] To reduce the violence in Mogadishu, the capital of Somalia, the United Nations issued a small $25,000 reward for his arrest. Despite the specialized forces and monetary incentives, General Aideed eluded capture. He eventually died in 1996, from battle wounds in the ongoing civil war, a few years after US and UN forces left the country. Thus, the US did not achieve its goal of capturing General Aideed, cutting its losses after the bloody battle in Mogadishu in October 1993. Though it was a part of UNOSOM II, the United States, as an independent intervener, withdrew almost all its troops early the next year, in March 1994.

The intervention met its initial goal of curtailing the famine but did little to improve the situation for those caught between warring factions. When the United States realized that humanitarian and political factors could not be decoupled, they targeted General Aideed as the instigator of random violence and mass killings. Yet, the United States failed in this objective, and Somalis were left to fend for themselves in an explosive situation. UNOSOM II was also forced to end soon after the United States left, due to a lack of commitment to peace by the warring parties and deteriorating political will of UN member states. Thus, both independently and as part of the UNOSOM II, the United States found itself on the losing end.[15]

Over the period of involvement in Somalia, 1992–1994, the United States lost forty-three troops from a combined total of 28,000.[16] While this pales in comparison to US casualties in other wars fought, such as Vietnam or World War II, the US public was not prepared to accept losses for a cause in which national interests were not at stake. The aversion to losses peaked after the infamous battle of Mogadishu (dramatized in the movie *Black Hawk Down*), in which US Army Rangers attacked the Olympic Hotel in Mogadishu in search of General Aideed. The firefight lasted seventeen hours and resulted in the deaths of eighteen American soldiers and the wounding of eighty-four others. Compounding the losses was the flagrant display of defiance by Somali gunmen, as they dragged the body of a US soldier through the streets of Mogadishu.

Public opinion polls revealed a general decline in support of the United States' involvement in Somalia, even before the battle of Mogadishu on October 3–4, 1993.[17] While the majority of Americans (79%) initially agreed with the presence of US troops in Somalia, support sharply declined to 43% in September and to 36% after the battle of Mogadishu.[18] Similar questions yielded this same trend. Asked if US military forces should be involved in Somalia, 74% of respondents answered affirmatively in December 1992, just after the mission began, compared with only 34% in October 1993.[19] Moreover, in January 1993, just over 70% of Americans polled thought US efforts in Somalia were worth the cost.[20] That figure fell to 50% in October, after the losses in Mogadishu. In fact, the majority of Americans (60%) agreed with the statement, "Nothing the US can accomplish in Somalia is worth the cost of even one more US soldier" (CNN/*Times*, 10/7/93).

In addition to domestic political costs, the mission in Somalia came at a huge monetary expense. In providing military and logistical support, as well as food and medical assistance, the United States spent approximately $2.2 billion in Somalia[21] Needless to say, these costs were more than the United States had expected to spend—or had ever spent— on a humanitarian mission.

Given these indicators, the outcome of the intervention leads me to expect that the United States would increase its commitment to contingent sovereignty, once the intervention began. A costly intervention with minor success would create a strong need to justify the intervention in these terms, relative to the preintervention discourse. Prior to the intervention, the discourse would reflect a healthy competition between contingent and absolute sovereignty. That is, the United States would exhibit elements of both in its discourse, particularly as it comes to terms with the end of the Cold War and establishing a "New World Order." Given the outcome of the intervention, I expect that the discourse would shift toward the international community's right *and* obligation to intervene in situations reflecting dire human suffering. That is, states failing in their obligations to their people and the international community's laws forfeit their right to absolute sovereignty.

### US' Stated Views on Sovereignty Before Intervention

To see if the United States' views on sovereignty changed, I must establish a baseline for comparison. I do this by examining speeches one year prior to its intervention. In this time period (1991–1992), there are several items on the UN Security Council's agenda that help uncover state's views on the intersection of sovereignty and human rights. These items include the situations in Iraq, Haiti, Somalia, Cambodia, and (the former) Yugoslavia. Before discussing the results of the content analysis of the associated speeches, I summarize the discourse, using representative statements to illustrate how sovereignty was conceived.

Prior to the intervention in Somalia, the United States encouraged states to treat their citizens humanely, citing international law.[22] For example, after the Persian Gulf War (1990–91), Iraq was widely condemned for the treatment of its citizens, particularly its minorities. The United States acknowledged the situation by declaring that it is "profoundly concerned" about those "suffering because of the brutality of the Iraqi regime."[23] Though the United States voted to condemn the Iraqi government in a Security Council resolution, no further action was taken beyond insisting that "Iraq meet its humanitarian responsibilities."[24] In the United States' view, states had obligations to meet, but it was not the international community's job to enforce them: "It is not the role or the intention of the Security Council to interfere in the internal affairs of any country."[25]

The United States considered the situation in the former Yugoslavia similarly. While admitting a "sharp deterioration in the most fundamental human rights and freedoms," the United States recognized the primacy of state borders.[26] Only if the fighting spilled over into other countries did the problems in Yugoslavia become a matter of international action. This focused the debate on one of protecting border integrity, rather than the dire human rights situation. In this respect, the United States argued that the international community had an obligation to maintain state borders, but it did not mention a responsibility to protect the people within those borders.

The United States continued this position in Haiti, though there was evidence of widespread human rights abuses, including politically motivated rapes, designed to impede the prodemocracy movement.[27] In its discussion of Haiti, the United States concentrated on reminding Haiti of its international obligations, as well as the international community's responsibility to denounce Haiti for its actions. For example, the United States condemned the attacks on innocent civilians as the military junta there came unlawfully to power.[28] In addition, the United States encouraged the international community to isolate Haiti because its government did not represent the democratic will of the people. Though the United States did not refer to the rights and obligations of the international community in Haiti, it did so in other concurrent situations.

While the majority of speeches stressed the obligations of states with regard to human rights, there was somewhat frequent mention of the obligations of the international community to step in if human rights were violated. In the United States' view, if a state, such as Iraq, was unwilling to comply, the United Nations should step in.[29] The United States emphasized the obligation of the international community to "get humanitarian assistance to those in Iraq who need it most" and was "confident that the United Nations will rise to the challenge."[30] With regard to Bosnia, the United States declared, "This flagrant disregard for human life and for a clear agreement requires a response from the international community."[31] Referring to the UN's mission in Cambodia (UNTAC) that was to ensure the recent political settlement, the United States argued for a central role of the United Nations, in which the United Nations would "assume responsibilities commensurate with the visions of its founders."[32] These responsibilities, among other things, included the duty of the United Nations to promote human rights.

As previously noted, the United States recognized the right of states to absolute sovereignty. However, this position is not constant, since, in a limited way, the United States also introduced the right of the international community to bypass state borders. For example, the United States approved seizing Iraq's frozen oil-related assets to pay not just for Iraq's debts from the Persian Gulf War but also for humanitarian relief efforts in Iraq.[33] In addition, with regard to the ethnic cleansing in Bosnia, the United States supported the right of the international community to judge perpetrators.[34] While the United States rarely mentioned such rights, these few instances indicate that the United States was not hostile to the idea in some cases.

Content analysis of all the relevant speeches in the year prior to the US intervention in Somalia clearly points to an emphasis on state obligations (see figure 4.1). In almost 80% of the US speeches at the UN Security Council, the United States urged states to comply with their international obligations and admonishes certain states for their violations. At the same time, the United States was mindful of the international community's obligation to interfere in state's internal affairs if these obligations were not met, reflected in just over 56% of the speeches. Rarely (11%), however, does the United States advocate the right of the international community to interfere in sovereign states. Together, these indicators reveal some leanings toward contingent sovereignty, though absolute sovereignty remains a strong competitor, as confirmed by some continuing references to the rights of states (22%).

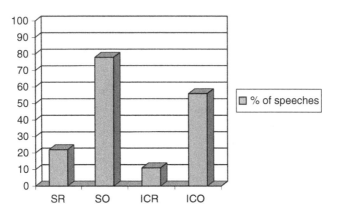

SR = State Rights, SO = State Obligations, ICR = International Community's
Rights, ICO = International Community's Obligations

FIGURE 4.1   US Conceptions of Sovereignty Before Military
Intervention

Will the United States continue with these views during and after the intervention in Somalia? The next section examines US discourse since the beginning of the intervention, by first providing a summary of these statements, and then comparing these with the baseline just established.

US' Stated Views on Sovereignty During and After Intervention

The United Nations Security Council authorized the US-led military intervention in Somalia on December 3, 1992. The resolution mandated the use of "all necessary means" to resolve "the human tragedy in Somalia."[35] From the beginning, the United States emphasized that the international community should address humanitarian crises. It described the United Nations as "vital to this cause."[36] In fact, throughout the intervention and even a year after, the United States consistently enunciated the humanitarian obligations of the international community: "we have the responsibility . . . [to] hold individuals accountable for their violations of international humanitarian law."[37]

In tandem with the discourse on the international community's obligations, the United States also frequently asserted the right of the international community to interfere if a state was not meeting its obligations. This included the right of the international community to judge those suspected of gross human rights abuses. As humanitarian situations arose in other countries demanding international attention, the United States explicity claimed that the international community had the right to use force: "we are authorizing a powerful military force."[38] While in some instances (Rwanda) it was simply too late, the fact remains that the United States espoused the right and obligation of intervention, though the international community lacked the will.

In terms of state's obligations, the United States continued its emphasis on the duty to comply with the norms and laws of the international community, including those regarding human rights. States were obliged to detain and arrest people suspected of gross human rights abuses, cooperate with the United Nations on such matters, and implement international laws in domestic legislation. What is striking, however, is the complete absence of references to state's rights. Absolute sovereignty, in which a state has ultimate authority over its internal affairs, is replaced by support for contingent sovereignty, represented by the dominant role of the international community to oversee human rights policies within states.

More concretely, the content analysis in figure 4.2 shows a marked decline in references to absolute sovereignty (from 22% to 0%),[39] but an increase in frequency of speeches referring to state's obligations (from 78% to 91%). In addition, stronger views concerning the role of the international

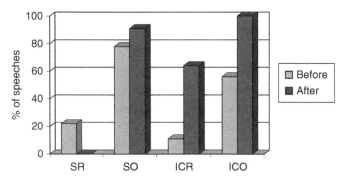

SR = State Rights, SO = State Obligations, ICR = International Community's

Rights, ICO = International Community's Obligations

FIGURE 4.2  US Conceptions of Sovereignty Before and After
Military Intervention

community permeate the speeches after the intervention began. When states
are unwilling or unable to do so, the United States affirmed in all its
speeches the obligation of the international community to interfere in
humanitarian crises (from 56% to 100%).[40] This increase was rivaled by a
significant nearly sixfold rise in references to the international community's rights (from 11% to 64%).[41] Thus, the evidence points to a change in
US views on sovereignty within the domain of human rights. The United
States reinforces contingent sovereignty to a greater extent than prior to the
Somali intervention.

This is consistent with my expectations. Because the intervention in Somalia was a high cost, low-success intervention, I expected that the United
States would increasingly embrace contingent sovereignty as the intervention went on. These results suggest that the outcome of the intervention
partially contributed to the changes in US conceptions of sovereignty.
While the United States was also seized with other humanitarian crises
during this time, Somalia was one of the first experiences (in the post–Cold
War world) that the United States had using military force to attempt to
remedy these kind of crises. In that respect, the intervention experience in
Somalia helped to shape the United States' ideas about the role of the international community in states' affairs.

## France

France began its mission to Somalia in December 1992, joining the US-led
efforts to end the famine. The French administration was divided on this
decision; some worried that France would overextend itself, given its UN

troop commitments in Cambodia and the Balkans.[42] However, considerable media attention had been given to the plight of Somalis in the days leading up to the intervention. Complementing this exposure was the lobbying of the high-profile Health and Humanitarian Action Minister, Bernard Kouchner.[43] Part of Mr. Kouchner's campaign for French involvement in Somalia was asking French schoolchildren to donate rice to Somalis (Allen and Styan 2000, 837). Though France denied the UN's request for military assistance in November 1992, by December, France changed its position, which coincided with the passage of UN Security Council Resolution 794 authorizing the use of force in Somalia to end the famine.

Similar to the United States, France sought to provide a military escort for the humanitarian operation, as well as stabilize the war-torn country. The French Minister of Defense Roland Dumas stated that "the first phase of the action consists in opening up humanitarian access corridors . . . in a second phase, the Blue Helmets will criss-cross the country and prepare the third phase, the national reconciliation and the rebuilding of the state."[44] In the first phase, France took part in the US-led UN mission (UNITAF), while it played its role as a UN member state in the latter phases as part of UNOSOM II (United Nations Operation in Somalia II).

As described in the US case earlier, the first phase of the intervention was successful in securing the humanitarian relief and transporting it to those in need.[45] As Mr. Kouchner declared, "Somalia was a big success. After this intervention, babies were not dying. So it was a success."[46] In addition, France's efforts at disarming the militias and securing the environment within its operational area succeeded (Guillot 1994, 37). At this time, the French scaled back their troops, from 2,000 to 1,100.

As part of the second UN operation in Somalia, French troops participated in UNOSOM II, which was supposed to oversee the reconciliation of the opposing sides and help rebuild the Somali state. France endorsed these goals but was not supportive of the United States' independent objective of capturing General Aideed. French Foreign Minister Alain Juppe said, "I don't know if the idea of killing Mr. Aideed at all costs is a solution to the problem."[47] France, in line with the UN, preferred to negotiate a settlement with all sides. Unfortunately, in this effort, UNOSOM II achieved little. Though there were two national disarmament and reconciliation conferences in January and March 1993, in which the warring parties agreed to a ceasefire, the agreements fell apart shortly thereafter as the fighting resumed.

The remaining French troops were withdrawn in December 1993, despite the protests of the United Nations. French Defense Minister Francois Leotard reasoned that "this operation has deviated from its assigned mission and is slowly being marked by unacceptable arrangements and military attitudes the Somalis do not understand."[48] While Mr. Leotard attempted to provide political cover for the early withdrawal, the fact remains that France left before achieving its goals. Somalia was not much better off than it had been.

Over the course of its presence in Somalia (1992–1994), France lost three soldiers.[49] Compared with the United States (forty-three casualties), the human cost of the intervention for France was quite low.[50] Moreover, there seemed little evidence of concern for the financial cost of the intervention to France in political discourse. If anything, the government of French President Mitterand was criticized for not doing enough. Humanitarian NGOs complained that "it is useless to feed people if snipers continue to kill them." (Guillot 1994, 35–36). However, public support for the intervention remained strong throughout. Initially, 82% of those polled supported France's involvement in this UN-mandated intervention (CSA/ La Vie, 12/10/92). Support for the deployment of French troops abroad continued after France's involvement in Somalia, with majorities reached on a range of polling questions related to support for peacekeeping (Sorenson and Wood 2005, 76).

Overall, France presents a case of a low-cost, low-success intervention in Somalia. Given these indicators, there is some dissonance between the outcome and the decision to intervene. Because the indicators of the intervention are not entirely consonant with France's views, I expect that there would be impetus for moderate change. Given France's support of contingent sovereignty, which implicitly guided France to intervene in the first place, I expect that France would lean toward reinforcing this view once the intervention began. Because cognitive dissonance does not consider situations with mixed indicators, these expectations are strictly exploratory, rather than confirmatory.

### France's Stated Views on Sovereignty Before Intervention

I review statements by France in the year prior to the intervention in order to establish a basis for comparison. During this time, the UN Security Council discussed several humanitarian situations in countries such as Iraq, Cambodia, and Somalia. As a member of the Council, France's views on the intersection of human rights and sovereignty norms can be seen in these speeches, which I will now summarize.

Regarding absolute sovereignty, France made no supportive statements about the right of states to independently govern their internal affairs. Rather, at least from the year prior to its intervention, France appeared to support contingent sovereignty. France frequently referred to states' obligations to the international community. In citing Iraq's violations of international humanitarian law, France discussed the United Nations' demands regarding human rights standards as "the minimum that the members of the international community must make in order to live up to the commitments they entered into."[51] With reference to human rights, France condemned "the failures of the government of Iraq to meet its obligations."[52]

At the same time, France reminded states not just of their obligations under international law but also to one another. For example, states must help other struggling states: "we call upon all states to do all in their power" to alleviate the suffering in Somalia, including contributing to relief efforts, supplying aircraft, and donating food.[53] This reflected France's sense of community, in that states are not just accountable to a "higher" body but also to one another.

The international community and its role was frequently the subject of France's remarks. France reminded the Council that it had consistently pursued humanitarian objectives because it was the responsibility of the international community to take a stand.[54] In France's view, "the international community can no longer, in an era when throughout the world democracy and respect for human rights are being reaffirmed, accept the flagrant violation of these values."[55] France regularly referred to the obligation of the international community to interfere in a state's affairs if unwilling or unable to comply with human rights norms; in such cases, "a firm reaction by the international community is essential."[56] In discussing the ongoing problems in Iraq, France stressed that "the international community cannot remain indifferent . . . It must do everything possible to prevent massive violations of human rights from continuing.[57] Regarding the continued abuses in Bosnia, France asserted that "the international community is duty bound to take action to allow humanitarian assistance to reach those for whom it is intended."[58]

After all, "human rights have triumphed . . . in the ideological struggle of the cold war,"[59] thereby charging the Council with the responsibility to "reaffirm faith in fundamental human rights."[60] In sum, France's conception of sovereignty prior to the intervention rested firmly upon contingent sovereignty; states must fulfill their international human rights obligations in order to remain sovereign.

The content analysis confirms this (see figure 4.3). As mentioned, none of the speeches refer to protecting state sovereignty when it comes to matters of human rights abuses. Rather, most speeches urged states to comply with their international obligations (70%). If states did not abide by human

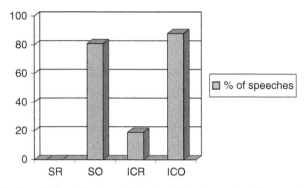

SR = State Rights, SO = State Obligations, ICR = International Community's

Rights, ICO = International Community's Obligations

FIGURE 4.3  France's Conceptions of Sovereignty Before Military
Intervention

rights norms, France strongly supported the idea that the international
community had the responsibility to interfere (80%). A relatively lesser
number of speeches mentioned the right of the international community to
address abuse under international law (20%).

France's Stated Views on Sovereignty During and After Intervention

Once the intervention began in December 1991, France continued to
espouse contingent sovereignty, reflecting the primacy of human rights.
We find that France continued to stress the international community as the
ultimate insurer of human rights norms. France insisted, "It is the duty of
the Council to react swiftly to ethnic cleansing."[61] Furthermore, the international community must be responsible for ensuring that perpetrators
were punished,[62] and that the international legal institutions (tribunals) for
this purpose were designed appropriately.[63] France solemnly acknowledged the heavy responsibility that the international community carried in
upholding human rights principles.

As for states, France implored them to comply with their international
obligations. For instance, during the break up of Yugoslavia, France continually reminded states that they must comply, warning that a lack of
compliance will receive a "clear cut reaction from the international community."[64] Even in times of war, France argued that states were obliged
"to follow the laws or customs of war."[65] In addition, states must comply
with international legal bodies: "all states are required to cooperate fully
with the Tribunal, even if this obliges them to amend certain provisions of
their domestic law."[66] Such a statement clearly cuts to the heart of a state's

sovereignty—the international community determines domestic laws. In fact, missing from all of France's speeches is any acknowledgment of states' rights.

France freely contended that the international community was empowered to tread on state sovereignty when necessary. It is in this area that France exhibits any change from its preintervention views on sovereignty. In creating the tribunals to investigate war crimes, for example, France drew upon the Council's legal right by "making use of its own powers."[67] Asserting these rights with reference to the human tragedies in Bosnia-Herzegovina, France approved the use of force to enforce the no-fly zone and warned that "we are not ruling out going even further if it proves necessary so to do."[68] Moreover, the resolutions that the Council passed were an "expression of the Council's authority" and the actions they embody, such as the use of force, and were "legitimate."[69] In sum, France asserted that the international community, represented by the UN Security Council, was endowed with certain rights in order to protect individual human rights.

In sum, France's conception of sovereignty exhibits elements of consistency and change (see figure 4.4). As the content analysis shows, France continued to disregard the importance of states' rights (from 0% to 0%). In terms of states' obligations, they retained their importance in French discourse to a similar extent as in preintervention discourse (from 81% to 80%). References to the international community's obligations to remedy gross human rights abuses also obtain similar levels (from 88% to 80%).

Amidst this uniformity, one substantively significant change does stand out. France more frequently referred to the international community's right

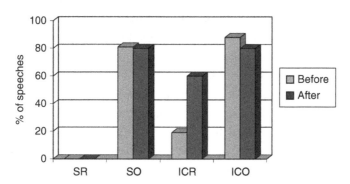

SR = State Rights, SO = State Obligations, ICR = International Community's Rights, ICO = International Community's Obligations.

FIGURE 4.4 France's Conceptions of Sovereignty Before and After Military Intervention

to interfere in humanitarian crises after the intervention began (from 19% to 60%).[70] This represents a dramatic change, reflecting an even stronger commitment to contingent sovereignty. One explanation could be the close relationship between "rights" and "obligations." Obligations are about what one is compelled to do, thereby implying a right to implementation. Within a context in which the international community was rebuilding international rules (early post–Cold War), France may have been compelled to more starkly state the norms of international behavior not merely as obligations, as in the preintervention period, but also as rights. Overall, the speeches given by France after the onset of intervention point to a relatively stronger view of contingent sovereignty than prior to the intervention.

## Supporters but Not Interveners: China and Russia

### China

While China abstained from voting in the UN Security Council on other peacekeeping missions, including those in Haiti and Rwanda, China supported the operations in Somalia (UNOSOM I, UNITAF, and UNOSOM II), but with reservations. China was concerned about setting a precedent for future peacekeeping operations, in which state sovereignty would not be observed by the international community (Fravel 113). China regarded the interventions in Somalia as "exceptions to the rule" because the situation in Somalia was "chaotic."[71] China's ambivalence about the intersection of human rights and sovereignty is evidenced by its lack of participation in the interventions.

To form expectations about how the Somali intervention might affect China's conceptions of sovereignty, despite its nonparticipation, it is important to consider China's culpability in the human rights policy domain, and thereby its self-interest. China had a long history of support for absolute state sovereignty, arguing that human rights were part of a state's internal affairs, not a subject for international debate.

For example, China had shocked much of the world with the use of force to quell the Tiananmen Square protests in 1989.[72] At this square in Beijing, protesters gathered from April 17 to June 5 to demand democratic reform, basic human rights, and government action against corruption. However, their protests were met with violence, resulting in at least several hundred civilian deaths (though other reports suggest several thousand).[73] Unfortunately, little changed within China and the following years were marked by continued reports of human rights abuses from international organizations monitoring the situation. In 1992, Human Rights Watch reported violent acts of repression by the Chinese government, including torture and murder of dissidents, forced labor, and abuse of political prisoners.[74] According the Political Terror Scale, which tracks levels of political violence across countries, China scored the highest level of terror in 1989 ("5" on a scale of "1" to "5"), and improved only slightly in the other years preceding the Somalia intervention (score of "4").[75] The scores for each year during and after the intervention stayed at about this level.[76]

Given that China is culpable of human rights abuses, I expect that it would continue to stress absolute sovereignty after the interventions. In order to maintain cognitive consistency between its internal and external practices, China will remain a strong supporter of states' rights to conduct their affairs as they see fit. If China were to lean toward contingent sovereignty in the international arena, it would create psychological discomfort. Absent a desire for change, the only way to avoid this is to promote international policies that are in line with domestic practices.

China's Stated Views on Sovereignty Before Somali Crisis

In order to detect changes in China's views on sovereignty, I establish a basis by which to judge whether change occurred.[77] I examine China's speeches on human rights and determine how China conceives of sovereignty within this policy domain. In the following section, I summarize these views through illustrative statements, and then I discuss the results of the content analysis from this period.

Prior to the intervention in Somalia, China made its views on the relationship between human rights and sovereignty clear through speeches given on a number of humanitarian crises, including in the former Yugoslavia and the treatment of Kurds in Iraq. In China's view, absolute sovereignty remained the most important principle governing international relations. In April 1991, China reminded the UN Security Council, "According to . . . the Charter, the Security Council should not consider or take action on questions concerning the internal affairs of any State."[78] In a later meeting that year, China again stated, "Here I wish to reiterate and emphasize that it is the consistent position of the Chinese government that a country's internal affairs should be handled by the people in that country themselves."[79] A state's domestic affairs were off-limits to the international community, and the international community was obliged to respect these rights per the UN Charter. Even in matters concerning gross human rights abuses, China claimed that states' rights must be respected. Only cases in which a state agreed to international interference would China consider intervention.[80]

For example, in first UN operation in Somalia (UNOSOM I), China declared that "it is our hope and belief that UN activities in Somalia will be conducted in accordance with the Charter . . . with full respect for Somali's independence and sovereignty."[81] In sum, when speaking about the place of human rights on the international agenda, China argued, "In essence, the issue of human rights falls within the sovereignty of each country. A country's human rights situation should not be judged in total disregard of its history and national conditions."[82]

During this time period, China rarely spoke about states' obligations to comply with the norms of the international community or the international community's obligation to help citizens victimized within states. Only at one time in the speeches under review did China concede that the international community had any obligations; that was to Cambodia, admitting that the Council was obliged to safeguard the Paris Agreements.[83] Further emphasizing China's fundamental belief in absolute sovereignty was the absence of any reference to the prerogative of the international community to remedy abuses within states.

A review of the content analysis confirms China's strong leaning toward absolute sovereignty (see figure 4.5). Out of all four categories, China most frequently mentioned protecting states' rights (63%). Few references were reflective of contingent sovereignty, as seen in the relatively small number of speeches concerning both state and international obligations to aid citizens exposed to humanitarian crises (13% each).

Having established China's conception of sovereignty as absolute, I now examine the extent to which these views change, if at all. Will states continue to be the ultimate authority for their own citizens, or will China

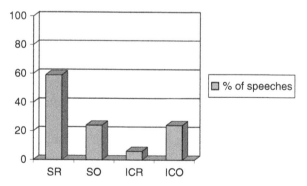

SR = State Rights, SO = State Obligations, ICR = International Community's

Rights, ICO = International Community's Obligations

FIGURE 4.5  China's Conceptions of Sovereignty Before Somali Crisis

allow for the expansion of international responsibilities? In the following section, I characterize the speeches given by China in the postintervention period to assess any change in conceptions of sovereignty, concluding with a discussion of whether my expectations match the empirical reality.

### China's Stated Views on Sovereignty After Somali Crisis

After the initial intervention began in Somalia (UNOSOM), China maintained its discourse regarding absolute sovereignty in the human rights arena.[84] It argued that human rights should not be a subject of the Council's discussions but rather delegated to other bodies: "Questions of human rights ought to be dealt with by the Commission on Human Rights."[85] This essentially meant that bodies with lesser authority (e.g., lacking power to enforce) should deal with human rights. In this way, China was indirectly able to protect its position on absolute sovereignty, since in other Council members' views, only the Council had the power to bypass state sovereignty.

When UN Security Council resolutions involved actions against human rights abuses within states, China repeatedly contended that it would not vote for the resolution unless it had the consent of the parties involved.[86] In the case of human rights abuses in the former Yugoslavia, China reaffirmed states' rights, reminding the international community that "the sovereignty, political independence and territorial integrity of the Federal Republic of Yugoslavia should be respected" and "the issue of Kosovo is an internal affair."[87] China held firmly to the notion of absolute sovereignty when it came to human rights.

At the same time, it made more frequent references to contingent sovereignty and acknowledged that the international community is responsible for alleviating large-scale human suffering. In Iraq, where many people were dying at the hands of a brutal regime, China acknowledged that the international community had to do something, though it did not have the right to use force to accomplish this task.[88] Similarly, in Bosnia, China believed that the Council had a duty to provide humanitarian relief, but not by invoking Chapter 7, which would legitimize using all necessary means.[89] Even in the case of genocide in Rwanda, China argued that the "international community should respect the sovereignty of states,"[90] though the international community could aid Rwanda if it was invited to do so. Together, the speeches indicate that China viewed absolute sovereignty as the main principle of international relations but allowed for some responsibility of the international community to enforce human rights. To guard against suspicions that China might be changing its views, China felt it necessary to remind the Council that China had not changed its position on human rights.[91]

When we examine the content analysis and compare it to the period prior to the intervention, we find that this is largely true (see figure 4.6). China still firmly stood behind absolute sovereignty, as reflected in the increase in its defense of states' rights in a majority of its speeches (from 59% to 73%). While a state's right to govern its internal affairs without outside interference dominates the speeches, there were negligible increases in two of the categories that reflect contingent sovereignty. With regard to a state being accountable to other states, China discussed this in 27% of its speeches, compared to 24% in the previous period. This increase is in tandem with a rise in the frequency of speeches that mention the international community's obligation to protect human rights (from 24% to 36%). However, there was no discussion of the international community's right to intervene in a state's internal affairs.

As expected, China remained a strong supporter of absolute sovereignty. A clear majority of the speeches emphasized that human rights fall within the purview of individual states. While China recognized that both states and the international community have *some* obligations to fulfill when it comes to protecting human rights, these speeches were few and came with qualifications. As a culpable member of the international community, China's conception of sovereignty did not experience much change, allowing it to maintain cognitive consistency with its own practices.

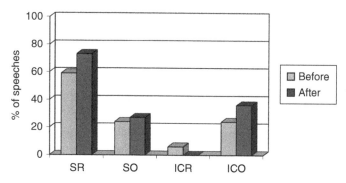

SR = State Rights, SO = State Obligations, ICR = International Community's Rights, ICO = International Community's Obligations.

FIGURE 4.6  China's Conceptions of Sovereignty Before and After Somali Crisis

Russia

Similar to China, Russia voted at the UN Security Council for the intervention in Somalia but did not participate in the mission. At the time of the deteriorating situation in Somalia, Russia was experiencing a great transition itself. On December 25, 1991, Mikhail Gorbachev resigned as leader of the Soviet Union, bringing hope to human rights activists everywhere. Among other things, the Soviet Union had imprisoned those who spoke out about the violations of human rights and suppressed religious expression. Though Gorbachev had been responsible for more progressive policies since his rise to power in 1986, by January 1991, there were protests against the apparent return of political repression.[92] The subsequent uprisings amidst Soviet military killings of citizens foreshadowed the fall of the Soviet Union later that year.

Russia (the former Soviet Union) had a history of human rights abuses under its repressive, communist regime, some of which endured through its political and economic transition. Russia maintained Soviet-style governments in many of the new republics. However, there were political movements to recognize past abuses and institutional incorporation of the principles of human rights, via constitutions and membership in the Conference on Security and Cooperation in Europe. The Somalia intervention coincided with this transitional phase in Russia, which reflected instability in Russia's compliance with human rights. Human Rights Watch noted a pattern of abuses associated with the political changes, often as a result of a continued struggle for power among locals.[93] In 1992, the year the intervention in Somalia began, Russia scored a "2" on a scale of "1" to "5", with "5" representing extreme terror in a country.[94] Russia continued at this low level of terror through 1993, and then jumped to higher levels of abuses, indicated by a "4" in 1994.

Given these indicators, I expect that prior to the intervention, Russia would initially support absolute sovereignty more than contingent sovereignty in the area of human rights. While not entirely discounting the role of the international community, I expect that Russia would initially maintain that human rights are a domestic matter, since it could not advocate human rights abroad while violating them at home. However, as Russia transitioned to democracy (ceased to be the Soviet Union), it would move toward contingent sovereignty, to the extent that its internal practices became consistent with international norms. Russia would especially have an interest in this because of its newness as a democratic member of the international community and need to build its reputation as such. Given the culpability measures, it appears that Russia was unable to maintain this record and relapsed into human rights violations toward the end of the Somalia interventions. At this stage, we should start to see a minor reemphasis on protecting states' rights in Russia's discourse. I still expect to see references to contingent sovereignty because Russia had publicly committed to a democratic, though turbulent, path and faced no threat of international intervention, given its power position.

### Russia's Stated Views on Sovereignty Before Somali Crisis

As with the other cases, I begin by establishing a baseline of comparison for Russia's views on sovereignty within the realm of human rights.[95] Prior to the first UN intervention in Somalia, several human rights situations were considered on the international agenda. Russia (or until December 1991, the Soviet Union) discussed its views on the relationship between human rights and sovereignty as these situations drew the attention of the UN Security Council.[96]

Initially, Russia seemed torn between absolute sovereignty and a greater role for the international community. For example, in April 1991, when the treatment of Iraq's citizens became the subject of the Council's deliberations, Russia stated, "In its approach to the problems that are brought before the United Nations, the Soviet Union firmly adheres to the principle of the inadmissibility of interference in the internal affairs of sovereign states."[97] Moreover, "the sovereignty, territorial integrity and political independence of Iraq must be ensured."[98] With regard to the crisis in Yugoslavia, later that year Russia reminded the Council that it was only because Yugoslavia had consented to the international community's help that it would vote for a resolution on humanitarian assistance.[99]

However, during this time period, and just as the Soviet Union officially dissolved and Russia retained its seat, its speeches began to refer more to states' obligations to follow international human rights norms. The newly elected President Yeltsin declared, "Our principles are clear and simple: primacy of democracy, human rights, and freedoms, legal and moral standards."[100] It became clear that Russia was signaling to the international community that it was rejecting its past practices. Yeltsin proclaimed human rights as a guiding principle: "I believe that these questions are not an internal matter of States, but rather their obligations under the UN Charter."[101] Russia's discourse continued to reaffirm sovereignty on the basis of meeting international standards of human rights. Russia reminded states with questionable practices, from Cambodia to Somalia to Iraq, that they were responsible for maintaining international human rights norms.[102]

In addition, speeches also more frequently discussed the international community's obligation to intervene in a state's internal affairs. Russia asserted, "The Security Council is called upon to underscore the civilized world's collective responsibility for the protection of human rights and freedoms."[103] For example, in its discussion of Iraqi human rights violations of its ethnic minority, the Kurds, Russia affirmed that the "Security Council is carrying out its responsibilities as given by the Charter."[104]

The results of the content analysis indicate that Russia placed a heavy emphasis on both states' and the international community's obligations (see figure 4.7). In its speeches, Russia most frequently cited states' responsibilities to comply with international norms (78%). Almost as often, Russia referred to the international community's duty to ensure that these norms were followed within states (67%). However, only rarely did Russia mention that interfering in states fell within the purview of the international community (22%). It also seldom advocated for states' rights (33%), and these were limited to its tenure as the Soviet Union.

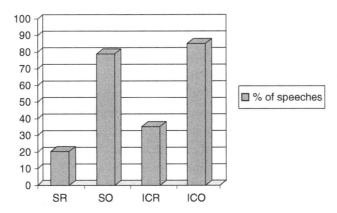

SR = State Rights, SO = State Obligations, ICR = International Community's Rights, ICO = International Community's Obligations

FIGURE 4.7 Russia's Conceptions of Sovereignty Before Somali Crisis

Russia's Stated Views on Sovereignty After Somali Crisis

After the UN intervention in Somalia began, Russia continued to emphasize the rights and responsibilities of the international community, when states cannot or will not meet minimum standards of human rights.[105]

For example, the United Nations was obliged to interfere in the former Yugoslavia, where innocent civilians were being slaughtered.[106] Russia even suggested that the international community set up a commission to identify and punish human rights abuses, which implies the right of the Council to bypass traditional notions of sovereignty through a system of international justice.[107] Russia later revisited this idea by cosponsoring a resolution that created a war crimes tribunal for Yugoslavia, declaring that the "entire international community" will punish those "who are grossly violating not only the norms of international law but even quite simply our human concepts of morality and humanity."[108]

In fact, when the most basic needs of citizens were not met by their government, Russia warned that "any political and military leaders who allow mass breaches of the norms of international humanitarian law" would be held accountable by the international community.[109] Though the speech was directed at the former Yugoslavia, Russia also cautioned that its position applied to other conflicts as well. In Russia's view, any actions that the Security Council took to alleviate human suffering within states were legally justified; the resolutions "reflect the responsibility with which the Security Council has consistently carried out . . . the duties incumbent upon it."[110] Even if it requires military force, the Security Council is not only obliged to help but also has the right. For example, Russia authorized the use of force in Somalia because the "crisis requires the use of international armed forces," and the Council had authorization to provide it.[111]

Though Russia continued to endorse contingent sovereignty, reflected in its promotion of states' obligations to international norms, and the international community's rights and obligations, Russia did make subtle references to absolute sovereignty toward the end of the intervention and after. In creating the war crime tribunal in Rwanda, Russia stated that it had cooperated because of requests from Rwanda.[112] Reinforcing this notion that states still had some authority in carrying out justice for international crimes, Russia noted that states did not "automatically" have to comply with requests of the tribunal.[113] Interestingly, in the last speech during this period, Russia also brought out an argument frequently used in the Cold War: "It is inadmissible for anyone, including . . . the Security Council itself, to attempt to make use of the sphere of international humanitarian law and human rights as an instrument for achieving political goals."[114] While these references to absolute sovereignty were very few, it is important to point out that Russia's internal situation seemed to be reflected in its external discourse, albeit muted.

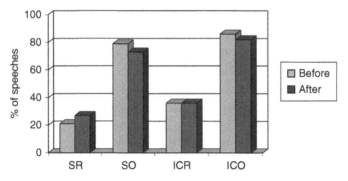

SR = State Rights, SO = State Obligations, ICR = International Community's
Rights, ICO = International Community's Obligations.

FIGURE 4.8  Russia's Conceptions of Sovereignty Before and After
Somali Crisis

Judging from the content analysis, it appears that Russia's views on sovereignty remained much the same (see figure 4.8). In its speeches, Russia continued to sometimes support the rights of the international community to intervene in states' affairs, though more often Russia is seen asserting the obligation of the international community to protect citizens around the world. This provides some evidence that Russia leaned toward contingent sovereignty, although this did not last throughout the period under study because of Russia's changing domestic situation. At the state level, Russia maintains that states must meet their international obligations to comply with human rights norms. At the same time, Russia infrequently cautions that state sovereignty must be respected. It appears that Russia was not quite ready to let go of the traditional notion of absolute sovereignty. On the whole, though, the results indicate that Russia allowed for a conditional view of sovereignty in the human rights domain.

## Discussion and Conclusion

Overall, the cases presented here demonstrate a shift away from absolute sovereignty toward contingent sovereignty. (see table 4.1). The analyses illustrate that states participating in the military intervention in Somalia more strongly reinforced contingent sovereignty once the intervention began. As per my expectations, the United Sates showed greater changes in its views on sovereignty than France because of the greater dissonance it experienced in the outcome of the intervention. Not only did the United

| | STATES' RIGHTS | | STATES' OBLIGATIONS | | INTERNATIONAL COMMUNITY'S RIGHTS | | INTERNATIONAL COMMUNITY'S OBLIGATIONS | |
|---|---|---|---|---|---|---|---|---|
| | BEFORE | AFTER | BEFORE | AFTER | BEFORE | AFTER | BEFORE | AFTER |
| **Military Intervention** | | | | | | | | |
| United States | 22 | 0* | 78 | 91 | 11 | 64** | 56 | 100** |
| France | 0 | 0 | 81 | 80 | 19 | 60** | 88 | 80 |
| **Noninterveners** | | | | | | | | |
| China | 59 | 73 | 24 | 27 | 6 | 0 | 24 | 36 |
| Russia | 21 | 27 | 79 | 73 | 36 | 36 | 86 | 82 |

NOTE: Numbers indicate percent of total speeches that mention a given category. The total number of speeches for each country is as follows (before; after): US (18; 11), France (16; 10), Russia (14; 11), China (17; 11). Statistically significant changes indicated by $*p < .10$; $**p < .05$.

States display greater changes in its commitment to contingent sovereignty as a result of the intervention (relative to changes in other states), but it also showed more dedication, in absolute terms, than the other states.

For its part, France remained fairly consistent in its views, though noticeable change occurred in its reinforcement of the rights of the international community. Because it encountered less dissonance from the intervention, France experienced less movement toward contingent sovereignty than the United States, though it was still clearly committed to an understanding of sovereignty that included compliance with human rights norms. The lesser change may result from the fact that France had less room to move, because it entered the intervention in Somalia from a position closer to contingent sovereignty than the United States.

The noninterveners, China and Russia, did not experience great changes in their views on sovereignty. At least partially because of the differences in their culpability, at least during this time period, Russia leaned more toward contingent sovereignty than China. However, what the aggregated results do not show (as in table 4.1), but was revealed in the case study, is that Russia's reinforcement of contingent sovereignty fluctuated according to its culpability. Because Russia was experiencing a bumpy transition to a free market democracy, its position on contingent sovereignty was inconsistent. When compared with the preintervention period, Russia more frequently espoused contingent notions of sovereignty after the intervention began. Toward the end of this period, however, Russia again fell back into a pattern of reinforcing states' rights.

In contrast, China's domestic situation was stable within the time period under study. Through both periods, China's views on sovereignty leaned toward absolute sovereignty. Indeed, once the intervention began, China continued to advocate for the right of states to be free of outside interference, though it concurrently recognized *some* responsibility of the international community to act in dire situations.

This examination of changes in states' understandings of sovereignty speaks more broadly to how responses to events influence the international normative structure, which guides states' behavior. The American and French intervention experiences in Somalia contributed to the growing prominence of contingent sovereignty. Their intense justification of the UN-approved intervention highlighted contingent sovereignty in the international community because it illustrated the willingness of leading states to invest resources and risk their own citizens' lives. France, the United States, and Russia, to some extent, pushed the trend toward contingent sovereignty, while China strongly pulled toward absolute sovereignty. Examining the various responses (intervention versus nonintervention) and discourse of the leading states helps to explain why human rights norms and state sovereignty norms continued to vie for dominance in the international community.

What are the implications of these changes for human rights and sovereignty? It is possible that the intervention, which was largely perceived as a failure, did little to hinder future states from committing human rights abuses. Finding the international community ill-equipped to adapt to these situations, especially the United States as the lone superpower, the outcome of the intervention in Somalia may have encouraged perpetrators that they would not be held accountable to external actors. This may have been the case with the Rwandan genocide in 1994. Despite the rise of human rights norms, the international community failed to act, illustrating that both ideational and material conditions must be met for an intervention to occur. At the same time, though, realizing the dedication of major states, and the leading superpower in particular, to human rights norms, other potential violators may also have been deterred from committing atrocities. After all, despite the lack of success, participation in the intervention seems to have enhanced states' commitment to contingent sovereignty, reflecting a movement toward a new normative context within which states act.

In sum, this chapter investigated changes in sovereignty conceptions in the context of human rights. The humanitarian crisis in Somalia provided an impetus for change, but it was the responses to the crisis that provided the mechanism for change or lack thereof. Cognitive dissonance theory provided a useful guide for expectations in this regard. Specifically, I found evidence that the outcome of the military intervention for the intervener influences, at least in part, the extent to which a contingent norm of sovereignty is accepted by a state. In addition, state culpability in a particular policy domain is a key factor to consider when explaining whether a non-intervener will adopt new conceptions of sovereignty.

# CHAPTER 5 | Sovereignty and Weapons of Mass Destruction

When certain regimes with a history of aggression and support for terrorism pursue weapons of mass destruction, thereby endangering the international community, they jeopardize their sovereign immunity from intervention—including anticipatory action to destroy this developing capability.

—RICHARD HAASS, *US State Department, Director of Policy Planning, 2003*[1]

THE DEVELOPMENT AND POTENTIAL use of weapons of mass destructions (WMD) have become major issues on the international agenda, concerns that are compounded by the increased threat of global terrorism by nonstate actors.[2] While nonstate actors operate outside the bounds of state sovereignty, and thus are outside the scope of this chapter, they nonetheless underscore the urgency with which states and the international community negotiate their rights and obligations vis-à-vis one another.

Overall, the growing consensus on norms regarding weapons of mass destruction illustrates the idea that certain weapons lack global legitimacy. What continues to be disputed, though, is the lengths that the international community should go in order to remedy situations of violations. As the conventions and treaties make clear, individual states have certain obligations to adhere to, while the community of states is tasked with monitoring and enforcing compliance. However, as made evident in the ongoing debates on possible responses to Iran's continued development of nuclear capabilities, especially Israel's increasing willingness to attack Iran's nuclear facilities, there is no consensus on how to handle states that disregard their international obligations in this policy domain.

At the same time, states do agree that Iran, and states like it, have obligations to the international community to fulfill. This suggests a movement toward contingent sovereignty, one in which states failing in these duties increasingly face international intervention. Given that necessary structural conditions are met, I argue that the extent to which other states adopt this view depends on the feedback from the intervention itself. As in the previous analyses, I propose that an unsuccessful and expensive intervention serves to more strongly reinforce interveners' dedication to contingent sovereignty. In addition, I expect that noninterveners who comply with international norms regarding WMD may espouse views of contingent sovereignty, though to a lesser extent than interveners. Though I enter the analyses with the same expectations as in earlier cases, the intervention under investigation is markedly different in that its justifications drew on false premises. As such, this case has the added benefit of drawing out an additional consideration for the possibility of normative change.

Using comparative case studies and content analysis of UN Security Council speeches by two of the leading interveners, the United States and the United Kingdom, as well as two noninterveners, France and Russia, I examine the first multilateral intervention in the post–Cold War period for the purpose of enforcing a contingent understanding of sovereignty that hinges on state compliance with international norms concerning weapons of mass destruction. I analyze states'conceptions of sovereignty prior to and during the Iraq intervention.[3] While the intervention continued past this, I only examine speeches through 2004, when an international consensus emerged about the lack of such weapons in Iraq, and the WMD justification for the war could no longer be used.

In the following section, I briefly review the history of the norms regarding weapons of mass destruction. Next, I discuss the international conditions that provide for the possibility of changes in states' understandings of sovereignty. I then analyze the United States' and the United Kingdom's views on sovereignty in light of their intervention in Iraq. This is followed by an examination of nonintervener's conceptions of sovereignty, as evidenced by France and Russia. I conclude with a comparative discussion of the findings.

## Norms Regulating Weapons

The idea that certain weapons should not be used arose out of the experiences of states in war. In fact, it can be traced back at least to 1675 in the Strasbourg Agreement between France and Germany, which prohibited the use of poison bullets in war.[4] This idea was broadened in scope and strength after states' experiences with chemical weapons in World War I. The extensive use of mustard gas during the war highlighted its devastating nature, causing lung damage and skin blisters, and led to a ban on the use of chemical and biological weapons in the 1925 Geneva protocol.[5] With large international support, the Geneva protocol reaffirmed two previous attempts to ban such weapons, the Treaty of Versailles (1919) and the Washington Treaty (1922), adding to them a ban on bacteriological warfare.

Though some states signed onto the protocol with reservations, allowing for retaliatory use, the main problem with the agreement stemmed from the focus on the *use* of biological and chemical weapons in war. The protocol failed to address the development, production, or stockpiling of such weapons. In addition, it did not provide a mechanism for verification. These weaknesses were largely addressed in the 1972 Biological Weapons Convention[6] (though it lacks a verification regime) and the 1992 Chemical Weapons Convention.[7] Most states are now parties to these conventions, including the major powers.

The evolving taboo on chemical and biological weapons coincides with strong norms against nuclear weapons. Though no treaty codifies their nonuse like the Chemical and Biological Weapons Conventions, their destructive capability makes their use today unthinkable, as the annihilation of Hiroshima and Nagasaki, Japan demonstrated. The power of nuclear weapons illustrated by the United States against Japan in World War II compelled the international community to limit the spread of nuclear materials and expertise through the Non-Proliferation Treaty (1968). Because nuclear energy is also employed for peaceful means, the International Atomic Energy Agency is responsible for inspecting states' nuclear power industries to guard against potential military applications. While there are only a handful of countries that possess nuclear arsenals, almost all states in the international system are a party to this treaty.

While this treaty limited the spread of nuclear weapons, it did not prohibit their testing. In 1996, the international community agreed on a Comprehensive Nuclear-Test-Ban Treaty to ban nuclear weapon test explosions. Though it has not yet entered into force, the norm against such testing is quite strong.[8] However, the responses to violations have varied, from condemnation to sanctions to potential use of force. For example, though they are not signatories to the treaty, India and Pakistan were unanimously condemned by members of the UN Security Council for their nuclear test explosions in 1998. North Korea also was admonished by the

UN Security Council, including its closest ally, China, for its nuclear testing in 2006.[9] However, the international community went further than condemnation as in the Indian and Pakistani cases. In the North Korean case, the UN Security Council agreed on limited economic and military sanctions, though the United States had initially pushed for the resolution to leave open the possibility for the use of military force.[10] The contrast in the responses to the various situations in India and Pakistan, and North Korea, represent the evolution of norms within individual states and the international community surrounding weapons of mass destruction.

## Conditions Conducive to Changes in Sovereignty

International conditions in the last twenty years set the stage for the possibility of contingent sovereignty in this issue area. Concerns about these weapons permeate the international system, elevating them to the top of the international agenda as the international community grapples with the associated rights and obligations. In particular, their potential use by renegade states and nonstate actors, such as terrorists, guarantees that norms regarding weapons of mass destruction remain a top long-term international issue.

That major powers are intimately involved with this issue also adds to its high profile. The willingness of the United States and Great Britain to go to war on the premise of Iraq's violation of international norms illustrates their understanding of not only states' rights and obligations, but also the international community's rights and obligations when it comes to weapons of mass destruction. While these states could have argued that they were defending human rights in Iraq, they instead chose to justify the war by claiming that Iraq breached its material obligations to halt its nuclear and chemical weapons programs. By militarily intervening, the United States and Great Britain (and their coalition partners) demonstrated that state sovereignty was contingent on meeting international obligations. Although no weapons were found, the intervention and the debate surrounding it contributed to the prominence of norms regarding weapons of mass destruction.

Contingent sovereignty, dependent on states adhering to WMD norms, is compatible with other norms within the global normative structure. Because these weapons threaten international peace and security, their prohibition dovetails with other prominent norms such as human rights norms and counterterrorism norms. For example, because weapons of mass destruction kill or injure indiscriminately, norms against their use are compatible with human rights norms. Moreover, the threat of their use by terrorists or renegade regimes makes norms governing such weapons highly compatible with those regarding counterterrorism.

In the larger picture, these norms share some common themes. Not only are they among the most prominent norms, they commonly reflect a respect for human life and a desire for peaceful relations among states and individuals. Moreover, these norms represent a shift toward contingent sovereignty since they all imply that the international community may take on certain state responsibilities if a state is unwilling or unable to fulfill their international obligations.

Global conditions are particularly conducive to movement toward contingent sovereignty because of the end of the Cold War and the post-9/11 environment. During the Cold War, norms about weapons of mass destruction developed but were not enforced. However, in only one instance were chemical weapons used (by Iraq in the Iran-Iraq war, 1980–88). Though states did not generally use such weapons, some states did successfully acquire them, motivated by perceived security concerns and prestige. However, given the Cold War nuclear standoff between the Soviet Union and the United States, there was no international consensus about how to prevent states from developing and possessing this category of weapons. For instance, a preemptive strike by a major power outside its sphere of influence may have led to World War III. In contrast, the post-Cold War period provides an opportunity to revisit questions about how to enforce norms against the development and spread of weapons of mass destruction.

Another global condition that contributes to the possibility of change is the post-9/11 environment. States now act within a hypersensitive security environment, driven by the global war on terrorism. That terrorists might acquire and use a weapon of mass destruction is not only a possible but also a plausible scenario. These actors add a level of unpredictability to the international system because they operate outside the bounds of traditional international relations. The threat of terrorism linked to weapons of mass destruction creates an environment in which the international community may be more willing to override states' rights, or absolute sovereignty, in favor of contingent sovereignty, in which the international community acts as ultimate enforcer of the norms regarding these horrific weapons. Together, these conditions suggest the opportunity for changes within states' understandings of sovereignty.

## Intervention in Iraq

Having defied the international community for twelve years, Iraq was the repeated subject of UN Security Council meetings. Because Iraq had been evasive about information regarding its weapons programs, and the disarmament conditions for peace set by the end of the Persian Gulf War (1990–91) were never fulfilled, the international community imposed increasingly stringent sanctions. However, the sanctions regime, including the oil-for-food program, did not motivate Iraq to comply with the demands of the UN Security Council. States grew impatient with Iraq and proposed different strategies to deal with it. Feeling the pressure, Iraq agreed to allow weapons inspectors back in, appeasing states like France who sought disarmament through inspections (Zartner 2006). For other states, like the United States, military action was increasingly the only sure way to "disarm" Iraq. Despite the strong opposition against an intervention, and the lack of approval from the United Nations, the US-led intervention commenced March 19, 2003.

## Enforcing WMD Norms? The United States and the United Kingdom

By taking military action in Iraq to enforce international norms on weapons of mass destruction, the United States and the United Kingdom committed to a contingent view of sovereignty, which has the potential to be reinforced or challenged, depending on the outcome of the intervention. Since they are both leading states in the international system, their experiences in Iraq help shape not only their own views but also the international community's perspective on conditions under which traditional sovereignty may be violated. I begin with the United States.

### United States

In February 2003, US Secretary of State Colin Powell went to the United Nations in hopes of persuading the international community to support military intervention in Iraq to halt its alleged development of weapons of mass destruction.[11] This effort was part of the Bush Doctrine, developed after 9/11, which created a US policy of preemption in matters related to international peace and security. Though regime change in Iraq had been a lingering argument since the Persian Gulf War, the suggested link between

Iraq and the al Qaeda terrorist network added fuel to the argument for war. While Powell's plea at the UN garnered some support, it did not attain official UN approval. In fact, it sparked great controversy among traditional allies of the United States. However, the United States was committed to act and the invasion of Iraq began in March of the same year.

Before the invasion, known as Operation Iraqi Freedom, the United States outlined several goals of the intervention. According to President Bush, the mission's objectives would be to "disarm Iraq of weapons of mass destruction, to end Saddam Hussein's support for terrorism, and to free the Iraqi people."[12] Upon commencement of the mission, President Bush alerted Americans that "at this hour, American and coalition forces are in the early stages of military operations to disarm Iraq, to free its people, and to defend the world from grave danger."[13]

Of these goals, only one came close to being accomplished. In terms of "freeing the Iraqi people," the intervention removed Saddam Hussein from power. Though he eluded coalition forces for some time, he was captured in December 2003. He was put on trial for crimes against humanity by the Iraqi Special Tribunal and was later executed in 2006 after being found guilty. Thus, one of the goals of the United States seemed fulfilled.[14]

In terms of Iraq's links to terrorism, via al Qaeda, no evidence has been found to support such a claim. In June 2004, a general consensus emerged about the myth of this connection when the 9/11 Commission, having had access to classified documents, could not locate information to substantiate collaboration between Iraq and al Qaeda.[15] Thus, there was little validity to the claim that Iraq had been party to the planning of the 9/11 attacks on America. Recently, for the first time, the US military publicly acknowledged this.[16] In fact, US forces seized over 600,000 official Iraqi documents during the invasion and upon analysis of these documents, found no connection between Iraq and al Qaeda: "This study found no 'smoking gun' between Saddam's Iraq and al Qaeda."[17]

Similarly, the objective of destroying weapons of mass destruction was found to be baseless. By 2004, scholars and defense experts agreed that no evidence of nuclear, chemical, or biological weapons, nor any type of missile delivery system, existed.[18] US Secretary of State Colin Powell even admitted that the claims he made at the United Nations were based on shaky assumptions.[19] In 2005, the Central Intelligence Agency's leading weapons inspector concluded the investigation, saying that it had "gone as far as feasible."[20] While military forces have found small stockpiles of degraded chemical weapons left over from the Persian Gulf War, they were not the weapons for which the coalition went to war in 2003.

Moreover, they did not support the claim that Iraq had an ongoing weapons program, since they dated back to 1990.

Overall, the United States encountered low success in meeting its goals. While in the eyes of the United States the people of Iraq were "freed," the other US objectives—destroying weapons of mass destruction and cutting Iraq's ties to al Qaeda—were simply not met. Nor could they have been. These objectives were based on the misuse and abuse of information, and thus fulfilling them proved impossible.

As the war in Iraq progressed, the human, financial, and domestic political costs increased beyond the expectations of the government. At any given time, the United States had between 130 000 to 168 000 troops in Iraq, making up a clear majority of the coalition forces.[21] In the first year, 2003, the United States lost 486 troops. This figure almost doubled in 2004 to 849, where it remained for the years following.[22] At the same time, the financial costs of the war increased. In 2003, the United States spent $50 billion for the war in Iraq, increasing to $70 billion in 2004.[23] The costs are even greater if one considers the opportunity costs.[24]

The human and financial costs had a strong effect on public opinion, particularly as citizens realized that they had been misled on the reasons for the war.[25] Just over a month into the war (late April 2003), when asked to weigh the benefits and costs of the war in Iraq, 70% of Americans felt that it was worth the cost, while 27% thought that it wasn't.[26] In a similar poll at the end of 2004, only 42% still believed the war in Iraq was worth it, while a majority (56%) considered the war not worth fighting.[27] The trend in calling the war a "mistake" is similar. At the onset of the invasion (March 2003), 75% of Americans judged the war to not be a mistake, and 23% considered that it was.[28] In contrast, by July 2004, a majority of Americans (54%) came to believe that the intervention was a mistake, while 45% continued to think that it was not.[29] Significantly, this was the first time in the post-Vietnam era that the public deemed a major deployment of US troops an "error."[30]

In sum, the unfavorable cost and success indicators suggest a situation of cognitive dissonance. Neither piece of information validated the decision to intervene, but this particular case is unusual. Under normal conditions, I would expect that after the United States intervened, it would demonstrate a stronger commitment to contingent sovereignty. Yet, the military intervention in Iraq lies in stark contrast to the interventions examined in the other chapters since the bases for those interventions were supported. No one doubted that a dire humanitarian situation in Somalia existed, nor did anyone suggest that Afghanistan was not linked to al Qaeda and terrorism more generally.

With regard to Iraq, however, no weapons of mass destruction were ever found; the war was based on false premises. Because of this, I expect the United States to discuss contingent sovereignty *less* frequently than it did prior to the war. That is, to maintain cognitive consistency, the United States will distance itself from the view that that the international community has an obligation and right to intervene to prevent the development or spread of weapons of mass destruction. However, I do expect that the United States would continue to assert that states should meet their international obligations, though the references to this may occur less often than previously.

US' Stated Views on Sovereignty Before Intervention

To see if US views on sovereignty have changed, I set as a baseline for comparison the period prior to the intervention. I examine speeches at the UN Security Council in the post–Cold War period, leading up to the military action in Iraq. Iraq was the focus on the majority of speeches related to weapons of mass destruction, but the nuclear tests of Pakistan and India (1998) also garnered an international response. Before discussing the results of the content analysis, I summarize the discourse related to the four categories of sovereignty I created and offer representative statements to show how sovereignty by the United States was conceived.

In the period prior to the intervention in Iraq, the United States almost always emphasized state obligations relating to weapons of mass destruction. In the first meeting of the UN Security Council after the dissolution of the Soviet Union, the United States reminded states that they must abide by the Nuclear Non-Proliferation Treaty and encouraged the new states from the former Soviet Union to comply with the treaty.[31] In addition, the United States offered aid to states to meet those obligations. If states violated international law, the United States forcefully warned that such states would find the international community acting "to compel them to observe international standards of behavior."[32] States not parties to the relevant treaties were urged to sign and ratify them. For example, when India and Pakistan tested nuclear weapons in 1998, the United States implored them to sign the Comprehensive Nuclear-Test-Ban Treaty: "both states should sign and ratify the CNTBT immediately."[33] Furthermore, the United States signaled that even though India and Pakistan had not been signatories to that treaty beforehand, they had risked their reputation by conducting the tests. The countries would find a way to "restore their standing" if they complied with the UN Security Council's demands, which were set forth in the resolution condemning the nuclear tests.[34]

This discussion of state obligations is similar to the many references about Iraq's violations. The United States repeatedly reminded the international community of Iraq's noncompliance with its post–Persian Gulf War obligations of disarmament and halting illegal weapons programs: "Iraq failed its responsibilities,"[35]; "No council member argues that Iraq has disarmed as required,"[36]; "Iraq is not fulfilling its responsibilities."[37] Moreover, the United States warned that "if the Security Council fails to act decisively in the event of further Iraqi violations," it would not constrain the United States from taking action of its own.[38] While primarily targeting Iraq, the United States was making a broader statement about sovereignty, in which states are bound by their international obligations. At no time during the period under investigation did the United States espouse views of absolute sovereignty in matters related to chemical, biological, or nuclear weapons.

Not surprisingly, then, the United States also argued that the international community had the obligation, and sometimes the right, to address violations of weapons norms. In a clear majority of speeches, the United States asserted that this sensitive domain required the international community to act. It declared, "What greater cause for this great body than to make certain the world has seen the last of these terrible weapons?"[39] For example, in speaking of Iraq's violations, "it must be the Council's purpose to ensure that the threat remains contained."[40] The United States claimed that the international community must "meet the challenge and stand firm . . . and hold Iraq to its commitments."[41] In order to enforce these commitments, the United States affirmed that the international community had the right to sanction states that did not conform: "sanctions are the leverage the international community has to get the government of Iraq to comply with Security Council resolutions."[42]

Yet, as the Iraq intervention drew near, the United States also claimed that the international community could go further, implying the use of force: "Our security rests upon us meeting our responsibilities, and if it comes to it, invoking the serious consequences called for in Resolution 1441."[43] In this regard, the United States was alleging a legal basis for intervention, by claiming that it fell within the rights of the international community. Thus, in the United States' view, not only did the international community have the right to sanction state violators of weapons norms, but they also had the right to violate state sovereignty when sanctions did not work.

Content analysis of all the relevant speeches prior to the US intervention in Iraq points to an emphasis on contingent sovereignty (see figure 5.1). In 82% of the US speeches at the UN Security Council, the United States argued that states had certain international obligations to fulfill, and that they would face consequences in the case of violations. Similarly, the United States frequently discussed the role of the international community in making the world safe from weapons of mass destruction. In 71% of the

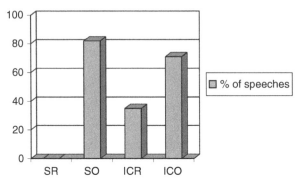

SR = State Rights, SO = State Obligations, ICR = International Community's
Rights, ICO = International Community's Obligations

FIGURE 5.1   US Conceptions of Sovereignty Before Military
Intervention

speeches, the United States emphasized the international community's responsibility to maintain international peace and security. However, in only 35% of the speeches, did the United States advocate the right of the international community to interfere in a state's affairs. Finally, as I mentioned earlier, no speeches mentioned a state's absolute right to sovereignty in connection with illicit weapons.

The next section investigates whether and how these views on sovereignty changed as a result of intervention. To provide a comparison to pre- and post-intervention, I first describe the discourse that follows the intervention and then compare those results to the baseline just established.

US' Stated Views on Sovereignty During the Intervention

The United States went to war in Iraq on March 19, 2003, with the primary goal of disarming Saddam Hussein's regime. With its growing commitment to intervene, the United States repeatedly discussed how Iraq had violated international norms for the past twelve years, since the end of the Gulf War. In order to keep the arms control and nonproliferation regimes credible, it was now time to take action on behalf of these norms. In the United States' view, state sovereignty was contingent on fulfillment of international obligations.

Yet, once the intervention began, the United States' views on contingent sovereignty weakened, with regard to the role of the international community. Though the United States made speeches regarding Iraq, in less than half, the United States asserted claims about the role of weapons of mass destruction norms in determining state sovereignty. While this is surprising in light of its fixation on these weapons prior to the war, it is not unexpected; evidence of a weapons program and weapons stockpiles were not found. Thus, the United States retreated from this argument.

The United States did continue to refrain from support for absolute sovereignty. Rather, the United States frequently persisted in discussing *state* obligations when it came to weapons of mass destruction: States "should keep the most dangerous weapons and materials and delivery systems out of the hands of nonstate actors and terrorists."[44] Moreover, states have obligations to fulfill UN resolutions, including implementing them into national law and adhering to arms-export controls.[45]

Though references to state obligations appeared in the majority of the speeches, it declined slightly compared with before the intervention. Sharper declines, however, were found in the United States' acknowledgement of the international community's obligations. This occurred only in July 2004, after the evidence for weapons of mass destruction in Iraq was found lacking, and the United States returned to associating WMD with terrorism. In its discussion of UNSC Resolution 1540 aimed to address the problem of non-state actors and WMD, the United States reiterated the obligation of the international community to "criminalize proliferation, secure sensitive materials and ensure export controls on weapons" in light of their potential use by terrorists.[46]

Outside of discussion pertaining to this specific resolution, the United States did not lobby for the international community's involvement. In fact, in tandem with its muted voice on obligations, the United States also barely mentioned rights of the international community. It acknowledged that the UN Security Council could create resolutions binding on states, implying that the Council had the right to interfere in states' domestic affairs, if necessary.[47] However, the United States stepped back from asserting the enforceability of the WMD resolution, stating that "the resolution is not about enforcement."[48] It further remarked, somewhat tellingly, that this resolution had a "forward-looking focus, it sets a standard for how nations should act in the future rather than judging past actions. It reinforces an objective of vital interest to all: that proliferation cannot be tolerated."[49]

The results of the content analysis highlight these changes, or lack thereof, with greater clarity (see figure 5.2). With respect to absolute sovereignty, no change occurred: the United States continued to refrain from advocating states' rights (from 0% to 0%). Results for changes in contingent sovereignty are mixed but point to an overall weakening of views on contingent

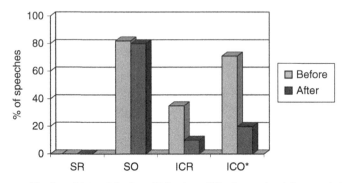

SR = State Rights, SO = State Obligations, ICR = International Community's
Rights, ICO = International Community's Obligations.

FIGURE 5.2 US Conceptions of Sovereignty Before and During
Military Intervention

sovereignty in this policy domain. While the United States spoke almost as
frequently about states' obligations to comply with international norms regarding
weapons of mass destruction (from 82% to 80%), it hardly mentioned
the obligations of the international community. In fact, the United
States only mentioned this in 20% of its speeches, compared with 71% of
its speeches prior to the intervention, which represents a dramatic downward
shift.[50] References to the international community's rights also decreased.
After the intervention began, only once did the United States support
the right of the international community to interfere in state's affairs
(from 35% to 10%). Thus, on the whole, the United States moved away
from its commitment to contingent sovereignty in the direction of absolute
sovereignty.

This fits largely with my expectations. Because no weapons of mass
destruction were found, the United States had to back away from its discussion
of the international community's right and obligation to intervene
for those purposes. However, it did not retreat completely from its position
on contingent sovereignty since it still recognized and encouraged states to
comply with international norms on illicit weapons. This change in
discourse allowed the United States to maintain cognitive consistency,
given that the public justification for the intervention proved false. The
indicators, costs and success, applied here to predict a situation of cognitive
dissonance, assumed that the normative justification for intervention
was legitimate. Thus, this case study shows the importance of legitimacy
for norm change to occur. The results indicate that an intervention built on
an erroneous argument can actually have the unintended consequence of
weakening a commitment to contingent sovereignty.

## United Kingdom

Amid much controversy, even within his own party, Prime Minister Tony Blair supported the United States' policy of firmness toward Iraq. In March 2002, Prime Minister Blair publicly announced that he agreed with the US' assessment of Iraq as posing a grave threat and would not rule out military action. Regarding Saddam Hussein, Prime Minister Blair asserted, "He is in breach of at least nine UN Security Council resolutions about weapons of mass destruction. He has not allowed weapons inspectors to do the job that the UN wanted them to do in order to make sure that he can't develop them."[51] This stance put Prime Minister Blair at odds with his party, and the British public, who were not convinced of the threat and argued for such a plan to be legitimized by the United Nations first. However, Blair was undeterred and continued to support the United States, despite his decreasing popularity. In February 2003, he even went as far as to propose a second UN resolution that would explicitly allow for military action, but this attempt failed. Despite the largest rebellion within his party since he came to office, including the resignation of three cabinet ministers, Blair committed his country to a US-led military action on March 19, 2003.

The United Kingdom set out with similar goals to the United States in the Iraqi intervention, or Operation Telic. According to the UK Ministry of Defense, "The prime objective remains to rid Iraq of its weapons of mass destruction and their associated programmes and means of delivery."[52] In subsequent statements, Prime Minister Tony Blair added the removal of Saddam Hussein's regime to the operation's goals: "If the only means of achieving the disarmament of Iraq . . . is the removal of the regime, then the removal of the regime of course has to be our objective."[53] Thus, the two central objectives were "to remove Saddam Hussein from power and ensure Iraq has disarmed of all chemical, biological and nuclear weapons programs."[54]

As I discussed in the US case, only one of these goals was met. Saddam Hussein was removed from power, tried for crimes against humanity, and executed. Pillars of the old regime fell: Saddam Hussein's sons were killed in battle; key figures surrendered or were captured (including Iraq's defense minister and Saddam Hussein's chief weapons advisor); and the Iraqi military was dismantled. Soon after the invasion, a new governing body, the Iraqi Governing Council, was created, which broadly represented the Iraqi public. In addition, new Iraqi police and military forces began training. There were virtually no signs left of Saddam Hussein's regime.

While coalition forces produced regime change, they were unable to uncover evidence of weapons of mass destruction. Suspicions grew as the intervention continued. By February 2004, the United Kingdom had commissioned an independent commission to assess the prewar intelligence claiming that Iraq had weapons of mass destruction.[55] In July 2004, Prime Minister Blair admitted, "I have to accept: as the months have passed, it seems increasingly clear that at the time of invasion Saddam did not have stockpiles of chemical or biological weapons ready to deploy."[56] Because of this, the United Kingdom failed in its efforts to find these weapons; it was impossible for the United Kingdom to remove banned weapons that did not exist. Thus, in terms of the extent of success achieved in Iraq, the evidence is mixed. Saddam Hussein was successfully removed from power, but no illicit weapons were ever found.

The United Kingdom has suffered human, financial, and domestic political losses because of the war in Iraq. At the onset, the UK contributed 46,000 troops to the invasion, but this later was dramatically reduced to less than half after two months.[57] In October 2003, the number of British troops in Iraq dropped to 10,000, where it would remain for the next few years.[58] In the first year of the war, fifty-three British troops lost their lives.[59] In 2004, this number was reduced to twenty-two casualties, partially due to the relatively small number of troops deployed.[60] On the financial side, the costs of the war increased as the war continued. According to the Ministry of Defense, the UK military action in Iraq cost for the financial year 2002–2003 was £847 million. In 2003–2004, the cost increased to £1,311 million, but declined in the next financial year, 2004–2005, to £910 million.[61] Thus, the total for the first several years was just over £3 billion. With no end in sight at the end of 2004, the war was proving very costly to the United Kingdom and its leaders.

According to polls conducted by the Pew Research Center, British support for the war declined from a majority of 61% in May 2003 to 43% in March 2004.[62] In the same polls, those believing that the United Kingdom should not have gone to war increased from 34% to 47%. Among other issues, the rise in negative opinion about the war translated to the voting arena. In the general election of 2005, Prime Minister Blair barely held onto power for a third term. Moreover, his party (Labour) lost seats in Parliament and retained a smaller majority than in previous elections. Public opinion continued to sour, and the war in Iraq was one of the main reasons that Prime Minister Blair agreed in 2006 to an early departure from his post.[63]

Similar to the situation in the United States, I expect that the changes in conceptions of sovereignty would be moderated by lack of evidence for weapons of mass destruction, a major justification for the war. According to cognitive dissonance, a costly but moderately successful war would yield expectations for the United Kingdom to reinforce contingent sovereignty to a slightly greater extent during the war than previously. Yet, the legitimacy of the war was called into question, which may take precedence over the indicators of cognitive dissonance, which predicts efforts to mold information to conform to a previous decision. Again, this assumes that there is a valid justification for the decision. In the case of the UK intervention in Iraq, this would lead me to expect the United Kingdom to dissociate itself with the right and obligation of the international community to intervene for the purpose of halting development and stockpiling of weapons of mass destruction. This allows it to maintain cognitive consistency. However, I do expect that they would continue to cling to support for states meeting their international obligations in this arena. The United Kingdom will move away from contingent sovereignty, though not to such an extreme that it endorses absolute sovereignty.

UK's Stated Views on Sovereignty Before Intervention

As I did in the previous case, I first summarize UK discourse prior to the intervention in order to establish a baseline for comparison. This discussion is based on UK speeches regarding the intersection of sovereignty and weapons of mass destruction. Again, the majority of the speeches are related to Iraq, while a few are dedicated to the nuclear tests by India and Pakistan (1998).

Regarding absolute sovereignty, the United Kingdom failed to support the rights of states in any of its speeches related to illicit weapons. Instead, the United Kingdom exhibited a contingent view of sovereignty. Throughout the speeches, it focused on the obligations of states to comply with the norms of the international community: "we all have to continue to exercise our responsibilities."[64] States, "all of them, without exception, must also be active in arms control" by implementing international treaties and "work for further measures of disarmament."[65] If states did not meet the established norms of the international community, they would face, at the very least, condemnation. This occurred in the case of the nuclear tests conducted by India and Pakistan (1998). The United Kingdom condemned "these actions," which "run counter to the will expressed by the 149 signatories of the Comprehensive Nuclear Test Ban Treaty."[66]

However, Iraq's violations drew more attention from the United Kingdom. Throughout the 1990s and up to the war in Iraq, the United Kingdom highlighted Iraq's noncompliance with UN Security Council demands and the terms of the Gulf War ceasefire: "Iraq remains in material breach of these obligations."[67] In order to avert intervention, Iraq was supposed to "cooperate fully with weapons inspectors, or face disarmament by force."[68] From these and other statements, the United Kingdom sent a signal to the community of states that it was serious about states meeting their obligations, and that they could not hide behind the shield of sovereignty.

In fact, the United Kingdom expressed the view that the international community had a "fundamental role to play" in safeguarding the world from destructive weapons.[69] One of the "most important responsibilities of the international community . . . is to hold Iraq to its obligations . . . this includes the threat posed by weapons of mass destruction."[70] The United Kingdom further argued that the international community would not be meeting its responsibilities if it ignored Iraq's defiance of UN resolutions.[71] Taking this a step further, the United Kingdom asserted that the international community had a right to bypass state sovereignty in the event of noncompliance. As it stated, "We back our diplomacy if necessary with the credible use of force."[72] In order to make UN resolutions meaningful, the United Kingdom believed that it was fully within the scope of the international community's right to enforce international peace and security with military action.[73]

Overall, preintervention discourse pointed to the United Kingdom's contingent notion of sovereignty (see figure 5.3). The content analysis demonstrates that the United Kingdom never endorsed absolute sovereignty for states. Rather, the analysis highlights the United Kingdom's emphasis on states meeting their obligations (88% of speeches). At the same time, it frequently argued that the international community had the responsibility to help states meet these obligations (71%), and in just under half the speeches (47%), the United Kingdom claimed that they could override state sovereignty in pursuit of these goals.

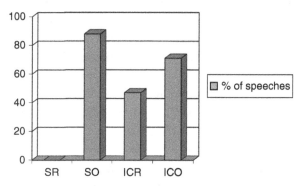

SR = State Rights, SO = State Obligations, ICR = International Community's Rights, ICO = International Community's Obligations

FIGURE 5.3  UK Conceptions of Sovereignty Before Intervention

Once the intervention began, the United Kingdom refrained from mentioning norms regarding weapons of mass destruction in most of its speeches. Even when the topic was Iraq, the United Kingdom largely focused on describing the situation to the Security Council in terms of progress on sanitation, employment, and education, among other things. In only one-third of the speeches did the United Kingdom discuss its views on norms about weapons of mass destruction.

Of these speeches, the United Kingdom continued, albeit to a lesser degree, to emphasize the importance of states meeting their responsibilities. In one speech, the United Kingdom defended the intervention by reminding the Security Council that its demands had never been carried out by Iraq.[74] More broadly, the United Kingdom stressed the "importance of arms control and disarmament obligations" of states.[75] While its discussion of states' responsibilities slightly declined from the previous period, it did continue to lean toward contingent sovereignty, although it did show support for absolute sovereignty in one speech.

The reduced commitment to contingent sovereignty is also seen in the United Kingdom's remarks about the role of the international community. The United Kingdom reminded the international community that in dealing with the threat of weapons of mass destruction, "it was not only appropriate for the Council to act, it was imperative to do so."[76] Because the consequences of inaction were perceived as untenable, the United Kingdom urged that the threat "required a global response."[77] Not only *should* the international community do something, it also had the *right* to act in preserving international peace and security. For example, in supporting a UN resolution that addressed weapons proliferation, the United Kingdom argued that the resolution would be binding on states and had a legal basis rooted in Chapter 7 of the UN Charter, which describes legitimate action that may be taken against threats to peace.[78]

The movement away from contingent sovereignty is more clearly seen in the content analysis. As seen in figure 5.4, all categories capturing contingent sovereignty declined. With regard to state obligations, the United Kingdom demonstrated a slight decline in such references, from 88% to 80% of the speeches. Mentions of the international community's obligations and rights also faced a similar decrease, from 71% to 60%, and 47% to 40%, respectively. The one change that stands out is within the category of states' rights, in which the United Kingdom reinforced states' rights in

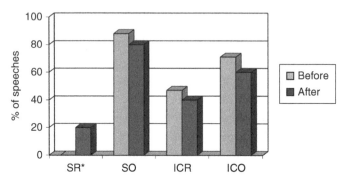

SR = State Rights, SO = State Obligations, ICR = International Community's
Rights, ICO = International Community's Obligations

FIGURE 5.4 UK Conceptions of Sovereignty Before and During
Military Intervention

several of its speeches after the onset of the war in Iraq (0% to 20%).[79] Overall, the results indicate that the United Kingdom moved toward absolute sovereignty after the intervention began.

As with the US case, these results are as I predicted. Since the weapons of mass destruction were not found, the United Kingdom largely avoided discussion of these norms. When it did so, it voiced contingent sovereignty less often relative to the preintervention discourse. The reinforcement of contingent sovereignty was muted because the action could no longer embody the norm it was based on. Instead, we find that the United Kingdom stressed absolute sovereignty with regard to weapons of mass destruction.

## War Protesters: France and Russia

### France

From the beginning, France strongly opposed the war. France preferred to continue diplomatic means to deal with the alleged weapons violations of Iraq. In fact, in February 2003, France proposed an alternative to using force by arguing at the UN Security Council for "extending and strengthening" United Nations weapons inspections.[80] France promised to veto any resolution that included the use of military force to compel compliance. This was consistent with domestic public opinion, with over 80% of the French strongly opposed to a war in Iraq.[81] When the intervention began anyway, President Chirac argued, "Whether, I repeat, it's a matter of the necessary disarmament of Iraq or of the desirable change of regime in that country, there is no justification for a unilateral decision to resort to war."[82] He thereby deemed the intervention illegal under international law. In this regard, despite agreeing that Iraq was not meeting its international obligations, France upheld an absolute notion of sovereignty; states had international responsibilities, but the international community also had the obligation to respect a state's sovereignty.

In considering France's lack of support for the use of military force, it might be useful to consider its own culpability regarding weapons of mass destruction and its interest in preserving Iraq's sovereignty. Examining these two interrelated areas help to form expectations about France's views on sovereignty after the war began.

In terms of culpability, France is not considered to be a violator of weapons of mass destruction norms. France has ratified all four relevant treaties—the Treaty on the Non-Proliferation of Nuclear Weapons, the Comprehensive Nuclear-Test-Ban Treaty, the Chemical Weapons Convention, and the Biological Weapons Convention—and is considered a responsible member in this regard in the international community.[83] In addition, it is a party to a number of export-control regimes, including the Australia Group and the Missile Technology Control Regime. Based on evaluations of the Arms Control Association, France has complied with its international obligations in the post–Cold War era and has even engaged in negotiations with Iran in order to dissuade Iran from developing a nuclear weapons program.

However, there has been some suggestion that France helped Iraq to evade UN weapons sanctions. For example, the chief UN weapons inspector found evidence of French companies selling illicit weapons to Iraq until shortly before the Iraq war began.[84] The assertions in the United States mounted, where it became difficult to separate fact from media frenzy.[85] In fact, France felt compelled to respond in a detailed letter to the US, outlining a list of unfair attacks and stories in US newspapers.[86] What is, perhaps, less controversial is the economic connection between Iraq and France.

It is well known that France had historical and commercial ties to Iraq.[87] For years, France had been Iraq's closest Western ally, which facilitated the development of an economic relationship. Though not officially cited as such, these interests could have provided strong reasons for avoiding war in Iraq. For example, Iraq still owed French companies millions of dollars for weapons sold to it during the Iran-Iraq war (1980–88). In addition, France was the largest exporter to Iraq, selling $650 million dollars worth of products in 2001. Most important, perhaps, French companies had potential contracts with Iraq to drill unexploited oil reserves, which would enter into force once Iraqi sanctions were lifted.

Given these mixed indicators, I expect that prior to the intervention, France would moderately support contingent sovereignty. Yet, once the intervention begins, I expect that France will lean toward absolute sovereignty because the intervention highlights the possible consequences of norm violations. Since France had interests in Iraq and was partially culpable in this policy domain, it will advocate for states' rights in order to keep its internal practices consistent with its external policies. However, I do expect that France will still advocate an active role for the international community in helping states meet their obligations.

### France's Stated Views on Sovereignty Before Iraq WMD Crisis

As with the previous cases, I first review statements by France in the time period prior to intervention to establish a basis for comparison. This period was marked by discussions in the UN Security Council of Iraq and its questionable compliance with weapons of mass destruction norms. However, there was also concern about India's and Pakistan's nuclear testing and its effects on the nonproliferation regime. It is within these speeches that France's understanding of sovereignty in this policy domain can be discerned.

France supported contingent sovereignty, evident by the lack of discussion of states' rights. France made no assertions that the international community should respect state sovereignty when it came to weapons of mass destruction. Rather, France focused almost entirely on encouraging states to comply with the laws of the international community. In early 1992, France stated, "Everyone must now participate in nuclear disarmament" and reminded states that there should be "universal adherence to the Treaty on Non-Proliferation of Nuclear Weapons."[88] When states failed to follow what France regarded as the norms of the world community, as in the cases of Pakistan and India, France "deplored and condemned these tests, which run counter to global efforts against nuclear proliferation."[89] In the Iraq situation, France continued to warn that "Iraq must comply" with its international obligations, including allowing weapons inspectors to monitor the status of its weapons programs.[90] France further cautioned that it wanted to "send a clear warning to Iraq that the Council will not tolerate new violations."[91] In France's view, states were beholden to their international obligations, implying limits to a state's absolute sovereignty.

These obligations were then to be monitored by the international community, though the enforcement mechanism relied primarily on states' own incentives for cooperation. Initially, rather than imposing (UN Charter) Chapter 7 obligations, which would allow for the potential use of force, France implored states to seek cooperation on matters related to weapons of mass destruction.[92] For example, with regard to India's and Pakistan's nuclear testing, France believed it was the "duty" of the international community to "encourage" these states to accede to the relevant conventions and seek a peaceful resolution to their differences.[93] The international community carried the same kind of responsibility in the situation in Iraq: it is the "Security Council's duty to place firmness and lucidity in the service of a common objective . . . the disarmament of Iraq."[94] For a time, France supported "giving peace a chance," advocating diplomatic measures that did not infringe on state sovereignty.[95]

However, as Iraq's defiance continued, France became more willing to discuss the use of force as "the final recourse."[96] "France has always said that we do not exclude the possibility that one day we might have to resort to force."[97] In the several months prior to the intervention, France also believed in "strengthening the role and authority of the Security Council" and emphasized the idea that the Council must act together.[98] If action, such as military force, was necessary, "the United Nations will have to be at the centre," and this would only be after all options had been considered.[99] Thus, France admitted that such an option fell within the purview of the international community, though it was not prepared to exercise this right in the case of Iraq.

In tangible terms, the content analysis demonstrates that France's speeches focused on a contingent view of sovereignty (see figure 5.5). In almost all the speeches (92%), France discussed the importance of states meeting their international responsibilities. At the same time, France also supported the international community's responsibility to monitor states' norm compliance and violations, especially in an area that threatened international peace and security (79% of speeches). Yet, a relatively small proportion of speeches (29%) actually illustrated France's recognition that the international community had a right to interfere within states in order to remedy norm violations. These results indicate that France had a moderate view of contingent sovereignty; it clearly was not supportive of sovereignty as a shield, but it also did not strongly advocate for the ultimate authority of the international community.

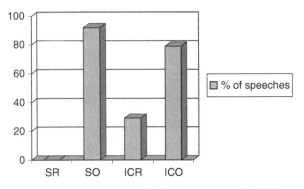

SR = State Rights, SO = State Obligations, ICR = International Community's
Rights, ICO = International Community's Obligations

FIGURE 5.5 France's Conceptions of Sovereignty Before Iraq
WMD Crisis

### France's Stated Views on Sovereignty After Iraq WMD Crisis

After the intervention began, France's discourse changed in some interesting ways. First, its commitment to absolute sovereignty dramatically
increased with regard to weapons of mass destruction. In particular, this
change relates to the situation in Iraq. France emphasized that the international community should be guided by "respect for the unity and territorial
integrity of Iraq, and the preservation of its sovereignty."[100]

Displeased with the US-led military intervention in Iraq, France
reiterated that states have ultimate authority, not the international community. In speaking of measures to ensure nonproliferation compliance,
France stated, "The Security Council cannot take those measures in their
stead, but it can decide that they do need to take them."[101] With this, France
acknowledged that there were limits to what the international community
could impose on states. In fact, France argued that states, as sovereign
entities, were "free to define the penalties, legal regulations and practical
measures to be adopted" when it came to resolutions passed by the
Council.[102]

France's strong emphasis on states' rights was paired with a decrease in
references to states' obligations. It mentioned the importance of states following through on their obligations less often than in the previous period.
France encouraged states to meet their disarmament obligations and
asserted that "measures to be taken to counter proliferation were the responsibility of states."[103] However, France more frequently referred to
states' rights to noninterference from the international community.

As such, there was little discussion of the right of the international community to intervene to aid a state in meeting its obligations. In one speech, France did mention the legal basis for the potential use of force in the event of noncompliance, implying that such a decision fell within the rights of the Security Council.[104] However, the majority of the speeches focused on what the international community should do to reduce the threat of illicit weapons. France continued to see the United Nations as having a significant role to play in keeping the world safe from weapons of mass destruction: "France is convinced that the UN, particularly the Security Council, must play its full role in the multilateral anti-proliferation effort."[105] The global community should work together to halt proliferation, including asking states to comply with necessary measures.[106]

The results of the content analysis indicate more clearly the changes in conceptions of sovereignty for France (see figure 5.6). Discussion of states' rights increased dramatically, from 0% to 75% of speeches, while references to states' obligations to the international community decreased from 86% to 50% of the speeches.[107] In addition, France reduced its discussion of the global community's rights, from 29% to 13%, which further establishes its movement toward absolute sovereignty. At the same time, however, France increasingly emphasized the international community's obligations to aid states in their compliance with norms regarding weapons of mass destruction (from 79% to 100% of speeches). This suggests that France did not fully retreat to the traditional understanding of absolute

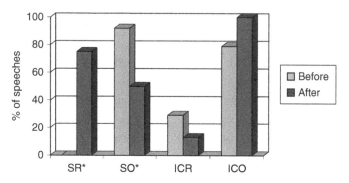

SR = State Rights, SO = State Obligations, ICR = International Community's
Rights, ICO = International Community's Obligations

FIGURE 5.6 France's Conceptions of Sovereignty Before and After Iraq WMD Crisis

sovereignty, though its movement along the sovereignty continuum in this direction matched my expectations.

## Russia

While Russia is a staunch ally of the United States and the United Kingdom in the global war on terrorism, it parted ways with them on matters of state noncompliance with norms on weapons of mass destruction. Like France, Russia made it clear that it would veto any UN Security Council resolution permitting the use of force in Iraq.[108] Siding with chief UN weapons inspector, Hans Blix, Russia argued that more time was needed for the UN weapons inspectors to accurately assess the status of Saddam Hussein's weapons programs. Though the United States went to extraordinary lengths to lobby Russia in particular, it was not swayed;[109] Russia reasoned that military action would violate international norms and lead to a broader crisis in the Middle East. While Russia fully agreed that Iraq was not in compliance with its obligations, it nevertheless was adamant against a US-led intervention.

Though Russia did not support intervention, it could still change its conception of sovereignty. However, this change hinges on its culpability in the policy domain. Russia would not support an intervention in which it was itself a violator of the norms the action was predicated on. Thus, before and after the intervention, Russia would support absolute sovereignty. Yet, if Russia was not guilty of violations, there exists a potential for it to change its notion of sovereignty, as we saw in the chapter on counterterrorism.

In the domain of weapons of mass destruction, Russia's record appears mixed. On the positive side, Russia has ratified all four of the major arms control agreements. In addition, it is a member of several export-control regimes, including the Nuclear Suppliers Group and the Missile Technology Control Regime. Russia is not a member of the Australia Group but asserts that it follows the group's rules and control list. As a leading state, Russia has used its influence to advocate transparency in Iran's nuclear programs and has been one of the key members in the North Korea disarmament talks.

On the negative side, Russia's adherence to the Biological and Chemical Weapons Conventions has been challenged by the United States, which maintains that Russia has offensive capabilities and has not fully disclosed the extent of its activities.[110] Moreover, with regard to proliferation, independent analysts and the United States have asserted that Russia has aided, knowingly or not, other states (India and Iran) with their nuclear and missile programs.[111] For example, Russia and Iran have an agreement to cooperate in the civil use of nuclear energy. As part of the agreement, Russia is aiding Iran in constructing a nuclear power plant in Bushehr and providing enriched uranium as nuclear fuel. While both countries argue that this cooperation is within the guidelines of the Nuclear Non-Proliferation Treaty, it is suspected that Iran will or is using Russia's help to develop nuclear weapons.[112]

Given Russia's mixed record regarding its adherence to weapons of mass destruction norms and considering its interest in maintaining absolute sovereignty for states in this regard, I do not expect Russia to alter its views on sovereignty because of the war in Iraq.[113] Rather, I expect Russia to maintain that states should live up to their international commitments, while reminding the international community of their obligation to respect states' sovereignty. In this way, Russia is able to maintain a comfortable level of cognitive consistency, keeping its internal practices in line with its international behavior.

### Russia's Stated Views on Sovereignty Before Iraq WMD Crisis

Russia's views on sovereignty prior to the intervention can be characterized as mixed: anchored by absolute sovereignty, but moderated by contingent notions of sovereignty. Russia held strongly to protecting states' rights and limiting the role of the international community in dealing with weapons of mass destruction. For example, while Russia condemned the nuclear tests of India and Pakistan, it also decided it was best to stay out of the countries' internal affairs and let them solve the problem amongst themselves.[114] Moreover, in discussing ways to achieve Iraqi compliance with UN resolutions, Russia argued that the Security Council should draft a resolution according to what was acceptable to Iraq, thereby giving Iraq ultimate authority.[115] In a later discussion, Russia asserted that "it is of fundamental importance that the resolution clearly confirms that all members of the United Nations respect the sovereignty and territorial integrity of Iraq."[116]

While Russia kept the issue of states' rights in the foreground of discussions, it also consistently advocated that states abide by their duties, as well as the international community. Russia implored states, members of the Security Council or not, to disarm and "adhere to their obligations."[117] Russia was very critical of the United States' and the United Kingdom's enforcement of the no-fly zone in Iraq: they "grossly violated the Charter of the United Nations, the principles of international law, and the generally recognized norms and rules of responsible behavior."[118] However, Russia did not condone Iraq's behavior, warning that "Baghdad must meet the demands of the United Nations that it eliminate its W.M.D. programmes."[119] Thus, states must comply with international standards, whether they are violating these norms or violating proper enforcement of these norms.

Russia also believed that the international community had a role in disarmament.[120] Because the United Nations was the "most suitable mechanism for settling the most burning issues," it had an "exceptional responsibility" to oversee state compliance and to act accordingly if necessary.[121] Because weapons of mass destruction posed a threat to international peace and security, it was incumbent upon the representatives of the international community, the UN Security Council, to compel states to disarm. Yet, this was to be carried out according to the principles of the UN Charter, which, in Russia's view, meant following the principle of noninterference in states' internal affairs.

As illustrated by the content analysis, Russia is not entirely committed to a contingent or absolute notion of sovereignty (see figure 5.7). A majority of speeches (59%) refer to respecting state sovereignty, while an even greater proportion of speeches (76%) mention support for states needing to meet their obligations. Similarly, Russia endorsed the international community's duty to maintain peace and security in 76% of its speeches. In only 6% of the speeches did Russia ever refer to any rights of the international community in this regard. Overall, Russia held mixed views of

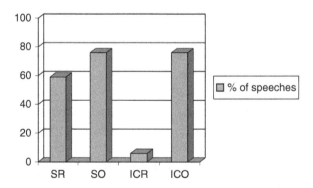

SR = State Rights, SO = State Obligations, ICR = International Community's
Rights, ICO = International Community's Obligations

FIGURE 5.7 Russia's Conceptions of Sovereignty Before Iraq
WMD Crisis

sovereignty when it considered the intersection of sovereignty and weapons of mass destruction norms.

### Russia's Stated Views on Sovereignty After the Iraq WMD Crisis

Russia's views on sovereignty remained relatively constant after the intervention began. It maintained a commitment to absolute sovereignty, discussing states' rights slightly more than in the prior period. Russia argued that the US-led intervention was illegal and violated Iraq's sovereignty: "an unprovoked military action has been undertaken, in violation of international law and in circumvention of the charter, against Iraq, a sovereign state and the member of the United Nations."[122] Russia was deeply concerned about helping Iraq regain its sovereignty and implored the coalition forces to do this as soon as possible.[123] In Russia's view, the intervention was not justified, and it sought repeatedly to return Iraq to a sovereign state.

At the same time, although to a lesser degree, Russia agreed that states were obligated to adhere to international norms. Iraq still had to comply with the standards that the international community had set for it in the peace settlement after the Gulf War. Indeed, all states were compelled to follow the rules of the international community: "we call on all States . . . to counter the proliferation of weapons of mass destruction."[124] This included enacting national legislation if necessary and creating compliance reports for the international community.

In terms of the international community's obligations, Russia continued to give it a large role in halting proliferation and disarmament. Almost all the speeches referred to the importance of the international community's efforts to safeguard the world from these destructive weapons: "the Security Council, as the body that bears primary responsibility for the maintenance of international peace and security, has fully shouldered its obligations by ensuring the deployment of international inspectors to Iraq."[125] More broadly, Russia acknowledged that "the world community is called upon to increasingly and actively address" the threats posed by weapons proliferation.[126] Thus, the Security Council should oversee "efforts to prevent the illicit acquisition of weapons of mass destruction," as well as always act collectively against such a threat.[127]

In these efforts, the Council was "entitled . . . to take appropriate measures in the area of international security, to include those that are legally binding."[128] Russia, though in a limited way, acknowledged the rights of the international community in this issue area. These rights included the ability to enact international laws and monitor states' compliance with these laws. However, references to such rights were mentioned only rarely.

As we can see from the results of the content analysis in figure 5.8, Russia did experience changes in its views of sovereignty. Russia increased its references to protecting state sovereignty once the intervention began but only slightly (59% to 69% of the speeches). Interestingly, however, two of the three categories representing contingent sovereignty also increased. The mentions of support for the international community's rights and its obligations both showed slight increases (from 6% to 15%, and 76% to 85%, respectively). The one area of decline among the categories was references to states' obligations, taking a rather dramatic drop from 76% to 54% of the speeches.

Substantively, Russia maintained a mixed view of sovereignty, espousing elements of absolute and contingent sovereignty. It may be that Russia theoretically supported a strong role for the international community in dealing with weapons of mass destruction, demonstrated by the increase in discourse surrounding the international community's rights and obligations. However, in the specific case of Iraq, Russia leaned strongly toward absolute sovereignty, reflected in a greater commitment to states' rights and a weakening emphasis on states' obligations. This evidence lends support to my assertion that Russia would be guided by self-interest in determining the conception of sovereignty it would embrace.

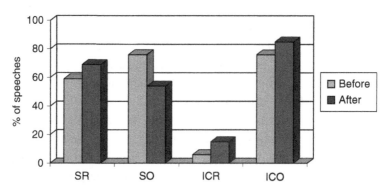

SR = State Rights, SO = State Obligations, ICR = International Community's Rights, ICO = International Community's Obligations.

FIGURE 5.8  Russia's Conceptions of Sovereignty Before and After Iraq WMD Crisis

# Discussion and Conclusion

The cases detailed in this chapter illustrate the consequences of an intervention built on false premises and conducted without a majority consensus from the global community. Within this context, the intervention resulted in the opposite of what was expected: weapons of mass destruction norms were subordinated to absolute sovereignty. Despite the situation of negative indicators (costs and success), which should have led to the reinforcement of contingent sovereignty, the interveners and the nonintervening states stressed a commitment to respecting states' rights with regard to weapons of mass destruction.

As illustrated in table 5.1, the states participating in the intervention muted their support for the rights and obligations of the international community to deal with the threats posed by weapons of mass destruction. In the case of the United States, these changes were statistically significant. The significant change toward absolute sovereignty in the United Kingdom's case was seen in their increased support for states' rights. Having found no evidence to confirm their assertions, both the United States and the United Kingdom distanced themselves from using weapons of mass destruction as justification for the ongoing intervention. In doing so, they negatively affected the norm upon which they acted, essentially weakening, rather than strengthening, the norm of absolute sovereignty.

TABLE 5.1 Conceptions of Sovereignty for Interveners and NonInterveners

| | STATES' RIGHTS | | STATES' OBLIGATIONS | | INTERNATIONAL COMMUNITY'Z RIGHTS | | INTERNATIONAL COMMUNITY'S OBLIGATIONS | |
|---|---|---|---|---|---|---|---|---|
| | BEFORE | AFTER | BEFORE | AFTER | BEFORE | AFTER | BEFORE | AFTER |
| **Military Intervention** | | | | | | | | |
| United States | 0 | 0 | 82 | 80 | 35 | 10 | 71 | 20** |
| United Kingdom | 0 | 20** | 88 | 80 | 47 | 40 | 71 | 60 |
| **Noninterveners** | | | | | | | | |
| France | 0 | 75** | 86 | 50* | 29 | 13 | 79 | 100 |
| Russia | 59 | 69 | 76 | 54 | 6 | 15 | 76 | 85 |

NOTE: Numbers indicate percent of total speeches that mention a given category. The total number of speeches for each country is as follows (before; after): US (17; 10); UK (17; 5); France (14; 8); Russia (17; 13). Statistically significant changes indicated by *p<.10; **p<.05.

This highlights an important issue in applying the theory of cognitive dissonance to military interventions that was not seen in the other chapters. The underlying assumption was that the norm could be legitimately applied. However, as we have seen here, when that assumption does not hold, the expected results are not borne out. This is not entirely surprising. Insights from cognitive dissonance also point to an innate desire to maintain cognitive consistency. Because the weapons of mass destruction explanation for war became delegitimized, leaders used other reasons to remain in Iraq, such as creating democratic institutions. In this way, leaders switched their support from one norm to another and in the process, attempted to regain the public's trust by creating a new legitimizing narrative.

The noninterveners, France and Russia, differed in how the intervention affected their views on sovereignty. France became more committed to absolute sovereignty, while Russia experienced little change in its views. The differences may be accounted for in their different starting points on the sovereignty continuum. Though they both leaned toward absolute sovereignty after the intervention began, only France had previously been an advocate of contingent sovereignty. Thus, we seem more change in France. As I suggested earlier, one explanation for these countries ultimately defending states' right may be that the target of intervention was Iraq. France and Russia had an economic interest in maintaining Saddam Hussein's regime. Another contributing factor was that each country had a mixed record of compliance with weapons of mass destruction norms. In light of the willingness of some states to use force to halt violations, France and Russia were compelled to reinforce absolute sovereignty in order to maintain congruence between their internal practices and external policies.

While these four cases (United States, United Kingdom, France, and Russia) demonstrate the extent to which actions influence conceptions of sovereignty within specific states, they also point to changes in the normative structure more broadly. Earlier, I suggested that several elements of the normative structure are critical for change: norm prominence, norm coherence, and environmental conditions. While these elements were ripe for contingent sovereignty to take hold, the lack of the intervention's legitimacy contributed to the downplaying of norms regarding weapons of mass destruction vis-à-vis absolute sovereignty. The intervention highlighted the virtues of state sovereignty within this policy domain, rather than one contingent on compliance with these norms.

Furthermore, the illegitimate intervention contributed to the breakdown of the contingent sovereignty norm's coherence with other norms. The United Kingdom and the United States essentially disconnected sovereignty contingent on compliance with international weapons norms from other norms that they had also used in justifying the war in Iraq. Though there were some later efforts to maintain a link between counterterrorism norms and weapons of mass destruction norms, the focus was on nonstate actors rather than state sponsors.

With regards to environmental conditions, the evidence in this chapter suggests that the intervention may have had the unintended consequence of promoting the development of weapons of mass destruction. Though the United States and the United Kingdom demonstrated the willingness to intervene on behalf of weapons violations, they were not able to convince the international community that such an action was appropriate, despite the alleged "evidence." States seeking to begin or to continue developing weapons of mass destruction likely recognize that the international community is not unified on how to deal with such a threat, and they may ascertain that they would be safe from military action. Furthermore, the United States and the United Kingdom, two of the most likely interveners, may not wish to take such risks again, given the outcome. Thus, some states may be encouraged to pursue illicit activities.

In addition, the intervention may have contributed to an increase in terrorism, especially given the lack of evidence found for weapons of mass destruction. This provided further justification for attacks against the West and "imperialist powers." Since the war began, terrorists have targeted countries, such as England, Pakistan, and Spain, for their support of the military action in Iraq. These attacks have wide-reaching impact, expanding the instability of the Middle East to the rest of the world.

While the military action of the United States and United Kingdom in Iraq have arguably more impact on the evolution of the normative structure, it is nevertheless important to consider the impact of Russia's and France's protest. The nonparticipation of these countries in the intervention and their emphasis on states' rights reinforced the prominence of absolute sovereignty over weapons of mass destruction norms. Absolute sovereignty is incompatible with other norms, and thus its reinforcement assigns it to the top of the hierarchical normative structure.

In sum, this chapter investigated changes in sovereignty conceptions in the context of weapons of mass destruction. The military intervention in

Iraq provided a potential impetus for change toward contingent sovereignty. However, because of the false premises of the intervention, the predictions of cognitive dissonance were not borne out. Rather, the evidence showed that the action reinforced absolute sovereignty in the cases of the interveners. As for the noninterveners, state culpability and self-interest were found to be important predictors of changes in attitudes toward sovereignty, providing support for an actor's desire to maintain cognitive consistency.

# CHAPTER 6 | Conclusion

Although R2P was originally intended to deal solely with situations of mass atrocity, if it becomes a standard part of global governance, the principles of R2P unbundled and applied in a different way may have lessons to teach about forging solutions to other shared problems so that the single sovereign state doesn't get in the way of collective efforts. This could lead to a new global architecture that would help us achieve shared objectives, thus escaping the Westphalian nation-state straitjacket that impedes real progress toward solutions to today's global risks.[1]

> —LLOYD AXWORTHY, Canadian Foreign Affairs Minister, and
> ALLAN ROCK, Canadian Ambassador to the United Nations, 2008

I HAVE TRIED TO illustrate how a social psychological approach might help explain how norms evolve. Though the predictions seem counterintuitive, the insights of cognitive dissonance help account for the development of contingent sovereignty in situations that would otherwise point to a reinforcement of absolute sovereignty. Leaders must rationalize their decisions to intervene and make sense of its outcome for their publics in order to maintain legitimate power. In the game of politics, leaders learn to handle a certain level of dissonance. However, the masses are less likely to tolerate dissonance, especially a dissonant situation that involves casualties. To reconcile the "failing" intervention with the desirability of the norm it was based on, leaders will emphasize the significance of that norm to the masses. Except for the special case of the intervention in Iraq, this preliminary investigation showed that the more arduous and costly the intervention, the more contingent sovereignty was reinforced. This is significant because traditional explanations guided by rational choice theory would have predicted the opposite: the more difficult the intervention, the *less* commitment there would be to contingent sovereignty.

## Importance of Action

Action endows ideas with meaning, both defining current understandings of a concept and aiding its development. While most social scientists only focus on the influence of ideas on action, this study completes the story by emphasizing how action shapes ideas, recognizing that the relationship between action and ideas (norms) is reciprocal. The case studies herein support my main argument: changes in political norms are facilitated, in part, by political actions.

The rights and obligations implied by state sovereignty are only meaningful when concrete actions, not just words, are marshaled on their behalf. Through actions, such as military interventions, the nature of sovereignty is exposed. Without actions to confirm or reshape the meaning of sovereignty, the evolving concept itself at any particular time remains unclear. Thus, not only do understandings of sovereignty shape the decision to intervene, but intervention itself determines the form of acceptable sovereignty. Across the empirical cases, each intervention suggested that significant change occurs as a result of action (though not for every state), given that the necessary conditions for change were met.

The importance of action in explaining change is often overlooked, especially within the norms literature. This research typically stops at the policy outcome, or the decision to intervene, in examining the impact of norms on the decision-making process. This is an important part of the process of norm change, but it does not tell the full story. Given the dynamic nature of norms, we must *also* understand how decisions and their outcomes feed back to the normative structure. This provides for a fuller, more complete explanation of norm change.

## Contingent Sovereignty and Military Intervention

To review, the first two empirical studies, on counterterrorism and human rights, demonstrated that a failing intervention, in which an intervener faced high costs with limited success, reinforced contingent sovereignty. In both cases, this meant that the intervener was more committed to making sovereignty dependent either on compliance with counterterrorism norms or with human rights norms during and after the intervention. Furthermore, interveners, more strongly than noninterveners, promoted the idea that the international community had the obligations, and sometimes the right, to intervene when states failed in these duties. For example, the United States more strongly reinforced contingent sovereignty, in which state sovereignty depended on living up to counterterrorism norms, after it intervened in Afghanistan, and France's promotion of sovereignty as conditional upon states meeting human rights standards increased after its involvement in Somalia.

Other leading states not involved in the intervention varied in how their notions of sovereignty were influenced by the intervention. Conceptions of sovereignty depended both on a state's culpability in a particular policy domain and on its self-interest. For instance, in the case of the intervention in Somalia, the changes in conceptions of sovereignty for Russia were closely tied to changes in its own domestic human rights situation. As Russia acted with varying levels of respect for civil and political rights at home, it vacillated between support for absolute and contingent sovereignty with regard to human rights.

While this illustrates the influence of culpability on views of sovereignty within an issue area, there is also evidence regarding the impact of culpability across issue areas. For example, though China held tightly to absolute sovereignty throughout the intervention in Somalia, it moved toward contingent sovereignty with regards to counterterrorism in the context of the global war on terror. This correlated positively with its culpability in each domain; China consistently violated human rights but adheres to its counterterrorism obligations.

The example of China highlights another important finding of the study. State views on sovereignty are complex. We might expect that how a state understands sovereignty in one domain would correspond to its views on sovereignty in another. If I had only focused on the United States, this assertion would be supported. But this is not necessarily so. France was a strong advocate for contingent sovereignty in terms of human rights norms, but those views did not carry over to the domain of weapons of mass destruction. Note that this also indicates that some states support contingent sovereignty when international security interests are not at stake, but will sometimes oppose it when they are (Russia supported the war in Afghanistan, but not the war in Iraq). A state's culpability in the relevant issue area helps to explain these nuanced views.

The final empirical chapter examined the military intervention in Iraq and added a new aspect to the investigation: the legitimacy of an intervention. Whereas there was arguably just cause in intervening in Somalia and

Afghanistan, the war in Iraq failed to validate the intervention's primary justification: the development and stockpiling of weapons of mass destruction. As information on the lack of evidence became public, leaders had to find new arguments: "The goal in Iraq [and Afghanistan] is for there be to democratic and free countries who are allies in the war on terror."[2] Leaders were forced to pull away from the justification concerning Iraq's possession of weapons of mass destruction, since it created a sharp dissonance between the initial rhetoric on the purpose of the war and the actual situation on the ground.

Interestingly, this resulted in a policy backfire; a policy of making sovereignty contingent on compliance with weapons of mass destruction norms reverted to one endorsing absolute sovereignty in this arena. Other relevant norms, such as democratic norms, may have been reinforced, but in the context of international norms regarding illicit weapons, not only did the intervention push noninterveners toward absolute sovereignty, the interveners themselves revised their views of sovereignty in that direction.

While the legitimacy of the intervention divides the last empirical chapter from the previous two, what remains similar across all cases of intervention is the importance that leading states attribute to norms. Every state has a stake in the constitution of the normative environment. This is not only evidenced in the positive efforts to redefine the normative environment via intervention but also in the negative responses to attempts at change. States avoid changes to sovereignty and to normative developments more generally, if this would force them to face the international consequences of their own culpability. Because states seek to maintain a good reputation in the international community, they will resist changes that reflect poorly on them. Moreover, it enables them to maintain cognitive consistency, in which their internal practices match their external policies. Nothing is more important to a state, and its leaders, than to maintain an environment in which its policies remain unchallenged.

Today, the international community is in the process of redefining sovereignty. Partially as a result of responses to international events, sovereignty is being pushed and pulled in different directions by states, with nonculpable states pushing it toward a contingent notion and culpable states pulling it back toward an absolute view. Because of this division, a norm cannot settle, or become internalized, in the international community without a broad consensus. Until all the leading powers transition from norm violators to norm compliers, an ideational polarization will pervade international relations within various policy domains.

## Minor Powers and Norm Change

While the focus in this book has been on ideational forces, I recognize that the international system remains characterized by hierarchy (Lake 2009). Material forces continue to play a role in determining who sets the rules of the game. The normative structure is largely determined by the actions and discourse of the major powers. In practice, major states have absolute sovereignty, even if they espouse contingent sovereignty for others. Powerful states dictate the rules for less powerful states, rules that they themselves might not abide by. Thus, the evolution in the norm of sovereignty applies to the majority of states, but not its most powerful—unless such a change also aligns with their self-interest.

The fact that minor powers are embedded in a hierarchy of international relations certainly constrains their ability to affect norm evolution but need not condemn them to irrelevance. Regionally, it may be that minor powers shape norms in a similar way, through their actions and discourse, and this in turn facilitates predictable behavior among states in a particular locale. In addition, there may be regional hegemons that act like major powers, and the implications of this study may have some import in explaining norm change within a region. Further, actions and their corresponding discourses by states like South Africa in sub-Saharan Africa and Brazil in South America may have more influence on the evolution of regional norms than on broader changes in international norms. If global change in a norm is sought by a lesser power, it may depend on its ability to influence a major power's actions. For example, one might suggest that coalition partners in the war in Afghanistan—like Germany—indirectly affected the normative shift toward contingent sovereignty in the policy domain of counterterrorism.

Since the war began, Germany has had the third-largest troop contribution, which peaked at 5,300 troops in 2011.[3] It would be interesting to compare the effects of intervention for Germany on its views of sovereignty with the changes exhibited by its major power counterparts. We might expect lesser powers involved in an intervention to adhere to contingent sovereignty more strongly to gain approval and recognition from the major-power interveners. Yet, they may also be less willing or able to accept the costs of intervention over time, thus impacting their support for contingent sovereignty. Moreover, Germany would be a particularly interesting case because of protests by German troops regarding Germany's involvement in the war in Afghanistan, greatly increasing the political cost at home.[4] Results of such a study would complement the findings presented here, by both broadening and deepening the examination of views on sovereignty and the mechanism of cognitive dissonance.

## Contingent Sovereignty as Desirable?

Some interventions reinforce norms that are inherently "good," such as contingent sovereignty emphasizing compliance with human rights norms.[5] A community of states that recognizes individual human rights as nonnegotiable is a goal worth pursuing for humanity. But other understandings of sovereignty may not be as straightforward to judge if we ask *for whom* the norm is "good." It would seem that those creating and maintaining the normative structure, the leading powers, are the primary beneficiaries of any changes to the norm of sovereignty (if such a consensus could be reached). Ideally, such changes would also be in the interest of other states, if it enhanced their security and well-being. But changes in sovereignty are not necessarily desirable for all. For example, sovereignty conditional on meeting counterterrorism norms would seem to increase international peace and security. However, it may also lead inadvertently to that which it is trying to prevent. By joining international counterterrorism efforts, states may themselves become targets of terrorism. For example, with one of the largest troop contingents in Afghanistan, Germany continues to face al Qaeda and other terrorist threats at home, with plots uncovered almost regularly by local and international intelligence.[6] And major powers are not immune from terrorist plots, either. From thwarted plans of suicide bombers in the nation's capital to a car bomb in New York's Times Square, the United States has uncovered more than a handful of terrorist plots against the homeland.[7] Thus, we might reconsider whether sovereignty contingent on fulfilling counterterrorism obligations reduces or contributes to terrorism.

At the same time, we might also wonder whether this form of sovereignty is "good" for citizens of the target state. In attempting to enforce counterterrorism norms in Afghanistan, as detailed in chapter 3, the interveners have lost a significant number of troops and invested hundreds of billions of dollars. At the same time, for the Afghans, there were 3,021 civilian deaths, 431 of whom were victims of suicide bombs, in 2011 alone. In the same year, 185,000 Afghans were displaced, the highest number in any year since the war began.[8] The right and obligation of the international community to intervene does not necessarily mean it is "good."

In addition, the invocation of contingent sovereignty risks being misused by states. The now widely accepted idea of the international community's responsibility to protect (R2P; see chapter 4) was invoked by Russia in its 2008 war with Georgia, when Russia claimed that there was an imminent threat of genocide. Russian Foreign Minister Sergei Lavrov argued, "According to our Constitution there is a responsibility to protect—the term which is very widely used in the UN when people see some trouble in Africa or in any remote part of other regions. But this is not Africa to us, this is next door. This is the area where Russian citizens live."[9] However, many in the international community found the claim baseless and strongly condemned Russia's course of action. As Gareth Evans, one of the architects of the R2P doctrine warned, "The Russia-Georgia case highlights the dangers and risks of states, whether individually or in a coalition, interpreting global norms unilaterally and launching military action without UN Security Council authorization."[10]

More broadly, if we consider whether the norm of contingent sovereignty is good, not just within one issue area, but as a concept embodying an increasing number of contingencies across issue areas, this may suggest that the probability of possible intervention increases as well (if there is not a corresponding increase in state compliance with those areas). Such a situation may not be necessarily a good thing for international security and peace. At the same time, it might lead to the irrelevance of sovereign states, in the sense that state governments no longer have much authority over their respective populations. Whether this is a positive development depends on one's perspective. Clearly, leaders of every state have a stake in the current world order, because any change to sovereign rights threatens their position of power, and powerful states may have more to gain from the current system than a revised one, which may include a supragovernmental structure. Citizens in disadvantaged countries may have more to gain as we move toward more contingencies on sovereignty, while those in highly advantaged countries may have more to lose as they bear much of the financial cost of enforcing the contingencies. From the global level, international security and peace would largely depend on the level of compliance in the issue areas that make sovereignty contingent, and the will and ability of the international community to enforce states' obligations. My point is that I do not assume that movement toward contingent sovereignty, within one or many issue areas, is necessarily a "good" thing.

## Current Intersections

The issue areas examined in this book remain pressing international concerns, recently demonstrated in Libya, Syria, Iran, and Pakistan. I will briefly discuss each of them here, in light of the evidence from the analyses.

Intervention on behalf of human rights is possible, though still clearly selective. The 2011 intervention in Libya lends support to the idea that contingent sovereignty based on human rights norms remains a dominant international norm. Supported by the United Nations and the Arab League, the intervention enforced a no-fly zone over Libya and protected its civilians from further violence and repression by the regime of Muammar al-Qaddafi. The Libyan intervention affirmed the responsibility to protect doctrine, declared at a United Nations summit meeting in 2005 (see chapter 4). In contrast to the intervention in Somalia discussed in chapter 4, military action in Libya was by most accounts very successful and of moderate cost: the United States spent $1.1 billion for its part in the intervention, a fraction of the cost of the wars in Afghanistan or Iraq, and suffered zero casualties.[11] In return, the al-Qaddafi regime was dismantled, Libyan citizens were saved from "imminent atrocity," the possibility of democratic transition now exists, and human rights norms were reinforced.[12]

While I argue that contingent sovereignty is more strongly reinforced when an intervention is arduous, the argument rests on the assumption that people prefer cognitive consistency. The fact that the initial justification for the Libyan intervention was reaffirmed by its success meant that no further legitimation was necessary. The findings suggest that such an outcome maintains the conditions necessary for contingent sovereignty to evolve, but may not further its entrenchment or internalization in the international community.

The ongoing case of Syria is a prime example. While the intervention in Libya involved an environment in which military action could safeguard human rights, the inaction of the international community in Syria demonstrates that contingent sovereignty still faces limitations—and not surprisingly. Strategic interests, especially, but not only of the major powers, continue to play a role. While Russia and China had no real ties to Libya and its leadership, they have material interest in Syria and a close relationship with Syrian President Bashar al-Assad. In fact, despite international condemnation of the regime's violent tactics against the democracy-seeking opposition, Russia pledged to provide the Assad government with more weapons.[13] However, with mounting international pressure as total deaths rose to 9,000 civilians, the United Nations Security Council was finally able to pass a resolution that allowed thirty UN observers to monitor the ceasefire agreement (the Annan Plan) brokered by former UN Secretary-General Kofi Annan.[14] Despite its vetoes on previous resolutions, Russia played a key role in persuading President al-Assad to agree to the Annan Plan, as well as moving the UN Security Council forward in passing a UN resolution on Syria. Although the ceasefire was violated by both sides, the fact that the major powers reached a consensus on the situation is at least some progress for human rights.[15] At the same time, the real test of sovereignty understood as the responsibility to protect human rights lies just ahead as the international community continues to consider further action. Though contingent sovereignty in this area points to the possibility of military intervention, such decisions must also take into account the practical ability of military action to make a difference. For example, the United States military has warned that an intervention in Syria "would be a daunting and protracted operation," very different than the one carried out in Libya.[16] The situation is further complicated by the fact that the Syrian opposition is fractious, and a civil war looms on the horizon. Thus, even if Russia and China agree in principle to a UN resolution authorizing military action, other factors must also be taken into account in the practical application of contingent sovereignty.

While sovereignty is evolving to include state compliance with human rights norms, the same cannot be said about the realm of weapons of mass destruction. As the case of Iraq in chapter 5 demonstrates, states continue to exercise absolute sovereignty when it comes to the development and possession of these weapons. The current situation with Iran makes this evident. Even though Iran has clearly violated its international obligations, the international community is not willing to intervene to compel Iran's compliance. Though international sanctions on Iran have been employed, Israel is the only state that has threatened military action against Iran's nuclear sites. The United States recently offered Iran a concession—allowing the enrichment of uranium up to 5% purity, if Iran complies with other UN restrictions.[17] This suggests that Iran has international obligations to keep, though the United States is not asserting the right of the international community to intervene. Thus, this situation leans more toward an understanding of sovereignty that is absolute than one predicated on meeting certain conditions.

In contrast, in the domain of counterterrorism, there is a strong push toward contingent sovereignty. As discussed in chapter 3, the war on terror in Afghanistan has created a growing consensus among the major powers that states must be willing and able to meet their counterterrorism obligations. The US infringement on Pakistan's territory is one example of a powerful state enforcing this understanding of sovereignty. The United States has been conducting a number of drone strikes in Pakistan, targeted at terrorists. While there has been some argument about whether these are actual violations of sovereignty—Pakistan has publicly opposed the strikes but privately permits them—the mission to kill Osama bin Laden is a clear case. As former Pakistani President Pervez Musharraf stated, "American troops coming across the border and taking action . . . is not acceptable to the people of Pakistan. It is a violation of our sovereignty."[18] However, most critics of bin Laden's death pointed to concerns about how he was killed or what was done with his body, not to violations of Pakistan's sovereignty. In fact, many lauded it as a victory in the war on terror, remaining silent on the issue of sovereignty—even the appointed leader of the international community. As the UN Secretary-General Ban Ki Moon declared, "the death of Osama bin Laden is a watershed moment in our common global fight against terrorism."[19] Only time will tell if is it also a "watershed" moment for sovereignty as traditionally conceived. The evidence from the pressing international issues examined in this book certainly suggest its evolution.

## Possible Constraints on Sovereignty's Evolution

While I have focused on particular kinds of military interventions as engines of normative change, we might also consider circumstances of military intervention that may impede the progress of norm evolution. In the future, military interventions to enforce international obligations may rely more and more on private military companies (PMC). States increasingly rely on PMCs to provide military and security services.[20] For example, the US Department of Defense has contracted over 28,000 private security personnel in Afghanistan and Iraq, representing the first time the United States has relied so heavily on private armed security forces. While the number of such personnel has declined in Iraq with the US draw down, the number more than tripled in Afghanistan, from 2009 to 2011.[21] Though plagued with legal and ethical issues, states find PMCs useful in a variety of ways, from escorting diplomatic convoys to engaging in combat. Russia is currently considering the use of PMCs. President Vladimir Putin stated: "I believe that such companies are a way of implementing national interests without the direct involvement of the state."[22]

However, if the use of PMCs in armed conflict continues to rise, it may have implications for the evolution of sovereignty. For example, what if a state engages in an internationally approved intervention that seeks to compel a state to comply with its international obligations? I have argued that when states are heavily invested and find themselves on the "losing" end of an intervention, they will be more dedicated to contingent sovereignty in the relevant policy domain. However, if the intervention relies more on PMCs than troops, the calculation of costs may change since the casualties incurred by PMCs are not generally made public. In this case, the political costs are arguably lower than if only the state's military personnel were used. Thus, government officials are not in the position of continually needing to legitimize the intervention. The effect, then, on the norm of contingent sovereignty may be less reinforcement, though the act of intervention may keep the norm from devolving to absolute sovereignty.

Thus, while the intervention may encourage the contingent sovereignty norm, it does so to a lesser degree than if the political costs were higher. Similarly, if we think about the use of unmanned aerial vehicles, or drones, in which the risk of casualties for the intervener is extremely low, the outcome for the norm of sovereignty would be the same. Contingent sovereignty would evolve more slowly because it would not be as strongly reinforced.

## Considerations for Policymakers

The actions of states influence the development of the normative structure that governs international relations. Much of this depends on the outcome of the action, illustrated by the cases of military intervention in this book. Leaders must take into account how different actions may change the "rules of the game" for the future. As illustrated in the cases of Somalia and Afghanistan, military intervention contributed to the rise of human rights and counterterrorism norms, respectively. In the case of Iraq, we saw how an intervention predicated on false reasoning failed in promulgating norms regarding weapons of mass destruction.

This is a lesson policymakers should consider when rationalizing an intervention to their domestic audience and their international partners. In order to maintain power, the intervention must be legitimate. Today, this means not only the support of the United Nations, but also compelling evidence that a reason exists to risk limited resources. The war in Iraq is a prime example of the problems incurred when those tenets are not followed. Had the United States focused on another reason, such as gross human rights abuses, there may have been more support for the intervention. Justifications for military action matter, and leaders should take them seriously. While much of the public may be unconcerned with international politics, war brings politics home, blurring the lines between domestic and foreign policy. This makes it all the more necessary for leaders to be transparent in their decision-making.

In addition to domestic effects, leaders should also consider the consequences of their actions abroad. Needless to say, actions taken by one state have an effect on other states not involved. While we might expect small states to be influenced in their beliefs by the actions of major powers, this study shows that major states are also affected by one another. And sometimes this occurs in unexpected ways. While the US-led intervention in Somalia did not affect China's adherence to absolute sovereignty, Russia did experience some change with regards to its increased support for the international community's right to intervene on behalf of human rights.

Of course, this can also work in the opposite direction than intended: France more strongly supported absolute sovereignty after the intervention in the case of Iraq. This suggests that an intervention affects the perceptions of other major powers regarding the rules of the game, and that sometimes these have unintended consequences. One might expect that a leading power would not be inclined to change its views when it is not participating, but the case of Iraq shows that France did not maintain its position on contingent sovereignty. Thus, leaders should consider the implications for their actions not just on their partners but on other major powers as well. They may not be able to or desire to impede an intervention, but the nonintervening leading states do have an influence on how the normative structure evolves.

In some ways, this study should offer encouragement to policymakers engaged in legitimate interventions to further international peace and security. While these interventions necessarily risk casualties, the findings here show that a "losing" outcome may not be interpreted as such when speaking of norms. A costly and unsuccessful war can encourage the development of a norm, at least as strongly as if it were a "winning" intervention. Thus, while obviously hoping for the best result when deciding to take action, even a poor outcome can be adequate if focusing solely on the normative consequences.

One must keep in mind that sovereignty is a fluid notion, ebbing and flowing as any other concept would. Just as "democracy" is understood differently than one hundred years ago, so, too, is "sovereignty." As the cornerstone of international relations, sovereignty may be held as a fixed *feature* of the state system but not a fixed *idea*. For policymakers, this means that they may attempt to change its current definition, according to the values and interests of their population, through intervention. This points to the importance of building a consensus in the international community about what exactly the rights and obligations of the state are and what role the international community should play in enforcing those rules. Misunderstanding the "division of responsibility" or forcing a new view of sovereignty may increase opportunities for international conflict and reduce opportunities for cooperation. Moreover, leaders of major states in the international system have a weighted responsibility in determining such outcomes. Because they represent major states, these leaders have a disproportionate say in the international system and have the ability through their actions to influence the development of the normative structure of which the state sovereignty norm is a central part.

## Final Thoughts

Conceptions of sovereignty are changing. For the first time since the consolidation of the nation-state system in 1648, changes in how sovereignty is understood internationally are apparent. While the Peace of Westphalia (1648) imbued states with sovereign equality and independence, the nature of the international system today represents a kind of sovereignty that recognizes the material and ideational interdependence of states, a sovereignty that ever more depends on fulfillment of widely accepted norms governing state behavior. Increasingly, the maintenance of international peace and security depends on the subordination of states' rights to the international community's values and goals.

The significance of changes in notions of sovereignty cannot be underestimated. State sovereignty has long been a core principle of international relations. It defines how states interact with one another, as well as directs states in their domestic relations. And the sovereignty norm is not just a guide for actors; it is also a part of the structural features of the international system. Just as patterns of power distribution affect the opportunity for international conflict or cooperation, so, too, do the norms regarding state behavior, and in particular, the norm of state sovereignty. Changes in ideas about sovereignty's substance influence the normative structure within which states operate. Moreover, that normative structure informs states about their material understandings of power. Thus, a better understanding of the scope, and limitations, of changes in conceptions of sovereignty are an important intellectual and practical pursuit.

The international community, reflecting an increasing commitment to shared values and interests, is reassessing the rights and obligations of states in the post–Cold War world. International events, such as the 9/11 US terrorist attacks and the humanitarian crisis in Somalia, provide impetus for renegotiating the "division of responsibility" between states and the international community. No longer can the international community stand by in the face of human suffering, nor can it fail to enforce international norms that have consequences for peace and security in the global system. Absolute sovereignty is losing legitimacy, as the international community is increasingly called upon to act as the guardian of individuals. Whether sovereignty continues on this path depends, in part, on the responses of the international community to future crises, and its ability to garner consensus. One thing remains certain: given its prominence and fluid nature, sovereignty will continue to be an intensely debated, controversial concept.

# NOTES

*Chapter 1*

1. Norms are social rules that govern what behavior is appropriate for a particular actor in a given social environment. Thus, norms that govern state behavior reflect internationally recognized rules about appropriate behavior for a state in the international arena.

2. In the case of the recent international intervention in Libya (2011), all three African states on the UNSC voted for intervention (South Africa, Gabon, and Nigeria), though the African Union could not come to an agreement.

3. For example, regarding the genocide in the Darfur region of Sudan, the UN representative from Ghana went so far to question the UN Security Council's decision to "invite" Sudan to consent to the deployment of UN troops, because the UNSC already has the right to send military troops. William O'Neill. 2006. "The Responsibility to Protect Darfur." *Christian Science Monitor*, Sept. 28. http://www.csmonitor.com/2006/0928/p09s01-coop.html (Oct. 24, 2006). The African Union did send a peacekeeping force to Sudan in 2004, which lasted until they encountered numerous attacks and ran out of funding in 2007. Colum Lynch. 2007. "African Union Force Low on Money, Supplies and Morale." *The Washington Post*, May 13. http://www.washingtonpost.com/wp-dyn/content/article/2007/05/12/AR2007051201567.html?hpid=moreheadlines

4. The Peace of Westphalia refers to the Treaties of Peace between Sweden and the Holy Roman Empire and between France and the Holy Roman Empire, Oct. 14, 1648.

5. Jean Bodin, 1955 [1576]. Other great thinkers at the time, such as Hugo Grotius (1625) held similar views.

6. This clearly is a European-centric notion of sovereignty, given that Islamic states, for example, theoretically operate under a higher moral law.

7. When decolonization began to take hold, this is one reason that once the colonies gained independence as states, they have been so protective of absolute sovereignty.

8. Despite Wilson's advocacy, the United States was not a member of the League of Nations.

9. The five permanent members of the UN Security Council are China, Russia (the former Soviet Union), the United States, France, and Britain.

10. Interesting to note is the fact that though humanitarian intervention could be justified in at least three cases during the Cold War, alternative claims were used, for example, India in East Pakistan 1971; Tanzania in Uganda, 1979; and Vietnam in Cambodia, 1979 (Finnemore 2003).

11. Interestingly, Soviet leader Nikita Krushchev compromised with Polish reformers, allowing Poland to follow its own socialist path. However, these reforms were short-lived and Poland continued to labor under Soviet domination.

12. President George Herbert Walker Bush used the term "New World Order" in an address to a joint session of Congress and the nation, Sept. 11, 1990, to discuss his vision for a post–Cold War world.

13. Also underlying this debate are concerns of material emancipation, as reflected in events in Kosovo (1999).

14. Chinese President Jiang Zemin. 2000. "Statement by President Jiang Zemin of the People's Republic of China at the Millennium Summit of the United Nations Sept. 6, 2000." Permanent Mission of the People's Republic of China to the UN. Sept. 6. http://www.china-un.org/eng/zt/qiannianfenghui/t39519.htm (Jan. 23, 2006).

15. Chinese President Jiang Zemin. 1999. "Security." Permanent Mission of the People's Republic of China to the UN. March 26. http://www.china-un.ch/eng/cjjk/cjjblc/jhhwx/t85322.htm (Jan. 23, 2006).

16. Chinese President Jiang Zemin. See footnote 14.

17. 2012. "Avoiding Civil War in Syria." *China Daily*. Feb. 6. http://www.chinadaily.com.cn/cndy/2012-2002/06/content_14540573.htm.

18. Russian President Putin. 2000. "The Foreign Policy Concept of the Russia Federation." *Federation of American Scientists*. June 28. http://www.fas.org/nuke/guide/russia/doctrine/econcept.htm (Jan. 24, 2006).

19. Ibid.

20. John Tagliabue. 2003. "A Nation at War: World Reaction; Wave of Protests, from Europe to New York." March 21. *New York Times*. http://www.nytimes.com/2003/03/21/world/a-nation-at-war-world-reaction-wave-of-protests-from-europe-to-new-york.html?scp=3&sq=putin%20sovereignty&st=nyt&pagewanted=2.

21. Voice of Russia. 2012. "In Syria, Russia Defends Justice and Sovereignty." The Voice of Russia. March 2. http://english.ruvr.ru/2012_03_02/67289916/.

22. 2011. "More Violence Will Not Solve Libyan Crisis." *China.org.cn*. April 7. http://www.china.org.cn/opinion/2011-2004/07/content_22306059.htm.

23. US Secretary of State Condoleezza Rice. 2007. "Remarks at the InterAction 2007 Annual Forum." L'Enfant Plaza Hotel, Washington, D.C., US Dept. of State, April 18. http://www.state.gov/secretary/rm/2007/apr/83213.htm (Jan. 24, 2006).

24. President Bill Clinton. 1999. "Clinton's Statement: Stabilising Europe." BBC. March 25. http://news.bbc.co.uk/2/hi/americas/303693.stm.

25. Quoted in Samantha Power. 2001. "Bystanders to Genocide." *The Atlantic*. Sept. http://www.theatlantic.com/magazine/archive/2001/09/bystanders-to-genocide/4571/.

26. President Barack Obama. 2011. "Remarks by the President in Address to the Nation on Libya." *The White House*. March 28. http://www.whitehouse.gov/the-press-office/2011/03/28/remarks-president-address-nation-libya.

27. UK Foreign Secretary Robin Cook. 2001. "Human Rights—A Priority of Britain's Foreign Policy." Global Policy Forum. March 28. http://www.globalpolicy.org/empire/humanint/2001/0328robincook.htm (Jan. 24, 2006).

28. Tony Blair. 1999. "The Blair Doctrine." *PBS*. April 22. http://www.pbs.org/newshour/bb/international/jan-june99/blair_doctrine4-23.html.

29. Paul Reynolds quoting Tony Blair. 2004. "Blair's 'International Community' Doctrine." *BBC*. March 6. http://news.bbc.co.uk/2/hi/uk_news/politics/3539125.stm

30. Cited in Catherine Guicherd. 1999. "International Law and the War in Kosovo." *Survival* (Summer): 28.

31. Nicholas Watt. 2011. "Nicolas Sarkozy Calls for Air Strikes on Libya if Gaddafi Attacks Civilians." *The Guardian*, March 11. http://www.guardian.co.uk/world/2011/mar/11/nicolas-sarkozy-libya-air-strikes; News Wires. 2012. "UN backed action in Syria is an option." *France 24*. May 29. http://www.france24.com/en/20120529-hollande-says-un-backed-military-intervention-syria-option-resolution-security-council-france.

32. Although some have questioned whether sovereignty in this sense has been a constant, or even a "norm" in the international system (Krasner 1999), compliance with the norm has arguably occurred more often than not. For example, Krasner asserts that sovereignty covaries over time with power and interests and is frequently violated. However, he provides no baseline from which to judge this (potential number of violations) and thereby his work suffers from selection bias. I would argue state sovereignty has, more often than not, served as an inviolate norm governing international relations.

33. Sciolino, Elaine. 2007. "French Leader Raise Possibility of Use of Force in Iran." *New York Times*. Aug. 28, A3.

*Chapter 2*

1. For more on the changing concept of intervention, Martha Finnemore (2003) offers an excellent analysis of changes in beliefs about the use of force.

2. Although I may use the terms *beliefs, ideas,* and *norms* interchangeably, I recognize that they are theoretically distinct, yet also overlap.

3. Strobe, Talbott. 2001. "America Abroad." *Time*, June 24. http://www.time.com/time/magazine/article/0,9171,160112,00.html (Jan. 4, 2004). See also Amitai Etzioni. 2004. *From Empire to Community: A New Approach to International Relations*. New York: Palgrave Macmillan.

4. I locate "contingent" sovereignty in the middle of the diagram for simplicity. However, it could lie anywhere between the two poles, depending on the number of contingencies that sovereignty encompasses at any particular time.

5. Of course, the use of force and state sovereignty are inextricably tied to one another.

6. In fact, one of the top international relations journals in the United States, *International Studies Quarterly,* offered a special edition on "Evolutionary Paradigms in the Social Sciences" in 1996.

7. Ann Florini (1996) uses these insights to examine the evolution of the norm of transparency in international security.

8. Interestingly, research suggests that a strategy of imitation of successful actors is actually more advantageous than rational choice in models of decision-making (Cohen and Axelrod 1984).

9. A supportive structure is a context in which the value is supported by various members of the international community, e.g., NGOs, political entrepreneurs, international organizations, and/or international law.

10. I use the terms *leading powers*, *leading states*, and *major powers* interchangeably.

11. As debate regarding UN Security Council reform demonstrates, these members are not representative of the international community. For example, countries from Latin America and Africa do not hold permanent seats.

12. China. 2001. UNSC Meeting. Sept. 12. http://unbisnet.un.org/. [Hereafter referred to as UNSC Meeting. All meetings were obtained from the UNBISnet website.] For the reasons given in this chapter, I refer to and cite the state as speaker, not the individual representative.

13. US. 1992. UNSC Meeting. Jan. 21.

14. For an excellent discussion of the utility of psychology in international relations theory, see J. M. Goldgeier and P. E. Tetlock. 2001. "Psychology and International Relations Theory." *Annual Review of Political Science* 4: 67–92.

15. An additional area to explore outside the scope of this study is vertical reproduction of norms, how norms are passed down through generations within states, which reflect status quo behavior.

16. For an excellent account of how secondary states come to be socialized by the hegemon, see G. John Ikenberry and Charles Kupchan. 1990. "Socialization and Hegemonic Power." *International Organization* 44(3): 283–315.

17. Leading powers are those states with the power relative to other states to determine which norms prevail through their actions.

18. These expectations are also consistent with the induced-compliance paradigm, which is a further refinement of cognitive dissonance (Festinger and Carlsmith 1959; Aronson and Carlsmith 1963).

19. I recognize that states may say other things in their justifications not necessarily related to sovereignty.

20. This aids in avoiding the individual's private beliefs that alternative methods, such as interviews, would elucidate.

21. To clarify, "rights" are defined as what an entity is allowed to do or something that falls within its purview, whereas "obligations" refer to duties or responsibilities that an entity should do.

22. US. 2001. UNSC Meeting. Nov. 12.

23. Shortly before the war, few states recognized Afghanistan as a legally sovereign entity, despite the fact that it continued to have a functioning government and institutions. The military intervention completed the demise of Afghanistan's sovereignty.

## Chapter 3

1. While the US intervention in Afghanistan might have been considered self-defense before al Qaeda was defeated there (late Nov. 2001), the purpose of the ongoing war is certainly counterterrorism.

2. US. 2002. UNSC Meeting. Sept. 11. http://unbisnet.un.org/. [Hereafter referred to as UNSC Meeting. All meetings were obtained from the UNBISnet website.]

3. While some might argue that state sovereignty was not at issue because the Taliban was only recognized at the point of intervention by Pakistan and Saudi Arabia, it still remains the case that Afghanistan was a state with governing institutions that exerted supreme political authority over a territory.

4. In order to collect the speech data, I used the search term "terrorism" as a topic in the UN's database of speeches, UNBISnet. The database contains all UNSC meetings from 1983 to the present. I use the universe of speeches, rather than a sample. For each country under investigation, there is an average of thirty-eight speeches meeting the above criteria and nine speeches prior to 9/11. I recognize that the number of speeches in the period prior to 9/11 is small. One would expect the number of speeches to be small in this issue area because the UNSC, as representatives of the international community, did not recognize the challenges of terrorism as an international threat to peace and security until 1999, shortly before the terrorist attacks of 9/11.

5. There are seven regional conventions on terrorism: the Arab Convention on the Suppression of Terrorism, 1998, deposited with the Secretary-General of the League of Arab States; Convention of the Organization of the Islamic Conference on Combating International Terrorism, 1999, deposited with the Secretary-General of the Organization of the Islamic Conference; European Convention on the Suppression of Terrorism, 1977, deposited with the Secretary-General of the Council of Europe; OAS Convention to Prevent and Punish Acts of Terrorism Taking the Form of Crimes Against Persons and Related Extortion that Are of International Significance, 1971, deposited with the Secretary-General of the Organization of American States; OAU Convention on the Prevention and Combating of Terrorism, 1999, deposited with the General Secretariat of the Organization of African Unity; SAARC Regional Convention on Suppression of Terrorism, 1987, deposited with the Secretary-General of the South Asian Association for Regional Cooperation; and Treaty on Cooperation Among States Members of the Commonwealth of Independent States in Combating Terrorism, 1999, deposited with the Secretariat of the Commonwealth of Independent States.

6. These include: 1963 Tokyo Convention on Offenses and Certain Other Acts Committed on Board Aircraft; 1970 Hague Convention for the Unlawful Seizure of Aircraft (followed by the 2010 Supplementary Protocol); 1971 Montreal Convention for the Suppression of Unlawful Acts Against the Safety of Civil Aviation; 1973 Convention on the Prevention and Punishment of Crimes Against Internationally Protected Persons, Including Diplomatic Agents; 1979 Convention Against the Taking of Hostages; 1979 Convention on the Physical Protection of Nuclear Material; 1980 Convention on the Physical Protection of Nuclear Material; 1988 Protocol for the Suppression of Unlawful Acts of Violence at Airports Serving International Civil Aviation, (supplements the 1971 Montreal Convention); 1988 Rome Convention for the Suppression of Unlawful Acts Against the Safety of Maritime Navigation (and the 2005 Protocol); 1988 Protocol for the Suppression of Unlawful Acts against the Safety of Fixed Platforms Located on the Continental Shelf (supplements the Rome Convention) (2005 Protocol); 1991 Convention on the Marking of Plastic Explosives for the Purpose of Detection; 1997 Convention for the Suppression of Terrorist Bombings; and 1999 Convention for the Suppression of the Financing of Terrorism; 2005 Convention for the Suppression of Acts of Nuclear Terrorism; 2010 Convention on the Suppression of Unlawful Acts Relating to International Civil Aviation.

7. This convention entered into force on July 7, 2007.

8. NewsMax.com. 2005. "UN Approves Global Anti-Terror Nuclear Treaty.", April 14. http://archive.newsmax.com/archives/articles/2005/4/13/150428.shtml (Aug. 15, 2012).

9. President George W. Bush. 2001. "Address to Joint Session of Congress." *The White House*. Sept. 20. http://www.whitehouse.gov/news/releases/2001/09/20010920-20010928.html (June 12, 2007).

10. These documents include the National Security Strategy of the United States of America 2002; the National Strategy for Combating Terrorism 2006; and the National Strategy for Homeland Security 2007. For more information, see "National Security Strategy 2010." *The White House*. http://www.whitehouse.gov/sites/default/files/rss_viewer/national_security_strategy.pdf.

11. AP. 2005. "Gen.: Taliban Still Grave Threat." Feb. 25. http://www.cbsnews.com/stories/2005/02/25/world/main676660.shtml (March 23, 2007).

12. J. Michael McConnell. 2008. *Annual Threat Assessment of the Director of National Intelligence*. Air War College. http://www.au.af.mil/au/awc/awcgate/dni/threat_assessment_5feb08.pdf.

13. Barack Obama. 2009. "Remarks by the President in Address to the Nation on the Way Forward in Afghanistan and Pakistan." *The White House*. Dec. 1. http://www.whitehouse.gov/the-press-office/remarks-president-address-nation-way-forward-afghanistan-and-pakistan.

14. Ibid.

15. Julian Barnes. 2010. "Afghan Taliban Getting Stronger, Pentagon Reports." *Los Angeles Times*. April 29. http://articles.latimes.com/2010/apr/29/world/la-fg-0429-us-afghan-20100429.

16. Ibid.

17. Yaroslav Trofimov. 2010. "UN Maps Out Afghan Security." *Wall Street Journal*. Dec. 26. http://online.wsj.com/article/SB10001424052970203568004576043842922347526.html.

18. UN Director of Communications in Afghanistan, Kieren Dwyer, quoted in ibid.

19. Ewen MacAskill and Patrick Wintour. 2011. "Afghanistan Withdrawal: Barack Obama Says 33,000 Troops Will Leave Next Year." *The Guardian*, June 22. http://www.guardian.co.uk/world/2011/jun/23/afghanistan-withdrawal-barack-obama-troops.

20. As of this writing, data for terrorist attacks in Afghanistan are only available through 2010.

21. Financial figures were not available for the three months of 2001 when the war began.

22. Gallup Poll. "Afghanistan." *Polling Report*. Nov. 8-11, 2001; July 19-21, 2004. http://www.pollingreport.com/afghan.htm. Exact question wording: "Thinking now about US military action in Afghanistan that began in Oct. 2001: Do you think the United States made a mistake in sending military forces to Afghanistan, or not?"

23. Ibid., Aug. 21-23, 2008; July 27-Aug. 1, 2010.

24. CNN/ORC Poll. "Afghanistan." *Polling Report*. Sept. 22-24, 2006; Dec. 17-19, 2010. http://www.pollingreport.com/afghan.htm.

25. US Department of Defense. 2006. *Five–Year Afghanistan Report*. http://www.defenselink.mil/home/dodupdate/For-the-record/documents/20062006d.html. (Oct. 14, 2007). The report states that there were less than 10,000 US troops in 2002, 13,000 in 2003, and around 21,000 troops from 2004–2006. In a subsequent report by Amy Belasco for the Congressional Research Service, *The Cost of Iraq, Afghanistan, and Other Global War on Terror Operations Since 9/11*, she states that in 2007, there were 24,600 troops;

in 2008, there were 32,500 troops; in 2009, 69,000 troops; and in 2010, there were 84,000 troops. http://www.fas.org/sgp/crs/natsec/RL33110.pdf. (March 29, 2011).

26. This characterizes the war from 2001–2010, before the death of Osama bin Laden in 2011.

27. US. 1992. UNSC Meeting. Jan. 21; March 31.

28. US. 1996. UNSC Meeting. Jan. 31.

29. US. 1996. UNSC Meeting, Aug. 16.

30. US. 2000. UNSC Meeting. Dec. 6.

31. Ibid.

32. US. 1998 UNSC Meeting. Aug. 13.

33. US. 1999. UNSC Meeting. Oct. 19.

34. US. 2001. UNSC Meeting. Sept. 12.

35. US. 2001. UNSC Meeting, Nov. 12.

36. US. 2002. UNSC Meeting. Jan. 18.

37. US. 2003. UNSC Meeting. Jan. 20; US 2010. UNSC Meeting. May 11; Sept. 27.

38. US. 2003. UNSC Meeting. April 4; July 23. US. 2006. UNSC Meeting. Feb. 21; May 30. US. 2007. UNSC Meeting. May 22; Nov. 14. US. 2009. UNSC Meeting. May 26.

39. US. 2003. UNSC Meeting. May 6.

40. US. 2003. UNSC Meeting. July 29. US. 2008. UNSC Meeting. US. December 9. United States. 2009. UNSC Meeting. May 26. US. 2010. UNSC Meeting. May 11.

41. US. 2005. UNSC Meeting. Jan. 18; July 20; Sept. 4.

42. In an ideal data world, I would have been able to increase the number of speeches on counterterrorism. However, I already use the universe of UNSC speeches that fit my broad criteria. The fact that the number of speeches is so small presents methodological challenges in ascertaining the statistical significance of the changes. Despite this, I did conduct difference of proportions tests to test for statistically significant changes in these categories. The only category that resulted in statistically significant changes was the international community's rights ($p<.05$).

43. UK Prime Minister Tony Blair. 2001. "Prime Minister's Statement on Military Action in Afghanistan." British Prime Minister's Office. Oct. 7. http://www.number10.gov.uk/output/Page1615.asp (Aug. 25, 2007).

44. The United Kingdom's proportion of total coalition deaths was 15% at the end of 2010.

45. To put these figures in perspective, British troop levels in Afghanistan for various years are: 3,300 in 2006, 7,700 in 2007, 9,000 in 2009, around 10,000 in 2010. "Information is not Beautiful: Afghanistan." *The Guardian*, Nov. 13, 2009. http://www.guardian.co.uk/news/datablog/2009/nov/13/information-beautiful-afghanistan. James Kirkup. 2010. "Hopes That Britain Could Reduce Afghan Troop Numbers Soon." Feb. 4. http://www.telegraph.co.uk/news/politics/7157207/Hopes-that-Britain-could-reduce-Afghan-troop-numbers-soon.html; BBC. 2007. "UK Soldier Killed in Afghanistan." July 25. http://news.bbc.co.uk/2/hi/uk_news/politics/4836760.stm (July 26, 2007).

46. ICM Research/Guardian Poll. Oct 26-28, 2001.Exact question wording: "Do you approve or disapprove of the military action by the United States and Britain against Afghanistan?" *ICM Research*. http://www.icmresearch.com/guardian-afghanistan-poll-1-10-10-01 (May 23, 2007); ICM Research/Guardian Poll. Sept. 27-28, 2006. Exact question wording: "Do you yourself support or oppose the British military operation in

Afghanistan?" *ICM Research*. http://www.icmresearch.com/bbc-afghanistan-poll-09-09-06 (May 23, 2007).

47. Nigel Morris and Kim Sengupta. 2009. "Voters Turn against War in Afghanistan." *The Independent*, July 29. http://www.independent.co.uk/news/uk/politics/voters-turn-against-war-in-afghanistan-1763227.html?printService=print.

48. BBC. "Public Opinion about the Afghan War Changes." http://www.bbc.co.uk/history/events/public_opinion_about_the_afghan_war_changes

49. Morris and Sengupta. 2009. "Voter Turn against War in Afghanistan." See note 47.

50. Rosa Prince. 2010. "General Election 2010." April 18. *The Telegraph*. http://www.telegraph.co.uk/news/election-2010/7603926/General-election-2010-war-in-Afghanistan-to-play-part-UK-in-campaign.html.

51. Paul Wood. 2007. "Afghanistan Warning Decoded." July 18. *BBC*. http://news.bbc.co.uk/2/hi/uk_news/politics/6903946.stm (July 26, 2007).

52. Nick Allen. 2009. "Liam Fox Says Britain Needs to Build Up Afghan Army in Order to Leave." *The Telegraph*. Aug. 23. http://www.telegraph.co.uk/news/worldnews/asia/afghanistan/6077155/Liam-Fox-says-Britain-needs-to-build-up-Afghan-army-in-order-to-leave.html.

53. BBC. "West Cannot Defeat al–Qaeda, says UK Forces Chief." Nov. 14. http://www.bbc.co.uk/news/world-middle-east-11751888. See also Caroline Gammell. 2008. "War in Afghanistan Cannot Be Won." *Telegraph*, Oct. 5. Brigadier Mark Carleton-Smith said, "We're not going to win this war. It's about reducing it to a manageable level of insurgency that's not a strategic threat and can be managed by the Afghan army." http://www.telegraph.co.uk/news/newstopics/onthefrontline/3139702/War-in-Afghanistan-cannot-be-won-British-commander-Brigadier-Mark-Carleton-Smith-warns.html.

54. UK Ministry of Defence. "PM Announces Troop Withdrawals from Afghanistan." July 6, 2011. http://www.mod.uk/DefenceInternet/DefenceNews/DefencePolicy-AndBusiness/PmAnnouncesUkTroopWithdrawalsFromAfghanistan.htm.

55. UK. 1992. UNSC Meeting. Jan. 21.

56. Ibid.

57. UK. 1992. UNSC Meeting. Jan. 21; March 31; UK. 1993. UNSC Meeting. Nov. 11.

58. UK. 1996. UNSC Meeting. Aug. 16.

59. UK. 1999. UNSC Meeting. Oct. 19.

60. Ibid.

61. UK. 2001. UNSC Meeting. Sept. 12.

62. UK. 2001. UNSC Meeting. Nov. 12.

63. UK. 2004. UNSC Meeting. May 25; UK. 2005. UNSC Meeting. April 25; UK. 2007. UNSC Meeting. Nov. 14.

64. UK. 2002. UNSC Meeting. Jan. 18; UK. 2004. UNSC Meeting. March 4,; May 25; Oct. 19. UK. 2005. UNSC Meeting. Jan. 18. UK. 2007. UNSC Meeting. Nov. 14. UK. 2010. UNSC Meeting. May 11.

65. UK. 2002. UNSC Meeting. April 15; UK. 2003. UNSC Meeting. April 4.

66. UK. 2002. UNSC Meeting. June 27.

67. UK. 2003. UNSC Meeting. Jan. 20.

68. UK. 2003. UNSC Meeting. May 6; UK. 2005. UNSC Meeting. April 25; UK. 2006. UNSC Meeting. May 30; UK. 2007. UNSC Meeting. Nov. 14; UK. 2008. UNSC Meeting. Dec. 9; UK. 2010. UNSC Meeting. May 10; Sept. 27.

69. UK. 2003. UNSC Meeting. July 23; July 29.

70. UK. 2004. UNSC Meeting. March 4.

71. UK. 2005. UNSC Meeting. Sept. 14. See also UK. 2004. UNSC Meeting. March 4; 2007. UNSC Meeting. Nov. 14; UK. 2008. UNSC Meeting. Nov. 12; UK. 2009. UNSC Meeting. Nov. 13.

72. UK. 2004. UNSC Meeting. May 25.

73. UK. 2004. UNSC Meeting. July 19. See also UK. 2007. UNSC Meeting. Nov. 14; UK. 2008. UNSC Meeting. Nov. 12.

74. UK. 2005. UNSC Meeting. Sept. 14; Aug. 4; Oct. 26; UK. 2008. UNSC Meeting. Nov. 12, Dec. 9; UK. 2009. UNSC Meeting. Nov. 13; UK. 2010. UNSC Meeting. May 11.

75. UK. 2010. UNSC Meeting. Sept. 27.

76. See note 42. In the case of the UK, all of the changes were statistically significant at p<.10.

77. 2004. "China Not to Give in to Terrorism." *China Daily*, June 12. http://www.chinadaily.com.cn/english/doc/2004-2006/12/content_338889.htm.

78. Hu Jintao. 2005. "Statement by President Hu Jintao of China at the Security Council Summit." *China at the United Nations.* Sept. 14. http://www.china-un.org/eng/zt/shnh60/t212914.htm

79. Kazakhstan, Kyrgystan, Russia, Tajikistan and Uzbekistan are also members. 2007. "Hu: Fighting Terrorism Important Mission of SCO." *People's Daily Online*, Aug. 18. http://english.people.com.cn/90001/90777/6242598.html.

80. China. 2001. UNSC Meeting. Nov. 12.

81. Some might argue that China is using a "terrorism" defense as political cover for committing human rights abuses, which would be an interesting avenue for a separate research project.

82. China has never made the Unites States' State Sponsors of Terrorism List, though I recognize that this is a partially politically motivated list.

83. China. 1992. UNSC Meeting. Jan. 21.

84. China. 1996. UNSC Meeting. Jan. 31.

85. China. 1996. UNSC Meeting. Aug. 16.

86. China. 1999. UNSC Meeting. Oct. 15.

87. China. 1999. UNSC Meeting. Oct. 19.

88. China. 2000. UNSC Meeting. Dec. 6.

89. China. 1999. UNSC Meeting. Oct. 19.

90. China. 2001. UNSC Meeting. Sept. 12.

91. China. 2001. UNSC Meeting. Sept. 12; Nov. 12.

92. China. 2001. UNSC Meeting. Nov. 12; China. 2002. UNSC Meeting. Jan. 18, April 15. China. 2004. UNSC Meeting. Jan. 12; May 25. China. 2005. UNSC Meeting. Jan. 18; April 25;, July 20; Oct. 26. China. 2006. UNSC Meeting. Feb. 21; May 30; Nov. 24. China. 2010. UNSC Meeting. Sept. 10.

93. China. 2002. UNSC Meeting. Jan. 18.

94. China. 2002. UNSC Meeting. June 27.

95. China. 2003. UNSC Meeting. Jan. 20; April 4; July 23; July 29. China. 2004. UNSC Meeting. March 4; July 19; Oct. 19. China. 2005. UNSC Meeting. April 25; Oct. 26.

96. China. 2010. UNSC Meeting. Nov. 15; See also China. 2001. UNSC Meeting. Nov. 12. China. 2003. UNSC Meeting. Jan. 20; Oct. 16. China. 2010. UNSC Meeting. Sept. 10.

97. China. 2008. UNSC Meeting. March 19. China. 2009. UNSC Meeting. Nov. 13. China. 2010. UNSC Meeting. Sept.10.

98. See note 42. The change in China's discourse on states' rights is close to statistical significance (p<0.13).

99. See note 42. This change in China's references to the international community's obligations is statistically significant at p<.05.

100. CNN. 2001. "Putin Urges Global Terrorism Fight." Oct. 3. http://articles.cnn.com/2001-10-03/world/gen.terrorism.putin_1_eu-russia-eu-plans-terrorism?_s=PM:WORLD.

101. In 2010, a Moscow subway bombing killed 39 people. A few days prior to this, there had been a suicide bombing in Dagestan that killed 12 people. Clifford Levy. 2010. "Medvedev Vows Harsh Tactics Against Militants." *New York Times*, April 1. http://www.nytimes.com/2010/04/02/world/europe/02moscow.html.

102. See Robert Moser and Matthew Shugart. 2004. "Russia: Answering Terrorism with Dictatorship." *The San Diego Union-Tribune*, Oct. 4. http://dss.ucsd.edu/~mshugart/sd-ut_russia.html. Pavel Baev. 2004. "Instrumentalizing Counterterrorism for Regime Consolidation in Putin's Russia." *Studies in Conflict and Terrorism* 27: 337–352.

103. Russia. 1992. UNSC Meeting. Jan. 21; March 31.

104. Russia. 1993. UNSC Meeting. Nov. 11.

105. Russia. 1996. UNSC Meeting. Jan. 31; Aug. 16.

106. Russia. 1996. UNSC Meeting. Aug. 16.

107. Russia. 1996. UNSC Meeting. Jan. 31.

108. Russia. 2000. UNSC Meeting. Dec. 6.

109. Russia. 1996. UNSC Meeting. Oct. 19; Russia. 2000. UNSC Meeting. Dec. 6.

110. Russia. 2001. UNSC Meeting. Sept. 12.

111. Russia. 2001. UNSC Meeting. Nov. 12.

112. Russia. 2002. UNSC Meeting. Jan. 18.

113. Ibid.

114. Russia. 2002. UNSC Meeting. Jan. 18, April 15, June 27, Oct. 4, Oct. 16., Russia. 2003. UNSC Meeting. Jan. 20, May 6. Russia. 2004. UNSC Meeting. Oct. 8. Russia. 2005. UNSC Meeting. April 25. Russia. 2006. UNSC Meeting. May 30. Russia. 2008. UNSC Meeting. March 19. Russia. 2009. UNSC Meeting. Nov. 11. Russia. 2010. UNSC Meeting. Nov. 15.

115. Russia. 2002. UNSC Meeting. Jan. 18.

116. Russia. 2002. UNSC Meeting. Jan. 18; June 27; Oct. 4. See also Russia. 2005. UNSC Meeting. Oct. 26. Russia. 2006. UNSC Meeting. Feb. 21. Russia. 2008. UNSC Meeting. March 19. Russia. 2009. UNSC Meeting. May 26.

117. Russia. 2003. UNSC Meeting. Oct. 16; May 6; July 23; April 4. Russia. 2004. UNSC Meeting. Jan. 12; March 4; May 25; Oct. 8. Russia. 2005. UNSC Meeting. July 20. Russia. 2006. UNSC Meeting. Feb. 21.

118. Russia. 2002. UNSC Meeting. Oct. 4. Russia. 2003. UNSC Meeting. April 4.

119. Russia. 2002. UNSC Meeting. Oct. 4.

120. Russia. 2002. UNSC Meeting. June 4.

121. Russia. 2004. UNSC Meeting. Oct. 8. See also Russia. 2005. UNSC Meeting. Sept. 14. Russia. 2006. UNSC Meeting. Sept. 28. Russia. 2008. UNSC Meeting. May 30. Russia. 2010. UNSC Meeting. Nov. 15.

122. US Department of State. 2002. *Patterns of Global Terrorism Report, Russia.* http://www.state.gov/s/ct/rls/crt/2002/html/19984.htm (Aug. 5, 2007).

123. MIPT Terrorism Knowledge Base. 2002. "Russia: 2002 Overview." http://www.tkb.org/MorePatterns.jsp?countryCd=RS&year=2002 (March 16, 2007).

124. Russia. 2010. UNSC Meeting. Sept. 27. See also Russia. 2005. UNSC Meeting. Sept. 14. Russia. 2009. UNSC Meeting. May 26.

125. See note 42. This represents a statistically significant change (p>.05).

126. See note 42. These changes in references to the international community's rights and obligations represent statistically significant changes (p<.05, p<.10, respectively).

*Chapter 4*

1. I consider the United States and France as "leading" interveners because they had the highest number of troops involved. I take into account the fact that the United States and France entered and withdrew from Somalia at different points in time.

2. In order to collect the speech data, I used the search terms "human rights" as a topic in the UN's database of speeches, United Nations Bibliographic Information System (UNBISnet). Because "human rights" does not capture all the relevant speeches, I also search for known situations of humanitarian crisis, such as "Bosnia" and "Rwanda." I analyze speeches preceding any intervention (1991–92), as well as speeches during and one year after the interventions in Somalia (UNOSOM, UNITAF, UNOSOM II), through 1995. For each country under investigation, there was an average of twenty-eight speeches meeting the above criteria, and fourteen speeches prior to intervention.

3. United Nations. 1996. "Fact Sheet No. 2 (rev.1), The International Bill of Human Rights." *Office of the High Commissioner for Human Rights.* http://www.ohchr.org/Documents/Publications/FactSheet2Rev.1en.pdf (Oct. 7, 2007).

4. Editorial. 2006. "The Shame of the United Nations." *New York Times.* Feb. 26. http://www.nytimes.com/2006/02/26/opinion/26sun2.html?_r=2&n=Top%2fOpinion%2fEditorials%20and%20Op%2dEd%2fEditorials&oref=slogin&oref=slogin (Nov. 3, 2007).

5. The most recent treaty is the International Convention for the Protection of All Persons from Enforced Disappearance (2006).

6. Yale University. "Cambodian Genocide Program." http://www.yale.edu/cgp/ (Oct. 7, 2007).

7. UN, Dept. of Public Information. 1997. "Somalia– UNOSOM I." http://www.un.org/Depts/DPKO/Missions/unosomi.htm (Sept. 3, 2007).

8. Don Oberdorfer and Kenneth J. Cooper. 1992. "Bush Sends Forces to Help Somalia," *Washington Post,* Dec. 5. http://pqasb.pqarchiver.com/washingtonpost/access/8540223.html?dids=8540223&FMT=ABS&FMTS=ABS&date=Dec+5%2C+1992&author=Oberdorfer%2C+Don%3BCooper%2C+Kenneth+J&pub=The+Washington+Post&edition=&startpage=A1&desc=Bush+Sends+Forces+to+Help+Somalia (Sept. 5, 2007).

9. Global Security. "Operation Restore Hope." http://www.globalsecurity.org/military/ops/restore_hope.htm (Sept. 3, 2007).

10. Scott Kraft. 1992. "Food Convoys Reaching Remote Hunger Zones." *Los Angeles Times.* Dec. 18. http://articles.latimes.com/1992-12-18/news/mn-2124_1_operation-restore-hope

11. Michael Gordon. 1992. "Mission to Somalia; UN Backs a Somalia Force as Bush Vows a Swift Exit; Pentagon Sees Longer Stay." *New York Times,* Dec. 4. www.nytimes.com/ (Sept. 4, 2007).

12. While the majority of the troops were sent home, the United States retained several thousand logistical troops in Somalia.

13. UN, Dept. of Public Information. "Somalia—UNOSOM II." See note 7.

14. Eric Schmitt. 1993. "U.S. Forces to Stay in Somalia to End Warlord Violence." *New York Times*, Aug. 28. www.nytimes.com/.

15. US General Accounting Office. 1994. *Peace Operations: Withdrawal of U.S. Troops from Somalia.* June. http://archive.gao.gov/t2pbat3/152098.pdf (Sept. 5, 2007).

16. US Defense Manpower Data Center, Statistical Information Analysis Division. "Worldwide U.S. Active Duty Military Deaths." http://siadapp.dmdc.osd.mil/personnel/CASUALTY/table13.htm (Sept. 17, 2007).

17. For an analysis of the casualties hypothesis in relation to Somalia, see James Burk. 1999. "Public Support for Peacekeeping in Lebanon and Somalia: Assessing the Casualties Hypothesis." *Political Science Quarterly* 114(1): 53–78.

18. *Time/*CNN polls. Jan. 13, Sept. 23, Oct. 7, 1993. Exact question wording: "In general, do you approve or disapprove of the presence of U.S. troops in Somalia?"

19. NBC/*WSJ*. Dec. 12-15, 1992. Exact question wording: "Should U.S. military forces be involved in the situation in Somalia, or should they not be involved?" NBC/*WSJ*, Oct. 6, 1993. Exact question wording: "Do you think U.S. military forces should be involved in the situation in Somalia, or should they not be involved?"

20. CBS/*NYT*. 1/12–14/93, 10/6/93. Exact question wording: "Given the [possible] loss of American lives and other costs involved, do you think sending U.S. troops to make sure food gets through to the people of Somalia is worth the cost, or not?"

21. US General Accounting Office. 1996. "Peace Operations: US Costs in Support of Haiti, Former Yugoslavia, Rwanda and Somalia." June 6. *Federation of American Scientists*. http://www.fas.org/man/gao/gao9638.htm

22. US. 1991. UNSC Meeting. March 11; April 5; Aug. 15. US. 1992. UNSC Meeting. Aug. 11; Oct. 2; Nov. 23. http://unbisnet.un.org/. [Hereafter referred to as UNSC Meeting. All meetings were obtained from the UNBISnet website.]

23. US. 1991. UNSC Meeting. April 5.

24. Ibid.

25. Ibid.

26. US. 1991. UNSC Meeting. Sept. 25.

27. See DeNeen L. Brown. 2004. "Political Rapes of 1991 Still Haunt Haitian Democracy Activists." *Washington Post*, March 21. http://www.latinamericanstudies.org/haiti/haunt.htm (Sept. 29, 2007).

28. US. 1991. UNSC Meeting. Oct. 3.

29. US. 1992. UNSC Meeting. Oct. 2.

30. US. 1991. UNSC Meeting. Aug. 15.

31. US. 1992. UNSC Meeting. Oct. 9.

32. US. 1992. UNSC Meeting. Feb. 28.

33. US. 1992. UNSC Meeting. Oct. 2.

34. US. 1992. UNSC Meeting. Oct. 6.

35. US. 1992. UNSC Meeting. Dec. 3.

36. US. 1992. UNSC Meeting. Dec. 12.

37. US. 1994. UNSC Meeting. Nov. 8.

38. US. 1995. UNSC Meeting. Dec. 15.

39. In an ideal data world, I would have been able to increase the number of speeches on human rights. However, I already use the universe of UNSC speeches that fit my broad criteria. The fact that the number of speeches is so small presents methodological challenges in ascertaining the statistical significance of the changes. Despite this, I did conduct difference of proportions tests to test for statistically significant changes in these categories. The decrease in references to states' rights is statistically significant at $p < .10$.

40. This change is statistically significant at $p < .05$.

41. This change is statistically significant at $p < .05$.

42. Alan Riding. 1992. "Mission to Somalia; French Fault 'Circus' Coverage of the Arrival of U.S. Troops." *New York Times*, Dec. 10. http://query.nytimes.com/gst/fullpage.html?res=9E0CE1D8163BF933A25751C1A964958260&scp=46&sq=france+somalia&st=nyt (Sept. 6, 2007).

43. Co-founder of the humanitarian organization, Doctors Without Borders, in 1971.

44. *Agence France Presse*, Dec. 14, 1992.

45. Diana Jean Schemo. 1993. "As Hunger Ebbs, Somalia Faces Need to Rebuild." *New York Times*, Feb. 7. http://query.nytimes.com/gst/fullpage.html?res=9F0CE7DC103BF934A35751C0A965958260&sec=&spon=&pagewanted=all (Sept. 4, 2007).

46. Interview with Tim Allen, 1999. Quoted in Tim Allen and David Styan. 2000. "A Right to Interfere? Bernard Kouchner and the New Humanitarianism." *Journal of International Development* 12: 858.

47. Sciolino, Elaine. 1993. "Pentagon Changes Its Somalia Goals as Effort Falters." *New York Times*. Sept. 28. http://query.nytimes.com/gst/fullpage.html?res=9F0CE2DC103CF93BA1575AC0A965958260&sec=&spon=&pagewanted=3 (Sept. 5, 2007).

48. Reuters. 1993. "French Defense Minister Francois Leotard criticized U.S. Military Methods in Somalia Thursday as Flawed by 'Faults and Excesses.'" Oct. 8.

49. United Nations. "Fatalities." United Nations Peacekeeping. http://www.un.org/en/peacekeeping/resources/statistics/fatalities.shtml (Sept. 15, 2007).

50. I was not able to find information on the financial cost of the Somalia intervention for France.

51. France. 1991. UNSC Meeting. April 5.

52. France. 1992. UNSC Meeting. March 11.

53. France. 1992. UNSC Meeting. March 17.

54. France. 1991. UNSC Meeting. Sept. 19.

55. France. 1991. UNSC Meeting. Oct. 3.

56. France. 1992. UNSC Meeting. May 30.

57. France. 1992. UNSC Meeting. Aug. 11.

58. France. 1992. UNSC Meeting. Aug. 13.

59. France. 1992. UNSC Meeting. Jan. 31.

60. France. 1991. UNSC Meeting. April 5.

61. France. 1995. UNSC Meeting. Dec. 21.

62. France. 1993. UNSC Meeting. May 25. France. 1994. UNSC Meeting. Nov. 8. France. 1995. UNSC Meeting. Feb. 27.

63. France. 1995. UNSC Meeting. Feb. 27.

64. France. 1992. UNSC Meeting. Oct. 9.

65. France. 1993. UNSC Meeting. May 25.

66. France. 1993. UNSC Meeting. May 25.

67. France. 1994. UNSC Meeting. Nov. 8.

68. France. 1993. UNSC Meeting. April 17.

69. France. 1995. UNSC Meeting. Dec. 15.

70. See note 39. This change is statistically significant at p<.05.

71. Paul Lewis. 1992. "Mission to Somalia; First U.N. Goal is Security; Political Outlook Is Murky." *New York Times*, Dec. 4. http://query.nytimes.com/gst/fullpage.html?res=9E0CE1D6113FF937A35751C1A964958260 (Sept. 17, 2007).

72. Protests also occurred in other cities throughout China.

73. Nicholas D. Kristof. 1989. "Beijing Death Toll at Least 300; Army Tightens Control of City But Angry Resistance Goes on." *New York Times*, June 5. http://query.nytimes.com/gst/fullpage.html?res=950DEFDA1E3FF936A35755C0A96F948260&scp=5&sq=tiananmen+deaths&st=nyt (Sept. 15, 2007).

74. Human Rights Watch. 1993. "China." http://www.hrw.org/reports/1993/WR93/Asw-05.htm (Sept. 26, 2007).

75. Mark Gibney, Linda Cornett, and Reed Wood. 2006. "*Political Terror Scale 1976–2006*." http://www.politicalterrorscale.org/ (Sept. 25, 2007). While they also code US State Department reports, the scores here are based on coding of the Amnesty International reports only. "Level 1: Countries under a secure rule of law, people are not imprisoned for their view, and torture is rare or exceptional. Political murders are extremely rare. Level 2: There is a limited amount of imprisonment for nonviolent political activity. However, few persons are affected, torture and beatings are exceptional. Political murder is rare. Level 3: There is extensive political imprisonment, or a recent history of such imprisonment. Execution or other political murders and brutality may be common. Unlimited detention, with or without a trial, for political views is accepted. Level 4: Civil and political rights violations have expanded to large numbers of the population. Murders, disappearances, and torture are a common part of life. In spite of its generality, on this level, terror affects those who interest themselves in politics or ideas. Level 5: Terror has expanded to the whole population. The leaders of these societies place no limits on the means or thoroughness with which they pursue personal or ideological goals."

76. In 1992, China received a 4; in 1993, China received a 3; and in 1994, China received a 4.

77. In China's case, this means the discourse before the initial UN operation in Somalia (UNOSOM I) in April 1992.

78. China. 1991. UNSC Meeting. April 5.

79. China. 1991. UNSC Meeting. Sept. 25.

80. China. 1991. UNSC Meeting. Sept. 25.

81. China. 1992. UNSC Meeting. March 12.

82. China. 1992. UNSC Meeting. Jan. 31. This meeting of the Security Council was important and unique in that it was the first time that all countries were represented by heads of state.

83. China. 1992. UNSC Meeting. Feb. 28. The Paris Agreements were aimed at settling years of conflict and horrific human rights violations in Cambodia.

84. In China's case, this means the discourse after the initial UN operation in Somalia (UNOSOM I) in April 1992.

85. China. 1992. UNSC Meeting. Aug. 11. China. 1995. UNSC Meeting. Nov. 9.

86. China. 1992. UNSC Meeting. Oct. 9. China. 1993. UNSC Meeting. Aug. 9. China. 1995. UNSC Meeting. Nov. 22.

87. China. 1993. UNSC Meeting. Aug. 9.

88. China. 1992. UNSC Meeting. May 30.

89. China. 1992. UNSC Meeting. Aug. 13.

90. China. 1995. UNSC Meeting. Dec. 15.

91. China. 1995. UNSC Meeting. Dec. 15.

92. "Soviet Repression—and Courage." 1991. *New York Times*, Jan. 23. http://query. nytimes.com/gst/fullpage.html?res=9D0CE2DF153AF930A15752C0A967958260&scp =1&sq=human+rights+soviet+union+russia&st=nyt (Oct. 3, 2007).

93. Human Rights Watch. 1993. "The Former Soviet Union." http://www.hrw.org/ reports/1993/WR93/Hsw-07.htm (Oct. 4, 2007).

94. The last available figures for Russia before that were those of the Soviet Union in 1987, at which time the situation reflected a 5.

95. In Russia's case, this means the discourse before the initial UN operation in Somalia (UNOSOM I) in April 1992.

96. Although Russia was undergoing political transition at this time, I refer in the text to the Soviet Union as "Russia" for the sake of clarity.

97. Soviet Union. 1991. UNSC Meeting. April 5.

98. Ibid.

99. Soviet Union. 1991. UNSC Meeting. Sept. 25.

100. Russia. 1992. UNSC Meeting. Jan. 31.

101. Ibid.

102. Russia. 1992. UNSC Meeting. Feb. 28; March 11; March 17.

103. Russia. 1992. UNSC Meeting. Jan. 31.

104. Russia. 1992. UNSC Meeting. March 11.

105. In Russia's case, this means the discourse after the initial UN operation in Somalia (UNOSOM I) in April 1992.

106. Russia. 1992. UNSC Meeting. May 30.

107. Ibid.

108. Russia. 1993. UNSC Meeting. May 25.

109. Russia. 1992. UNSC Meeting. Oct. 6.

110. Russia. 1992. UNSC Meeting. Aug. 13.

111. Russia. 1992. UNSC Meeting. Dec. 3.

112. Russia. 1994. UNSC Meeting. Nov. 8.

113. Russia. 1994. UNSC Meeting. Nov. 8.

114. Russia. 1995. UNSC Meeting. Dec. 21. Russia. 1995. UNSC Meeting. Dec. 21.

*Chapter 5*

1. Richard Haass, "Existing Rights, Evolving Responsibilities," remarks to the School of Foreign Service and the Mortara Centre for International Studies, Georgetown University, Washington, US Department of State. Jan. 15, 2003. http://2001-2009.state.gov/s/p/ rem/2003/16648.htm

2. "Weapons of mass destruction" refer to nuclear, chemical, and biological weapons, which have the ability to inflict enormous casualties and cause great damage. UN. "Disarmament: Weapons of Mass Destruction." United Nations Office of Disarmament Affairs. http://www.un.org/disarmament/ (Jan. 23, 2008). Some sources also include radiological weapons or conventional weapons, see US Department of Defense. *U.S.*

*Department of Defense Dictionary.* http://www.dtic.mil/doctrine/jel/new_pubs/jp1_02. pdf (Jan. 31, 2008), but for my purposes, I will limit the discussion to how the term is most commonly used.

3. In order to collect the speech data, I used the search terms that capture "weapons of mass destruction" as a topic in the UN's database of speeches, UNBISnet. I examine speeches preceding the intervention (1990–2003), as well as speeches during the intervention (through 2004). For each intervener and nonintervener under investigation, there is an average of twenty-five speeches meeting the above criteria, with sixteen speeches prior to intervention. Note that only speeches that discussed this issue domain in conjunction with the norm of sovereignty were examined.

4. Tejal Chandan and Ramesh Thakur. 2006. "Policy Brief, No. 8, 2006." United Nations University. http://www.unu.edu/publications/briefs/policy-briefs/2006/PB8-06. pdf (March 22, 2008).

5. Protocol for the Prohibition of the Use in War of Asphyxiating, Poisonous or other Gases, and of Bacteriological Methods of Warfare, 1925.

6. Convention on the Prohibition of the Development, Production and Stockpiling of Bacteriological (Biological) and Toxin Weapons and on Their Destruction, 1972.

7. Convention on the Prohibition of the Development, Production, Stockpiling and Use of Chemical Weapons and on Their Destruction, 1992.

8. While the majority of the countries have ratified the treaty, all forty-four countries possessing nuclear capabilities must ratify it before it can come into force.

9. BBC. 2006. "North Korea Claims Nuclear Test." Oct. 9. http://news.bbc.co.uk/2/ hi/asia-pacific/6032525.stm (April 3, 2008).

10. Arms Control Association. 2006. "North Korean Test Provokes Widespread Condemnation." Nov. http://www.armscontrol.org/act/2006_11/NKTest.asp (March 24, 2008).

11. CNN. 2003. "Transcript of Powell's U.N. Presentation." Feb. 6. http://www.cnn. com/2003/US/02/05/sprj.irq.powell.transcript/index.html (April 22, 2008).

12. President Bush. 2003. "President Discusses Beginning of Operation Iraqi Freedom." *The White House*. March 22. http://www.whitehouse.gov/news/releases/2003/03/ 20030322.html (April 22, 2008).

13. President Bush. 2003. "President Bush Addresses the Nation." *The White House*. March 19. http://www.whitehouse.gov/news/releases/2003/03/20030319-20030317.html (April 22, 2008).

14. While the United States may regard this as success, freeing the Iraqis from their tyrant regime, it is important to note that Iraqis' initial views were divided on the invasion: 43% saw the coalition as liberators, while another 43% saw them as occupiers. By May 2004, those views changed dramatically: only 19% still said that they viewed coalition forces as liberators. See Ted Galen Carpenter. 2004. "More Iraq Hawk Myths Bite the Dust." *Cato Institute*, May 18. http://www.cato.org/pub_display.php?pub_id=2655 (April 12, 2008).

15. Walter Pincus and Dana Milbank. 2004. "Al Qaeda–Hussein Link is Dismissed." *Washington Post*, June 17. http://www.washingtonpost.com/wp-dyn/articles/A47812-42004Jun16.html (April 12, 2008).

16. Jonathan Karl. 2008. "Pentagon Report on Saddam's Iraq Censored?" *ABC News*, March 18. http://blogs.abcnews.com/rapidreport/2008/03/pentagon-report.html (April 13, 2008).

17. Kevin M. Woods, with James Lacey. 2007. "Iraqi Perspectives Project, Saddam and Terrorism: Emerging Insights from Captured Iraqi Documents." *Institute for Defense Analyses* Jan. http://abcnews.go.com/images/Politics/Saddam%20and%20Terrorism%20Redaction%20EXSUM%20Extract.pdf (April 1, 2008).

18. CNN. 2004. "Report: No WMD Stockpiles in Iraq." Oct. 7. http://www.cnn.com/2004/WORLD/meast/10/06/iraq.wmd.report/ (March 30, 2008). See also, Joseph Cirincione, Jessica T. Mathews, George Perkovich, with Alexis Orton. 2004. "WMD in Iraq: Evidence and Implications." Carnegie Endowment for International Peace, Jan. http://www.carnegieendowment.org/files/Iraq3FullText.pdf (April 2, 2008).

19. BBC. 2004. "Powell Admits Iraq Evidence Mistake." April 3. http://news.bbc.co.uk/2/hi/middle_east/3596033.stm (March 30, 2008).

20. AP. 2005. "CIA's Final Report: No WMD Found in Iraq." April 25. http://www.msnbc.msn.com/id/7634313/ (April 13, 2008).

21. Bryan Bender. 2003. "Number of Troops in Iraq to Expand." *Boston Globe*, Nov. 6. http://www.boston.com/news/nation/articles/2003/11/06/number_of_troops_in_iraq_to_expand/ (March 15, 2008).

22. Icasualties.org. "Iraq Coalition Casualty Count." http://icasualties.org/oif/Default.aspx (April 3, 2008).

23. Amy Belasco. 2008. "The Cost of Iraq, Afghanistan, and Other Global War on Terror Operations Since 9/11." *Congressional Research Service*, April 11. http://www.fas.org/sgp/crs/natsec/RL33110.pdf (April 2, 2008).

24. See, for example, Center for American Progress. 2004. "The Opportunity Costs of the Iraq War." Aug. 25. http://www.americanprogress.org/issues/2004/08/b171438.html (March 13, 2008); Linda Bilmes and Joseph Stiglitz, 2005. "The Economic Costs of the Iraq War." Information Clearing House. http://www.informationclearinghouse.info/article11495.htm (March 14, 2008).

25. Public opinion on the war has fallen largely along partisan lines. For an excellent study on the war and US public opinion, see Ole Holsti, 2011. *American Public Opinion on the War in Iraq*. Ann Arbor: University of Michigan Press.

26. ABC/*Washington Post*. April 27-30, 2003. Exact question wording: "All in all, considering the costs to the United States versus the benefits to the United States, do you think the war with Iraq was worth fighting, or not?" *Polling Report*. http://www.pollingreport.com/iraq2.htm (April 12, 2008).

27. ABC/*Washington Post*. Dec.16-19, 2004. Exact question wording: "All in all, considering the costs to the United States versus the benefits to the United States, do you think the war with Iraq was worth fighting, or not?" *Polling Report*. http://www.pollingreport.com/iraq2.htm (April 12, 2008).

28. *USA Today*/CNN/Gallup Poll Results. March 24-25, 2003. Exact question wording: "In view of the developments since we first sent our troops to Iraq, do you think the United States made a mistake in sending troops to Iraq, or not?" *USA Today*. http://www.usatoday.com/news/politicselections/nation/polls/usatodaypolls.htm (April 14, 2008).

29. *USA Today*/CNN/Gallup. July 8-11, 2004. Exact question wording: "In view of the developments since we first sent our troops to Iraq, do you think the United States made a mistake in sending troops to Iraq, or not?" *USA Today*. http://www.usatoday.com/news/politicselections/nation/polls/usatodaypolls.htm (April 14, 2008).

30. Susan Page. 2004. "Poll: Sending U.S. Troops to Iraq a Mistake." *USA Today*. May 24. http://www.usatoday.com/news/politicselections/nation/polls/2004-2006-24-poll_x.htm.

31. US. 1992. UNSC Meeting. Jan. 31. http://unbisnet.un.org/. [Hereafter referred to as UNSC Meeting. All meetings were obtained from the UNBISnet website.]

32. Ibid.

33. US. 1998. UNSC Meeting. June 6.

34. Ibid.

35. US. 1998. UNSC Meeting. Dec. 16.

36. US. 1999. UNSC Meeting. Dec. 17.

37. US. 2000. UNSC Meeting. March 24.

38. US. 2002. UNSC Meeting. Nov. 8.

39. US. 1992. UNSC Meeting. Jan. 31.

40. US. 2001. UNSC Meeting. June 26.

41. US. 2002. UNSC Meeting. Oct. 17.

42. US. 2000. UNSC Meeting. March 24.

43. US. 2003. UNSC Meeting. Feb. 14.

44. US. 2004. UNSC Meeting. Dec. 9.

45. US. 2004. UNSC Meeting. April 28.

46. Ibid.

47. US. 2004. UNSC Meeting. April 22; April 28.

48. US. 2004. UNSC Meeting. April 22.

49. Ibid.

50. In an ideal data world, I would have been able to increase the number speeches on WMD. However, I already use the universe of UNSC speeches that fit my broad criteria. The fact that the number of speeches is so small presents methodological challenges in ascertaining the statistical significance of the changes. Despite this, I did conduct difference of proportions tests to test for statistically significant changes in these categories. The decrease in references to states' rights is statistically significant at $p<.05$.

51. Michael Gordon. 2002. "A Nation Challenged." *New York Times*, March 12. http://query.nytimes.com/gst/fullpage.html?res=9500E2DF1439F931A25750C0A9649 C8B63&scp=1&sq=iraq+blair&st=nyt (March 22, 2008).

52. UK Ministry of Defense. 2003. "Iraq: Military Campaign Objectives." http:// www.operations.mod.uk/telic/objectives.pdf (April 22, 2008).

53. CNN. 2003. "Blair: We Must Unite Behind Our Troops." March 19. http://edition. cnn.com/2003/WORLD/meast/03/19/sprj.irq.blair.vote/index.html (March 12, 2008).

54. UK Prime Minister Tony Blair. 2003. "Tony Blair Speaks to House of Commons." *CNN*. March 24. http://edition.cnn.com/TRANSCRIPTS/0303/24/se.09.html (March 30, 2008).

55. BBC. 2004. "Iraq WMD Inquiry Details Unveiled." Feb. 3. http://news.bbc. co.uk/2/hi/uk_news/politics/3453305.stm (April 2, 2008).

56. BBC. 2004. "Blair Defiantly Insists War Was Right." July 14. http://news.bbc. co.uk/2/hi/uk_news/politics/3893987.stm (April 2, 2008).

57. CNN. 2007. "1,600 Troops to Leave Iraq." Feb. 21. http://www.cnn.com/2007/ WORLD/meast/02/21/uk.iraq.troops/index.html (April 2, 2008).

58. BBC. 2006. "UK Troops Numbers to Fall." March 13. http://news.bbc.co.uk/2/ hi/uk_news/4801624.stm (April 2, 2008).

59. Icasualties.org. "Iraq Coalition Casualty Count." http://icasualties.org/oif/Default.aspx (April 3, 2008).

60. Note that the number of casualties was similar in 2005 and 2006, twenty-three and twenty-nine casualties, respectively.

61. UK Ministry of Defense. "Defense Fact Sheet: Operations in Iraq: Facts and Figures." http://www.mod.uk/DefenceInternet/Templates/Factsheet.aspx?NRMODE= Published&NRNODEGUID=%7bF0BB1DF1-A9C7-4E17-96E7-B3301B06E45F%7d &NRORIGINALURL=%2fDefenceInternet%2fFactSheets%2fOperationsFactsheets% 2fOperationsInIraqFactsandFigures%2ehtm&NRCACHEHINT=Guest#mc7 (April 22, 2008).

62. The Pew Research Center for the People and the Press. Feb. 23-29, 2004. "A Year after Iraq War." Exact question wording: "On the subject of Iraq, did Great Britain make the right decision or the wrong decision to go to war in Iraq?" http://people-press.org/ reports/display.php3?PageID=796.

63. Note UK Prime Minister Blair did not leave office until 2007, endorsing Gordon Brown as his successor.

64. UK. 2001. UNSC Meeting. June 26.

65. UK. 1992. UNSC Meeting. Jan. 31.

66. UK. 1998. UNSC Meeting. June 6. Note also that the United Kingdom believed a violation of a norm had occurred, while conceding that it was not technically a violation of international law, since the states were not parties yet to the CNTBT. Thus, the states only encountered "condemnation" (though individual states did sanction them).

67. UK. 2002. UNSC Meeting. Oct. 17.

68. UK. 2003. UNSC Meeting. Feb. 5.

69. UK. 1995. UNSC Meeting. Jan. 18.

70. UK. 1999. UNSC Meeting. Dec. 17.

71. UK. 2002. UNSC Meeting. Oct. 17.

72. UK. 2003. UNSC Meeting. March 7.

73. UK. 2003. UNSC Meeting. Feb. 14.

74. UK. 2003. UNSC Meeting. March 27.

75. UK. 2004. UNSC Meeting. April 22; Dec. 9.

76. UK. 2004. UNSC Meeting. April 28.

77. UK. 2004. UNSC Meeting. Dec. 9.

78. UK. 2004. UNSC Meeting. April 28.

79. See note 50. This change is statistically significant at p<.05.

80. Julia Preston, with Steven Weisman. 2003. "Threats and Responses." *New York Times*, Feb. 12. http://query.nytimes.com/gst/fullpage.html?res=9B0DEEDA163AF931 A25751C0A9659C8B63&scp=4&sq=france+un+iraq&st=nyt (April 3, 2008).

81. Alan Riding. 2003. "Threats and Responses." *New York Times*, Feb. 23. http:// query.nytimes.com/gst/fullpage.html?res=9403E0D7113DF930A15751C0A9659C8B6 3&scp=8&sq=french+ties+to+iraq&st=nyt (April 3, 2008).

82. Elaine Sciolino. 2003. "Threats and Responses." *New York Times*, March 19. http://query.nytimes.com/gst/fullpage.html?res=9A01E7D81231F93AA25750C0A9659 C8B63&scp=2&sq=france+un+iraq&st=nyt (April 3, 2008).

83. See, also, Arms Control Association. 2007. "Arms Control and Proliferation Profile." http://www.armscontrol.org/factsheets/franceprofile.asp (April 2, 2008).

84. Craig Whitlock and Glenn Frankel. 2004. "Many Helped Iraq Evade U.N. Sanctions on Weapons." *Washington Post*, Oct. 8. http://www.washingtonpost.com/wp-dyn/articles/A16142-12004Oct7.html (April 3, 2008).

85. Justin Vaisse. 2003. "Anonymous Sources: The Media Campaign Against France." *Brookings*, July 1. http://www.brookings.edu/articles/2003/07france_vaisse.aspx (April 3, 2008).

86. CNN. 2003. "French cite examples of what they call false stories." May 15. CNN: *Inside Politics*. http://www.cnn.com/2003/ALLPOLITICS/05/15/french.list/ (April 3, 2008).

87. John Laurenson. 2003. "Ties with Iraq: French Industry Stands to Lose." *International Herald Tribune*, March 7. http://www.iht.com/articles/2003/03/07/edlauren_ed3_.php.

88. France. 1992. UNSC Meeting. Jan. 31.

89. France. 1998. UNSC Meeting. June 6.

90. France. 1999. UNSC Meeting. Dec. 17.

91. France. 2002. UNSC Meeting. Oct. 17.

92. France. 2001. UNSC Meeting. June 26.

93. France. 1998. UNSC Meeting. June 6.

94. France. 2002. UNSC Meeting. Oct. 17.

95. France. 2002. UNSC Meeting. Nov. 8.

96. France. 2003. UNSC Meeting. Feb. 5.

97. France. 2003. UNSC Meeting. Feb. 14.

98. France. 2002. UNSC Meeting. Nov. 8.

99. France. 2003. UNSC Meeting. Feb. 5.

100. France. 2003. UNSC Meeting. March 19; March 27; May 22.

101. France. 2004. UNSC Meeting. April 24.

102. France. 2004. UNSC Meeting. April 22.

103. Ibid.

104. Ibid.

105. France. 2004. UNSC Meeting. April 28.

106. France. 2004. UNSC Meeting. April 22; Dec. 9.

107. Both of these changes represent a statistically significant change at $p<.05$ and $p<.10$, respectively.

108. John Tagliabue. 2003. "Threats and Responses." *New York Times*, March 6. http://query.nytimes.com/gst/fullpage.html?res=9803E5D7123FF935A35750C0A9659C8B63&scp=1&sq=russia+iraq&st=nyt (April 2, 2008).

109. Michael Wines. 2003. "Threats and Responses." *New York Times*, March 1. http://query.nytimes.com/gst/fullpage.html?res=9F03E7D9103CF932A35750C0A9659C8B63&scp=4&sq=russia+iraq+law&st=nyt (April 6, 2008).

110. Arms Control Association. 2007. "Arms Control and Proliferation Profile: Russia." Nov. http://www.armscontrol.org/factsheets/russiaprofile.asp (April 4, 2008).

111. Ibid.

112. Global Security. 2006. "Weapons of Mass Destruction: Bushehr." Feb. 19. http://www.globalsecurity.org/wmd/world/iran/bushehr.htm (April 3, 2008).

113. Some have argued that Russia's economic interests prevented them from supporting the war. At the time of intervention, Iraq owed Russia $8 billion dollars. In addition, Russia had multibillion dollar contracts in Iraqi oil fields.

114. Russia. 1998. UNSC Meeting. June 6.
115. Russia. 1999. UNSC Meeting. Dec. 17.
116. Russia. 2002. UNSC Meeting. Nov. 8.
117. Russia. 1998. UNSC Meeting. June 6.
118. Russia. 1998. UNSC Meeting. Dec. 16.
119. Russia. 1998. UNSC Meeting. Dec. 17.
120. Russia. 1995. UNSC Meeting. Jan. 18.
121. Russia. 2003. UNSC Meeting. Feb. 14.
122. Russia. 2003. UNSC Meeting. March 27.
123. Russia. 2003. UNSC Meeting. May 22; July 22; Aug. 14.
124. Russia. 2004. UNSC Meeting. April 22.
125. Russia. 2003. UNSC Meeting. March 19.
126. Russia. 2004. UNSC Meeting. April 22.
127. Russia. 2004. UNSC Meeting. April 28.
128. Russia. 2004. UNSC Meeting. April 22.

*Chapter 6*

1. Lloyd Axworthy, former Foreign Affairs Minister of Canada, and Allan Rock, former Canadian Ambassador to the United Nations. 2008. "Breathe New Life into R2P." *Global Centre for the Responsibility to Protect*, Jan. 29. http://www.globalcentrer2p.org/pdf/R2POp-edAxworthy.pdf.

2. Mark Sandalow. 2004. "Record Shows Bush Shifting on Iraq War." *San Francisco Chronicle*. Sept. 24, 2004.

3. German Federal Government. 2011. "Fewer German Troops in Afghanistan as of 2012." Dec. 14. http://www.bundesregierung.de/Content/EN/Artikel/_2011/12/2011-12-14-mandat-isaf-absenkung-obergrenze-personal_en.html.

4. Mail Foreign Service. 2010. "German Troops in Afghanistan Call on Angela Merkel to Explain Why They're at War." *Daily Mail*. April 21. http://www.dailymail.co.uk/news/article-1267802/German-troops-Afghanistan-Angela-Merkel-explain-theyre-war.html.

5. While this conception of sovereignty may be reinforced and considered a good thing, it may also be that the intervention itself has negative consequences for the people it is trying to help. The discussion here is focused solely on the norms.

6. Tom A. Peter. 2010. "Al Qaeda Plot in Europe Possibly Revealed by German Terror Suspect." *Christian Science Monitor*. Sept. 29. http://www.csmonitor.com/World/terrorism-security/2010/0929/Al-Qaeda-plot-in-Europe-possibly-revealed-by-German-terror-suspect. David Crawford. 2011. "German Authorities Intensify Search for Terrorist Suspects." *Wall Street Journal*. May 2. http://online.wsj.com/article/SB10001424052748703703304576297302521541540.html. AP. 2012. "Germany: Loner Terrorists are Greatest Threat." April 27. *Fox News*. http://www.foxnews.com/world/2012/04/27/germany-loner-terrorists-are-greatest-threat/.

7. Charlie Savage. 2012. "FBI Arrests Man in a Suspected Terrorist Plot Near the US Capitol." *New York Times*. Feb. 18. http://www.nytimes.com/2012/02/18/us/arrest-reported-in-suicide-bomb-plot.html. Deborah Feyerick. 2010. "Times Square Bomb Plotter Sentenced to Life in Prison." *CNN*, Oct. 5. http://www.cnn.com/2010/CRIME/10/05/new.york.terror.plot/index.html.

8. UN Assistance Mission in Afghanistan. 2012. *Afghanistan: Annual Report 2011: Protection of Civilians in Armed Conflict. United Nations High Commissioner for Refugees*. Feb. http://www.unhcr.org/refworld/docid/4f2fa7572.html.

9. Ministry of Foreign Affairs of the Russian Federation. 2008. "Interview by Minister of Foreign Affairs of the Russian Federation Sergey Lavrov to BBC." *Russian Federation at the United Nations*. Aug 9. www.un.int/russia/new/MainRoot/docs/off_news/090808/newen2.htm.

10. Gareth Evans. 2009. "Russia, Georgia and the Responsibility to Protect." *Amsterdam Law Forum* 1 (2). http://ojs.ubvu.vu.nl/alf/article/view/58/115.

11. Jessica Rettig. 2011. "End of NATO's Libya Intervention Means Financial Relief for Allies." *US News and World Report*. Oct. 31. http://www.usnews.com/news/articles/2011/10/31/end-of-natos-libya-intervention-means-financial-relief-for-allies.

12. Marc Lynch. 2011. "What the Libya Intervention Achieved." *Foreign Policy*. Oct. 27. http://lynch.foreignpolicy.com/posts/2011/10/27/what_the_libya_intervention_achieved.

13. "Syria." *New York Times*. April 30, 2012. http://topics.nytimes.com/top/news/international/countriesandterritories/syria/index.html.

14. BBC. 2012. "UN Security Council Passes Plan to Deploy Syria Monitors." April 14. http://www.bbc.co.uk/news/world-middle-east-17715354.

15. On ceasefire violations, see for example: 2012. "Syria Violence Kills 23 Despite Truce." *Kuwait Times*. May 1. http://news.kuwaittimes.net/2012/05/01/syria-violence-kills-23-despite-truce-9-family-members-killed-in-single-attack/. 2012. "More Than 34 Children Killed in Syria Since Ceasefire." *Telegraph*. May 1. http://www.telegraph.co.uk/news/worldnews/middleeast/syria/9239095/More-than-34-children-killed-in-Syria-since-ceasefire.html.

16. Elisabeth Bumiller. 2012. "Military Points to Risks of a Syrian Intervention." *New York Times*. March 11. http://www.nytimes.com/2012/03/12/world/middleeast/us-syria-intervention-would-be-risky-pentagon-officials-say.html?pagewanted=all.

17. Paul Richter. 2012. "US Signals Major Shift on Iran Nuclear Program." *Los Angeles Times*. April 27. http://articles.latimes.com/2012/apr/27/world/la-fg-iran-nuclear-20120428.

18. Ashish Kumar Sen. 2012. "Musharraf: Bin Laden Mission Violated Pakistan." *Washington Times*. May 2. http://www.washingtontimes.com/news/2011/may/2/musharraf-bin-laden-mission-violated-pakistan/.

19. Reuters. 2011. "UN Chief Ban Hails bin Laden Death as "'Watershed.'" May 2. http://www.reuters.com/article/2011/05/02/us-binladen-un-idUSTRE7414W720110502.

20. Peter W. Singer. 2003. *Corporate Warriors: The Rise of the Privatized Military Industry*. Cornell: Cornell University Press. Deborah D. Avant. 2005. *The Market for Force: The Consequences of Privatizing Security*. New York: Cambridge University Press.

21. Moshe Schwartz. 2011. "The Department of Defense's Use of Private Security Contractors in Afghanistan and Iraq." *Congressional Research Service*, May. *Federation of American Scientists*. http://www.fas.org/sgp/crs/natsec/R40835.pdf. The report also notes that private security personnel are 2.75 times more likely to be killed in Afghanistan than US uniformed personnel.

22. Konstantin Bogdanov. 2012. "Russia May Consider Establishing Private Military Companies," *Rianovosti*. April 13. http://en.rian.ru/analysis/20120413/172789099.html.

# REFERENCES

Adler, Emmanuel. 1997. "Seizing the Middle Ground: Constructivism in World Politics." *European Journal of International Relations* 3 (3): 319–363.

Allen, Tim, and David Styan. 2000. "The Right to Interfere?: Bernard Kouchner and the New Humanitarianism." *Journal of International Development* 12 (6): 825–842.

Allison, Graham, and Philip Zelikow. 1999. *Essence of Decision: Explaining the Cuban Missile Crisis.* 2nd ed. New York: Longman.

Aronson, Elliot, and J. Merrill Carlsmith. 1963. "Effect of Severity of Threat on the Valuation of Forbidden Behavior." *Journal of Abnormal and Social Psychology* 66:584–588.

Aronson, Elliot, and Judson Mills. 1959. "The Effect of Severity of Initiation on Liking For a Group." *Journal of Abnormal Social Psychology* 59:177–181.

Ashley, Richard. 1984. "The Poverty of Neorealism." *International Organization* 38 (Spring): 225–286.

Axelrod, Robert, and Robert Keohane. 1985. "Achieving Cooperation under Anarchy: Strategies and Institutions." *World Politics* 38 (1): 226–254.

Banerjee, Sanjoy. 1991 "Reproduction of Subjects in Historical Structures." International Studies Quarterly 35 (1): 19–37.

———. 1997. "Narration and Structuration: Reproduction of the international system 1989–2002." Paper presented at International Studies Association, Chicago.

Barkin, J. Samuel, and Bruce Cronin. 1994. "The State and the Nation: Changing Norms and the Rules of Sovereignty in International Relations." *International Organization* 48 (1): 107–130.

Beauvois, Jean-Leon, and Robert-Vincent Joule. 1996. *A Radical Dissonance Theory.* London: Taylor and Francis.

Berggren, William A., and John A. Van Couvering 1984. *Catastrophes and Earth History.* Princeton: Princeton University Press.

Biersteker, Thomas J., and Cynthia Weber. 1996. "The Social Construction of State Sovereignty." In *State Sovereignty as a Social Construct*, edited by Thomas J. Biersteker and Cynthia Weber, 1–20. Cambridge: Cambridge University Press.

Black, David. 1999. "The Long and Winding Road: International Norms and Domestic Political Change in South Africa. In *The Power of Human Rights: International*

*Norms and Domestic Change*, edited by Thomas Risse, Stephen C. Ropp, and Kathryn Sikkink, 78–108. Cambridge Studies in International Relations: Cambridge University Press.

Bodin, Jean. 1955 [1576]. *Six Books of the Commonwealth*. Abridged and translated by M. J. Tooley. Oxford: Blackwell Publishing.

Brehm, Jack W. 1956. "Postdecision Changes in the Desirability of Alternatives." *Journal of Abnormal and Social Psychology* 52:384–389.

Bueno de Mesquita, Bruce. 1981. *The War Trap*. New Haven: Yale University Press.

———. 2000. *Principles of International Politics*. Washington, DC: CQ Press.

Bull, Hedley. 1977. *The Anarchical Society*. New York: Columbia University Press.

Bull, Hedley, and Adam Watson. 1982. *The Expansion of International Society*. Oxford: Clarendon Press.

Burris, C.T., Eddie Harmon-Jones, and W.R. Tarpley. 1997. "By Faith Alone: Religious Agitation and Cognitive Dissonance." *Basic and Applied Social Psychology* 19:17–31.

Carr, Caleb. 2002. *The Lessons of Terror—A History of Warfare Against Civilians: Why It Has Always Failed and Why It Will Fail Again*. New York: Random House.

Chen, Dingding. 2005. "Explaining China's Changing Discourse on Human Rights." *Asian Perspective* 29 (3): 155–182.

Clunan, Ann. 2006. "The Fight against Terrorist Financing." *Political Science Quarterly* 121 (4): 569–596.

Cohen, M. D., and Robert Axelrod. 1984. "Coping with Complexity: The Adaptive Value of Changing Utility." *American Economic Review* 74:30–42.

Cohen, S. ed. 1996. *L'opinion, l'humanitaire et la guerre: Une perspective comparative*. Paris: Foundation pour les etudes de defense.

Converse, Philip E. 1964. "The Nature of Belief Systems in Mass Publics." In *Ideology and Discontent*, edited by D. E. Apter, 206–61. London: Free Press of Glencoe.

Cronin, Bruce. 1998. "Changing Norms of Sovereignty and Multilateral Intervention." In *Collective Conflict Management and Changing World Politics*, edited by Joseph Lepgold and Thomas G. Weiss, 159–180 Albany: State University of New York Press.

CSA/La Vie. 1992. "Les Francais et l'operation militaire en Somalie et une eventuelle operation a Sarajevo." *CSA*. December 10. http://www.csa.fr.com.

Dawkins, Richard. 1977/1989. *The Selfish Gene*. New York: Oxford University Press.

Deng, Francis M., Sadikiel Kimaro, Terrence Lyons, Donald Rothchild, and I. William Zartman. 1996. *Sovereignty as Responsibility: Conflict Management in Africa*. Washington, DC: Brookings Institution.

Dewey, John. 1929/1923. *The Quest for Certainty: A Study of the Relation of Knowledge and Action*. New York: Milton, Balch.

Evans, Gareth, and Mohamed Sahnoun. 2002. "Intervention and State Sovereignty: Breaking New Ground." *Global Governance* 7 (2): 119–126.

Farkas, Andrew. 1996. "Evolutionary Models in Foreign Policy Analysis." *International Studies Quarterly* 40 (3): 343–361.

Feldman, Stanley. 2003. "Values, Ideology, and the Structure of Political Attitudes." *Oxford Handbook of Political Psychology*, edited by David O.Sears, Leonie Huddy, and Robert Jervis, 477–510. New York: Oxford University Press.

Festinger, Leon. 1957. *A Theory of Cognitive Dissonance*. Evanston, IL: Row, Peterson.

Festinger, Leon, and J. M. Carlsmith. 1959. "Cognitive Consequences of Forced Compliance." *Journal of Abnormal and Social Psychology* 58:203–210.

Festinger, Leon, Henry W. Riecken, and Stanley Schachter. 1956. *When Prophecy Fails: A Social and Psychological Study of a Modern Group That Predicted the Destruction of the World*. New York: Harper and Row.

Fink, Carole. 2004. *Defending the Rights of Others: The Great Powers, the Jews, and International Minority Protection, 1878–1938*. New York: Cambridge University Press.

Finnemore, Martha. 1996. *National Interests in International Society*. Ithaca: Cornell University Press.

———. 1998. "Military Intervention and the Organization of International Politics." In *Collective Conflict Management and Changing World Politics*, edited by Joseph Lepgold and Thomas G. Weiss, 181–204. Albany: State University of New York Press.

———. 2003. *The Purpose of Intervention: Changing Beliefs about the Use of Force*. Ithaca: Cornell University Press.

Finnemore, Martha, and Kathryn Sikkink. 1998. "International Norm Dynamics and Political Change." *International Organization* 52 (Autumn): 887–917.

Fischer, Markus. 1992. "Feudal Europe: 800–1300. Communal Discourse and Conflictual Practices." *International Organization* 46 (Spring): 427–466.

Florini, Ann. 1996. "The Evolution of International Norms." *International Studies Quarterly* 40 (3): 363–389.

Fowler, Michael, and Julie Marie Bunck. 1995. *Law, Power and the Sovereign State: The Evolution and Application of the Concept of Sovereignty*. University Park: Pennsylvania State University Press.

George, Alexander, and Andrew Bennett. 2005. *Case Studies and Theoretical Development in the Social Sciences*. Cambridge: MIT Press.

Giddens, Anthony. 1984. The Constitution of Society: outline of the theory of structuration. Cambridge: Cambridge University Press.

Gillespie, Thomas. 1993. "Unwanted Responsibility: Humanitarian Intervention to Advance Human Rights." *Peace and Change* 18 (3): 219–246.

Goertz, Gary. 2003. *International Norms and Decision Making: A Punctuated Equilibrium Model*. Oxford: Rowman and Littlefield.

Goertz, Gary, and Paul Diehl. 1992. "Toward a Theory of International Norms: Some Conceptual and Measurement Issues." *Journal of Conflict Resolution* 36 (4): 634–664.

Goldstein, Judith, and Robert O. Keohane, eds. 1993. *Ideas and Foreign Policy*. Ithaca: Cornell University Press.

Gould, Stephan J. and Niles Eldredge. 1977. "Punctuated equilibria: the tempo and mode of evolution reconsidered." *Paleobiology* 3 (2): 115–151.

———. 1993. "Punctuated Equilibrium Comes of Age." *Nature* 366: 223–227.

Gross, Leo. 1948. "The Peace of Westphalia, 1648–1948." *American Journal of International Law* 42 (1): 20–41.

Grotius, Hugo. 2001 [1625]. *De Jure Belli ac Pacis*. Trans. A. C. Campbell. Kitchener, Canada: Batoche Books.

Guillot, Philippe. 1994. "France, Peacekeeping and Humanitarian Intervention." *International Peacekeeping* 1 (1): 30–43.

Hall, Rodney Bruce. 1999. *National Collective Identity: Social Constructs and International Systems*. New York: Columbia University Press.

Harmon-Jones, Eddie, and Judson Mills, eds. 1999. *Cognitive Dissonance: Progress on a Pivotal Theory in Social Psychology*. Washington, D.C.: American Pyschological Association.

Hay, Colin. 2002. *Political Analysis*. New York: Palgrave.

Heider, Fritz. 1958. *The Psychology of Interpersonal Relations*. Hillsdale, NJ: Erlbaum.

Hill, Norman. 1976. *Claims to Territory in International Law and Relations*. Westport, CT: Greenwood Press.

Hobbes, Thomas. 1914 [1651]. *Leviathan*. London: J.M. Dent.

Holsti, Ole. 1969. *Content Analysis for the Social Sciences and Humanities*. Reading: Perseus.

———. 2011. *American Public Opinion on the War in Iraq*. Ann Arbor: University of Michigan Press.

Hopf, Ted. 2002. *Social Construction of International Politics: Identities and Foreign Policies*. Ithaca: Cornell University Press.

Hyde, Susan. 2006. "Observing Norms: Explaining the Causes and Consequences of Election Monitoring." Ph.D. diss. University of California, San Diego.

Ikenberry, G. John. 1993. "Creating Yesterday's New World Order." In *Ideas and Foreign Policy*, edited by J. Goldstein and R. Keohane, 57–86. Ithaca: Cornell University Press.

———. 2001. *After Victory: Institutions, Strategic Restraint, and the Rebuilding of Order after Major Wars*. Princeton: Princeton University Press.

International Commission on Intervention and State Sovereignty. 2001. *The Responsibility to Protect*. Ontario: ICISS.

Jackman, Robert W. 1993. *Power Without Force*. Ann Arbor: University of Michigan Press.

Jackson, Robert H. 1990. *Quasi-states: Sovereignty, International Relations and the Third World*. Cambridge: Cambridge University Press.

James, William. 1995 [1907]. *Pragmatism*. New York: Dover.

Jervis, Robert. 1976. *Perception and Misperception in International Politics*. Princeton: Princeton University Press.

Johnson, Gary. 1997. "The Evolutionary Roots of Patriotism." In *Patriotism in the Lives of Individuals and Nations*, edited by Daniel Bar-Tal and Ervin Staub, 45–90. Chicago: Nelson Hall.

Kant, Immanuel. 1998 [1795]. *Perpetual Peace*. NJ: Prentice Hall.

Keck, Margaret E., and Kathryn Sikkink. 1998. *Activists Beyond Borders*. Ithaca: Cornell University Press.

Keohane, Robert, and Joseph Nye. 1977. *Power and Interdependence*. Toronto: Little, Brown.

Keren, Michael, and Donald A. Sylvan. 2002. *International Intervention: Sovereignty Versus Responsibility*. London: Frank Cass.

Kier, Elizabeth. 1995. "Culture and Military Doctrine." *International Security* 19 (Spring): 65–93.

Klotz, Audie. 1995. *Norms in International Relations: The Struggle against Apartheid*. Ithaca: Cornell University Press.

Kowert, Paul, and Jeffrey Legro. 1996. "Norms, Identity and Their Limits: A Theoretical Reprise." In *The Culture of National Security*, edited by P. J. Katzenstein, 451–497. New York: Columbia University Press.

Krasner, Stephen D. 1988. "Sovereignty: An Institutional Perspective." *Comparative Political Studies* 2 (April): 66–94.

———. 1999. *Sovereignty: Organized Hypocrisy*. Princeton: Princeton University Press.

Lake, David. 2009. *Hierarchy in International Relations*. Ithaca: Cornell University Press.

Larsen, Eric V. 1996. *Casualties and Consensus: The Historical Role of Casualties in Domestic Support for U.S. Military Operations*. Santa Monica, CA: RAND.

Lawson, Letitia, and Donald Rothchild. 2005. "Sovereignty Reconsidered." *Current History* (May): 228–235.

Legro, Jeffrey W. 1997. "Which Norms Matter? Revisiting the 'Failure' of Internationalism." *International Organization* 51: 31–63.

———. 2000. "The Transformation of Policy Ideas." *American Journal of Political Science* 44 (3): 419–432.

Levite, Ariel E., Bruce W. Jentleson, and Larry Berman, eds. 1994. *Foreign Military Intervention: The Dynamics of Protracted Conflict*. New York: Columbia University Press.

Maoz, Zeev. 1989. "Joining the Club of Nations: Political Development and International Conflict, 1816–1976." *International Studies Quarterly* 33 (2): 199–231.

March, James, and Johan P. Olsen. 1998. "The Institutional Dynamics of International Political Orders." *International Organization* 52: 943–969.

Mayhew, David. 1974. *Congress: The Electoral Connection*. New Haven: Yale University Press.

Maynard Smith, John. 1978. *The Evolution of Sex*. Cambridge: Cambridge University Press.

McDermott, Rose. 1992. Prospect Theory in International Relations: The Iranian Rescue Mission. *Political Psychology* 13 (2): 237–263.

Meyer, J. 1980. "The World Polity and the Authority of the Nation-State." In *Studies of the Modern World System*, edited by A Bergesen, 109–137. New York: Academic Press.

Miller, J. 1984. "The Sovereign State and its Future." *International Journal* 39:284–301.

Mills, Kurt. 1998. *Human Rights in the Emerging Global Order: A New Sovereignty?* New York: St. Martin's Press.

Modelski, George. 1996. "Evolutionary Paradigm for Global Politics." *International Studies Quarterly* 40 (3): 321–342.

Morgenthau, Hans. 1948. *Politics Among Nations*. New York: Alfred A. Knopf.

Mueller, John. 1989. *Retreat from Doomsday. The Obsolescence of Major War*. New York: Basic Books.

Nadelmann, Ethan. 1990. "Global Prohibition Regimes: The Evolution of Norms in International Society. *International Organization* 44 (4): 479–526.

Nincic, Djuric. 1970. *The Problem of Sovereignty in the Charter and the Practice of the United Nations*. The Hague: Martinus Nijhoff.

Nincic, Miroslav. 2005. *Renegade Regimes: Confronting Deviant Behavior in World Politics*. New York: Columbia University Press.

North, Robert C., Ole R. Holsti, M. George Zaninovich, and Dina A. Zinnes. 1963. *Content Analysis. A Handbook with Applications for the Study of International Relations*. Northwestern University Press.

Oye, Kenneth. 1985. "Explaining Cooperation under Anarchy: Hypotheses and Strategies." *World Politics* 38 (1): 1–24.

Paris, Roland. 2001. "Human Security: Paradigm Shift or Hot Air?" *International Security* 26 (2): 87–102.

Pew Research Center for the People and the Press. 2002. "Americans and Europeans Differ Widely on Foreign Policy Issues: Bush's Ratings Improve But He's Still Seen as Unilateralist." Released April 17, 2002. http://people-press.org/reports/display.php3?PageID=452 (March 23, 2006).

———. 2004. "A Year After Iraq War Mistrust of America in Europe Ever Higher, Muslim Anger Persists." http://people-press.org/reports/display.php3?ReportID=206 (March 23, 2006).

Philpott, Daniel. 1996. "On the Cusp of Sovereignty: Lessons from the Sixteenth Century." In *Sovereignty at the Crossroads? Morality and International Politics in the post-Cold War Era*, edited by L. E. Lugo, 37–62. New York, Rowman and Littlefield.

———. 1997. "Ideas and the Evolution of Sovereignty." In *State Sovereignty: Change and Persistence in International Relations*, edited by Sohail H. Hashmi, 15–48. University Park: Pennsylvania Press.

———. 2001. *Revolutions in Sovereignty: How Ideas Shaped Modern International Relations*. Princeton: Princeton University Press.

Pierson, Paul. 1996. "The Path to European Integration: A Historical Institutionalist Analysis." *Comparative Political Studies*. 29 (2): 123–163.

Politis, Nicolas. 1935. *La Neutralite et la Paix*. Paris: Hachette.

Price, Richard, and Nina Tannenwald. 1996. "Norms and Deterrence: The Nuclear and Chemical Weapons Taboos." In *The Culture of National Security: Norms and Identity in World Politics*, edited by Peter J. Katzenstein, 114–152. Ithaca: Cornell University Press.

Ray, James Lee. 1998. *Global Politics*. 7th ed. Boston: Houghton Mifflin.

Risse, Thomas, Stephen C. Ropp, and Kathryn Sikkink. 1999. *The Power of Human Rights. International Norms and Domestic Change*. Cambridge: Cambridge University Press.

Rosenau, James N. 1995. "Sovereignty in a Turbulent World." In *Beyond Westphalia? State Sovereignty and International Intervention*, edited by Gene M. Lyons and Mastanduno, 191–227. Washington, DC: Johns Hopkins University Press.

Ruggie, John. 1990. Memo prepared for the SSRC-sponsored conference on ideas and foreign policy, Stanford, CA, Jan. 18–20, 1990. As quoted in Judith Goldstein and Robert O. Keohane, eds., "Ideas and Foreign Policy: An Analytic Framework" in *Ideas and Foreign Policy: Beliefs, Institutions and Political Change*. Cornell: Cornell University Press.

Santa-Cruz, Arturo. 2005. *International Election Monitoring, Sovereignty, and the Western Hemisphere: The Emergence of an International Norm*. New York: Routledge.

Scannella, Patrizia, and Peter Splinter. 2007. The United Nations Human Rights Council: A Promise to Be Fulfilled." *Human Rights Law Review* 7 (1): 41–72.

Schwarz, Norbert. 1998. "Warmer and More Social: Recent Developments in Cognitive Social Psychology." *Annual Review of Sociology* 24:239–264.

Searle, John. 1995. *The Construction of Social Reality*. London: Penguin Press.

Shultz, Thomas R., and Mark R. Lepper. 1996. "Cognitive Dissonance Reduction as Constraint Satisfaction." *Psychological Review* 103:219–240.

Skocpol, Theda, and John Ikenberry. 1983. "The Political Formation of the American Welfare State in Historical and Comparative Perspective." *Comparative Social Research* 6:87–148.

Snyder, Richard C., H. W. Bruck, and Burton Sapin. 1962. *Foreign Policy Decision Making: An Approach to the Study of International Politics*. New York: Free Press.

Sorenson, David S., and Pia Christina Wood, eds. 2005. *The Politics of Peacekeeping in the Post–Cold War Era*. New York: Frank Cass.

Thomson, Janice E. 1990. "State Practices, International Norms, and the Decline of Mercenarism." *International Studies Quarterly* 34 (1): 23–47.

———. 1995. "State Sovereignty in International Relations: Bridging the Gap between Theory and Empirical Research." *International Studies Quarterly* 39 (2): 213–233.

Thucydides. 1910 [431 BCE]. *The Peloponnesian War*. Translated by J. M. Dent. New York: E.P. Dutton.

United Nations Bibliographic Information System. "Index to Speeches." http://unbisnet. un.org/.

Van Evera, Stephen. 1984. "The Cult of the Offensive and the Origins of the First World War." *International Security* 9 (Summer): 58–107.

———. 1991. "American Intervention in the Third World." *Boston Review* (October). http://bostonreview.net/BR16.5/vanevera.html.

Von Frentz, and Christian Raitz. 1999. *A Lesson Forgotten: Minority Protection under the League of Nations: The Case of the German Minority in Poland, 1920–1934*. New York: St. Martin's Press.

Walt, Stephen. 1987. *The Origins of Alliances*. Ithaca: Cornell University Press.

Waltz, Kenneth N. 1979. *Theory of International Politics*. New York: McGraw-Hill.

Wendt, Alexander. 1999. *Social Theory of International Politics*. Cambridge: Cambridge University Press.

Zaller, John R. 1990. "Political Awareness, Elite Opinion Leadership, and the Mass Survey Response." *Social Cognition* 8 (1):125–153.

Zartner, Dana Falstrom. 2006. "Thought Versus Action: The Influence of Legal Tradition on French and American Approaches to International Law." *Maine Law Review: Symposium Issue on French and American Perspectives on International Law* 58 (2): 337–376.

# INDEX

modern state system, 6–7
  *See also* nation-state system
Mogadishu, 85, 86
Moon, Ban Ki, 152
morality and moral law, 7–9, 16, 26, 44,
    57, 75, 83, 103, 105, 157
Moscow, 71
motivation, interaction with cognition, 35
  *See also* cognitive dissonance/
    consistency
Mozambique, 15
Mubarak, Hosni, 55, 62
Mumbai, 49
Musharraf, Pervez, 152
mustard gas, 112

Nagasaki, 112
Napoleon, 9
nation-state system, 1
  absolute sovereignty as core principle
    of statehood and international
    relations, 17, 21, 22, 26, 27, 35,
    37, 38, 39, 41, 49, 50, 58, 63, 65,
    66–68, 70–71, 75, 155
  modern material and ideational
    interdependence of states, 155
  obligations to one another, 94
  Peace of Westphalia, 6, 9, 26, 143, 155
  self-interest of nation-states, 17, 145
  state control *vs.* state authority, 18
  structure *vs.* agency, 18
  as unitary actors, 17
nationalism, extreme, 18
Nazi Germany, 11, 18
necessary conditions for normative
    change, 29–33, 44, 47, 82, 144
neoliberalism, 18
neorealism, 17, 18, 24
Netherlands, 9
new visions of sovereignty. *See* fluid
    nature of sovereignty
NGOs (non-governmental organizations),
    93
Nice, 9
Nigeria, 5
no-fly zones, 96, 135, 150

non-proliferation treaties, 112, 118, 129,
    130, 135
non-state actors' use of weapons of mass
    destruction, 110, 113, 114, 121
nonculpability. *See* culpability
North Caucasus, 71
North Korea, 48, 112, 113, 134
Northern Ireland, 47
nuclear weapons
  Cold War standoff, 11–13, 114
  non-proliferation treaties, 112, 118,
    130, 135
  Nuclear Suppliers Group, 134
    *See also* weapons of mass
      destruction
Nuremburg trials, 11

Obama, Barack, 16, 52
oil-for-food sanctions, 115
Operation Anaconda, 52
  *See also* Afghanistan
Operation Enduring Freedom, 51
  *See also* Afghanistan
Operation Iraqi Freedom, 116
  *See also* Iraq
Operation Restore Hope, 84, 85
  *See also* Somalia
Operation Telic, 123
  *See also* Iraq
Organization of African Unity (OAU), 2,
    62, 80, 157, 161
outcomes *vs.* ideas, 26

Pakistan, 68, 77, 149, 151, 160
  death of Osama bid Laden in, 52, 151
  weapons of mass destruction, 112,
    113, 118, 125, 126, 130, 131, 135,
    141
Pan Am flight, 55, 62, 67, 72
Pankisi Gorge of Georgia, 75
Paris Agreements, 99
patriotism, 19, 29–30
Peace of Westphalia, 6, 9, 26, 27, 143,
    155
  Westphalian states. *See* nation-state
    system